SOCIAL AND EMOTIONAL DEVELOPMENT:
The Preschooler

edited by Norbert B. Enzer
with Kenneth W. Goin

Published by

 WALKER AND COMPANY
720 Fifth Avenue
New York, NY 10019

for

The Frank Porter Graham Child Development Center
The University of North Carolina, Chapel Hill

Acknowledgments

We are indebted to the following people, who with great patience and care, assisted in the development of this manuscript: Pascal Trohanis, David Lillie, and Rosemary Epting. We are also in the debt of Janet Peterson (UNC Printing) for her assistance in rendering the figures in Chapter 10 and to Timothy Toney for setting the manuscript's type.

Material in this book was developed with funds from a United States Office of Education Grant. Points of view or opinions herein do not necessarily represent official Office of Education position or policy.

First published in the United States of America in 1978 by the Walker Publishing Company, Inc.

Cloth ISBN: 0-8027-9048-8
Paper ISBN: 0-8027-7122-X

Library of Congress Catalog Card Number: 77-80360

Printed in the United States of America

10   9   8   7   6   5   4   3   2   1

Contents

Foreword

The education of children has for many years been focused on developing intellectual abilities. In the past several decades, however, it has become increasingly clear that the emotional status of a child as well as his ability or inability to interact with others are major prerequisites for intellectual development. This fact is nowhere more clearly illustrated than by very young children, especially if handicaps are present, who have difficulty in learning the most basic skills because of deficiencies in emotional and social development.

This book was prepared to familiarize those who work with young children with the area of social and emotional development—from theoretical issues to treatment regimens. It should be especially useful to teachers and paraprofessionals who serve in day care and mental health programs and to personnel serving in nursery schools for normal and handicapped youngsters, in other special education facilities, and in health programs.

The contributors to *Social and Emotional Development* offer a number of perspectives on social and emotional growth in preschool children, perspectives that are infrequently found in one volume. We felt that a book which included the expertise available in education, psychology, and psychiatry would be more important to a practitioner's general understanding of normal and abnormal development than would be a very specialized treatment of the issues from one field. The constitution of this book therefore, includes a variety of materials. Development and Disturbance, Part One, reviews normal social and emotional growth, disturbances affecting that growth, assessment of disturbances, and treatment. Part Two, Handicaps, examines the nature of disturbances when they are related to four conditions: mental retardation, and neurological, hearing, and vision impairments. Treatment, Part Three, is a look at psychiatric, psychoeducational, and behavioral approaches to remediation.

Readers will find that this book is a useful starting point for parent and staff education programs and for planning and developing preschool programs. The volume may also be a valuable resource for college students preparing for careers which involve working with children in the one-through-six age range. We hope that the book will be of service to these and many other readers.

Development and Disturbance

CHAPTER *1*

Normal Social and Emotional Development of the Preschool-Age Child

Elizabeth A.W. Seagull and David J. Kallen

PART I

INTRODUCTION

This chapter gives a brief overview of some of the important experiences which occur in the life of a child between the time he is born and the time of first entry into school. In this chapter, we are more concerned with emotional and social development than with cognitive or intellectual development. This is not because cognitive experiences before school entry are not important. Clearly they are, and the cognitive skills with which a child first enters school will be one of the important determinants of what and how rapidly he learns. But the cognitive aspects of early child development have been well dealt with elsewhere, and the learning experiences created by schools are oriented toward the development of cognitive and intellectual skills. It is our position that the noncognitive experiences children have prior to school entry are major determinants of what they will learn in school, and what they are willing to learn. It is also our belief that the way the school and its teachers interact with children has a major effect on emotional and social development. Thus, in this chapter we will trace some

ELIZABETH A.W. SEAGULL is a Pediatric Psychologist and an Associate Professor in the Department of Human Development, College of Human Medicine at Michigan State University, East Lansing. Her primary interests include: emotional development of ill and hospitalized children, children's rights, and the development of positive parenting abilities.

DAVID J. KALLEN is Assistant Chairman and a Professor in the Department of Human Development, College of Human Medicine, Michigan State University, East Lansing. His major interests include: nutrition and development, contraceptive behavior among unmarried college students, and the social psychology of health care systems.

of the important events which lead Jane or Johnny to be who they are when they first experience a formal educational setting. In the process, we will attempt to suggest ways in which the staff of preschool programs might interact with children to facilitate this development.

Our view of the events which are important is informed by our perspective of how children develop into who they are. This perspective includes the following important points:

1. *The branching concept of development.* We view development much like a tree with an almost infinite number of branches. In our view, experiences are mediated by later experiences, some of which are more important that others. From this point of view, the impact of an important event in the life of a child stems from the fact that it sets the child off on one branch or another, not that it has a necessarily determinant impact on the rest of his life. It has impact because it may lead to later experiences which reinforce the meaning of that early event for the child. Later events may modify the impact of that early event rather than reinforce it.

For example, if Johnny becomes seriously ill during infancy and has to spend a long time in the hospital, he may be quite unresponsive to his caretakers. This is partly because of the changes in his life—the need to deal with a variety of strangers, the relative impersonality of the hospital, and the lack of energy caused by the illness itself. If he does not play and smile, if he does not do all those things which "good infants" are expected to do, his mother may come to feel that he isn't much fun, or that he really is not a very responsive child. When he gets home, his mother may play with him less than she would have if he had not been hospitalized, thus reinforcing the branch which the hospitalization created. On the other hand, if Johnny's mother is alert to his smiles and responds positively to them, and takes extra care to do those things which lead him to smile or to interact with her, he may branch onto a track more nearly like that which he would have been on had he not been ill.

Or, take another example. Jane is the youngest of four children with a busy mother. In order to keep her life organized, mother finds it easier to do things for Jane than to let Jane do things for herself. At the same time, Jane's brothers and sisters are impatient with her and make fun of her when she is unable to do something she wants to do. By the time Jane first attends school she is likely to have a poor idea of her own capabilities and be less willing to try difficult things than some of her classmates. Her teacher may reinforce the message given by mother and siblings by assigning Jane only the easiest tasks or by becoming impatient or punishing when she will not try something. This will in turn reinforce Jane's view of herself as inept and unworthy and will reduce even further her level of aspiration (Lewin, 1951). If, on the other hand, the teacher gives Jane a series of things to do which she can do, encourages her to try them, and reinforces her when she succeeds, Jane may branch onto a track in which she develops a much more positive image of who she is and what she can do.

Thus, each event builds on the base of past experience. Important events can be viewed as branching points in which the child may continue along the same track or may be moved to a different track. By the same token, at a given time, two children may appear to be on the same track, but have gotten there in quite different ways.

2. *The interactive nature of development.* To us, development is an interactive phenomenon. By this we mean that beginning at birth, and perhaps before birth, the infant and the child are active initiators and responders who exert influence on others and on the events which influence them. They are not merely passive recipients of influence from others (Lewis and Rosenblum, 1974). What they do, of course, will be influenced by their physical makeup, by past events in their lives, by their growing perception of who they are, and by the nature of those with whom they interact. This view does not deny the general helplessness and dependency of infancy and early childhood. After all, a three-week-old baby cannot force others to do his bidding (although some mothers appear to act as if they could). However, even the three-week-old infant can be more or less active, more or less demanding, more or less responsive to others, and consequently influence the way others respond to him. At the same time, other people will act in various ways toward the infant, delighting in some performances and thereby increasing the chances that the behavior will be repeated, or ignoring the behavior so that the infant does not have much sense that it is worth repeating.

This is not to suggest that infants or young children act in the purposeful intentional way that adults do or that they consciously attempt to influence others. We cannot ask infants what they are trying to do; we can only infer it from what they do under different circumstances. When three-month-old Jane coos and babbles at the sound of her mother's voice, she does not think, "Oh goody, I'm going to get mama to talk to me more." But her babbles are likely to encourage responses from mama which reinforce Jane's babbling. Mama likes to hear Jane babble to her and likes doing things that make Jane happy. Jane feels pleasure in the sound of the familiar voice, and in the interaction with mama. Charlie may be less likely to respond to mama's voice but may take great delight in the sight of her face, breaking into a big smile every time he sees it. While Jane's mother may be able to keep her quiet and happy by talking to her from another room, Charlie's mother may have to move him around with her so that he can keep her in view most of the time. Whichever occurs, it is clear that both babies are influencing what happens to them through a true process of interaction.

3. *Uniqueness versus commonality.* The branching concept of socialization which informs our approach suggests that each individual is the result
of a series of unique experiences, and that a full understanding of that
individual requires an understanding of the whole series of unique events
which have transpired up to the present time. For many purposes this is
true. Yet, many individuals have highly similar experiences which lead to
similar patterns of development. In this chapter we will be looking largely
at the commonalities of experience and outcomes. In other words, we are
less concerned with the specifics of Johnny, who may be your pupil, with
his own special character and unique needs, than how all the Johnnies
got to be who they are. To do this, we will look at some of the kinds of
experiences infants and children have in general, and at how variations in
these experiences lead to different outcomes. We have attempted to
synthesize data from many sources, putting it together in ways that appear
to make sense to us and to be helpful to the reader. We are aware of
certain problems in doing this; particularly, the fact that some of the ways
we see the data fitting together have not yet been tested. Some of the
consequences we discuss must be inferred from the behavior of children,
rather than from a full understanding of the processes involved. For
example, when we talk about the development of a self-image of competence in a year-old infant, that self-image has not been measured directly.
What we are really saying is that certain experiences lead some children, at
a year of age, to behave as if they have a self-image of competence. We
have been careful not to assume that because an adult would interpret an
event in a given way that children would give the event the same interpretation. For example, when a grandparent dies, a young child may respond
in much the same way as when a favorite toy is lost. It may be difficult for
the child; but the concerns about death and the mourning which char-
acterize adults may not be part of the child's repertoire of response, and it
would be an error to interpret the child's behaviors and responses as if
they were. As adults, we are so far from the experiences and world view of
young children that it is easy to fall into the error of assuming their
responses are the same as ours, or that events have the same meaning for
them as for us.

4. *Social class versus the immediate environment.* In the past several
years much has been written about the effects of social class on child
rearing and on differences in the development of children in different
social classes and ethnic groups. Valuable information about how children
are reared and the consequences for the child of different rearing styles
was gained when developmental psychology left the university nursery
school and moved into the "real world," and when sociologists began
looking at both middle- and lower-class patterns of rearing children. In our
view, however, it would be a mistake to assume that social class position

causes the outcome. Rather, for our purposes, social class is a locator variable. By this we mean that the life conditions of a given social class at a particular point in time are such as to increase the probability that a given socialization pattern will be found in that segment of our society. However, it is the immediate environment in which the child develops which has the impact on his life. For example, there is a good deal of evidence to suggest that lower-class parents employ physical discipline as a primary method of punishment while middle-class parents are more likely to use verbal inductions and loss of love techniques to achieve the same ends. The latter techniques are more likely to lead to an internalization of the standards the parent is attempting to teach. Physical punishment is more likely to lead the child to believe that the problem is not with the act but with getting caught, and that he has paid the price for his misdeed and is free to do it again (Bronfenbrenner, 1958). It is the techniques of child rearing which are differentially distributed by social class and not the social class position per se which has the important influence on the child. The match is not perfect. Middle-class children whose parents use physical punishment extensively are apt to behave in ways which are similar to lower-class children; while lower-class children whose parents use loss of love techniques extensively are apt to develop the same level of internalization of standards as middle-class children. Thus, in this chapter we will discuss the various events which impinge on the child and the effect they have on him or her; we will not attempt in any great degree to relate them to social class patterns of behavior.

In Part II of this chapter we will discuss some of the important areas in which major "branching" in a child's emotional and social development may occur. In Part III, we will focus more on the important developmental happenings and activities in the life of the average preschool-age child. We will also discuss the implications of different types of responses to these behaviors for the overall emotional and social development of the child.

PART II

(Who goes there? A brief overview of important events between birth and first school experience.)

CONSTITUTION AND INTERACTIVE FIT

Ever since Craig was born he was rather inactive. He was content lying in his crib, looking at the world, not moving very much and sleeping a lot. Although his birth weight was average, he gained weight rapidly, and by three months was clearly a chubby baby. Craig's mother, however, was always on the go, always trying to interest Craig in something. Bruce, on the other hand, was active from the day he was born, was always moving, and took great delight in his mother's tickling him. He would squeal with pleasure every time he was touched, but it took him a long time to settle down after a play session.

Beginning at birth, infants differ on a number of dimensions, and their major caretakers differ in their preferred means of approaching children and in the modalities they use when making physical, emotional, or verbal contact with the infant. The fit between the constitutional nature of the child and the modality and means of approach generally preferred by the caretaker has important implications for the development of the child (Thomas, Chess, and Birch, 1968). Thus, the early interactive fit between infant and caretaker is one of the first major branching points in development.

According to Escalona (1968), the first important dimension on which infants differ is *activity*. Activity refers to the general amount and vigor of body motion typically shown by the infant in a wide variety of situations. In the example given at the beginning of this section, it is clear that Craig has a low activity level while Bruce has a high level. Although activity level can change through time, it appears to be an important determinant of the infant's response to situations in which he is stimulated.

The extent to which the infant likes to be cuddled or otherwise restrained is related to, but different from, activity level. Although it is traditional to comfort an infant by cuddling, some infants, and particularly those who are advanced in their motor development, resist it, often to the distress of mothers and grandmothers.

Infants also differ in their *reactivity to sensory stimulation* in general and to specific kinds of stimulation in particular. Again, in the earlier example, Bruce was highly sensitive to tactile stimulation. Other infants respond differently to sound or sight or movement.

Escalona suggests that infants may differ in the *strength of the boundaries* they have with the external world, and in the strength of the boundaries they have within their inner world. Strength of the boundary refers to the degree of stimulation which is necessary to create an awareness of that stimulation in the infant. Some infants have generally high boundaries, and it takes a fairly strong stimulation to have an impact on them; others have weak boundaries and are consequently bombarded by stimulation. Most infants, of course, have strong boundaries to some kinds of stimulation and weak boundaries to others. There are also differences among children in the internal boundaries. This refers to stimulation which originates from within the child—i.e., his perception of hunger pangs or other bodily states. Thus, infants' perceptions of stimulation of various kinds depend both on the strength of the boundaries separating them from the world and on the intensity of the stimulation they receive.

Infants' responses to stimulation, then, are determined by a number of different variables which interact to produce them: general activity level, reactivity, and sensitivity to internal states such as hunger and differential need for sleep. Thus, for example, if Bruce has a weak boundary to external tactile stimulation and is active and reactive, his mother's touching him provides a strong stimulus to which he responds strongly. However, if he has a strong boundary to auditory stimulation, it will take a very loud noise indeed to create a response in him.

Mothers differ in the ways they prefer to interact with their infants. Some mothers are active, demanding a response, preferring to touch and speak to their infants rather than letting them watch the world. Other mothers are more phlegmatic, providing gentler stimulation to their children, taking a calmer approach, and thus providing them more opportunities to explore the limits of their capabilities.

Escalona suggests that there are three important factors which act together in determining the behavior of an infant. These are: (1) the characteristics of each modality and the sensitivity of the child to that modality; (2) the mother's usual practices in stimulating or soothing the child, and particularly the use, and intensity of use, of each modality; and (3) the response and reaction that the infant has to stimulation in each modality.

Emotional, social, intellectual, and cognitive development require appropriate stimulation and adequate learning opportunities. The adequacy and appropriateness of a given child's experience is a function of the interaction between the preferred patterns of behavior of the mother (or other major caretakers) and the constitutional nature of the infant. That is, if the child is relatively unreceptive to stimulation and the mother's pattern of behavior is a relatively quiet, leave-the-child-alone approach, the child may be understimulated. If, on the other hand, the mother is relatively active and insistent in her approach to the child, who is unreceptive to stimulation, he may receive an adequate amount of stimulation. If the child is sensitive to internal and external stimulation, a forceful, insistent approach may provide too much stimulation and result in a child who is overreactive.

THE DEVELOPMENT OF ATTACHMENT
AND THE BEGINNINGS OF THE SELF

Studies of children in institutions and studies of children in normal families suggest that for adequate development the infant needs both appropriate levels of perceptual and somatosensory stimulation and appropriate mothering. Children who fail to thrive, either at home or in an institution, appear to suffer from both stimulus and maternal deprivation (Yarrow, 1965). They also tend to be children who do not provide responses to the caretaker which would tend to cement the bonding relationship.

When Jane was brought into the hospital at the age of three-and-a-half months, she weighted eight-and-a-half pounds and was only eighteen inches long. This was less than an increase of a pound-and-a-half over her birth weight, and one inch in length. The first two days in the hospital Jane didn't do anything but lie in her crib. When her mother was asked to feed her, she put Jane in her lap with a hand under her head and simply held the bottle in her mouth. There was no eye contact and no verbal interaction between Jane and her mother. Jane did not smile or respond in other ways to her mother or to the nurses, doctors, medical students, or other people who came into her room. Mother reported that Jane was not a very interesting child. Careful interviewing of mother revealed that Jane was left in her crib most of the time, that mother almost never held her and fed her only if she cried.

In the hospital, Jane was held and talked to frequently. She was given a mobile to look at and was carried and rocked often. She quickly gained weight. As she gained weight, she began to take more of an interest in her environment and to respond more to people around her. By the end of two weeks, she was smiling, and her mother was beginning to return the smile and to respond in other ways to Jane's behaviors.

Failure to thrive in infancy is the result of a breakdown of the attachment relationship between mother and child. In the normal infant-mother pair, this relationship begins early with the first look at the child by mother and is built by the continued interaction between the mother and the child. The nature and adequacy of the bonding relationship is a second major branch point on the tree of socialization.

Ainsworth and her associates (Bell and Ainsworth, 1972; Stayton, Ainsworth, and Main, 1973; Stayton and Ainsworth, 1973) report that the quality of a mother's response has a major impact on the development of the attachment relationship. Prompt appropriate responses on the part of the mother lead to a strong attachment, a sense of security, and the development of a sense of competence on the part of the infant.

Initially, the cry is the major signal used by the infant to indicate a need for interaction with the caretaker. The cry may indicate pain, hunger, boredom, a desire for interaction, or any one of a number of other needs. The new mother must learn to interpret the meaning of the cry; to determine if the baby is hungry, in pain, needs holding, or is expressing some other need. One difficulty with the interpretation of the child's cry is that the act of feeding also generally involves holding, moving the child, and other forms of stimulation. Mothers differ in the promptness with which they intervene when the infant cries, in the sensitivity they have to the child's feeding needs, and in their general response to the child's initiations of verbal or visual contact. One group of mothers may be said to show appropriate behavior. They intervene quickly when the child requests intervention, they are sensitive to demands for feeding, and they know when feeding is completed, a rest period is desired, a burp requires attention, and so on. As the child grows older, they offer verbal or visual contact when demanded. Other mothers prefer to let the child cry longer. They are less sensitive to feeding needs, giving too much to eat at some times and too little at others, failing to maintain requested verbal or visual contact, and generally responding on their own rather than the infant's terms.

These differences in maternal behavior result in quite different children. The child whose mother responds appropriately develops a strong sense of attachment to the mother. Such children cry less frequently and are able to tolerate the mother leaving the room both at home and in strange situations. They are more likely to explore their environment. At between nine months and a year of age, they are more obedient to verbal commands from the mother and begin to show evidence of having developed internal controls. They behave in ways consistent with a self-image of competence.

Ainsworth suggests that these behaviors in response to appropriate maternal behavior have survival value in the development of a species in which exploratory behavior is useful and in which responsiveness to maternal commands protects the infant from predators. At the same time, when the mothers are appropriately responsive to children, the children develop a sense that their actions can have a meaningful impact on what happens to them. Children of less responsive mothers, on the other hand, are less likely to get feedback which suggests that their behaviors have much of an effect, and therefore they become more dependent on mother and less willing to let her out of sight. They do not develop an expectation that mother will return when she is needed. Because mother's interventions are inconsistent and, at times, not responsive to the needs of the children, her commands are less likely to be obeyed. After all, if nothing one does has a predictable consequence, one is free to do as one likes.

The development of the attachment relationship, or bonding, is a two-way street. Just as the infant is dependent on mother's actions to develop a strong bond, a sense of competence, and a feeling of security in the relationship, so also do mothers and other caretakers respond to the actions of their children. Earlier we suggested that children who experience an episode of failure to thrive often do not respond in appropriate or rewarding ways to their mothers. When physical problems intervene to keep the child in the hospital for an extended period after birth, the bonding process may be severely disrupted. When a child is continually fussing, does not smile, or is unresponsive in other ways, the mother does not receive the reciprocal responses from the child which promote the development of her attachment to the infant.

Problems in the attachment relationship may be acute for infants born with various handicaps, and particularly those which involve visual or auditory communication. Selma Fraiberg suggests, for example, that children who are blind from birth do not smile when their mother approaches. But this lack of smiling is often perceived by the mother as a rejection of her. Teaching the mother to provide verbal or tactile stimulation for the blind child becomes another way of eliciting the smiling response, and other responses which promote attachment. Clearly, the development of attachment, the cementing of the social bond, depends on true interaction.

The extent to which the mother is able to make an appropriate response to the child is in part a function of the fit between mother and infant. The fussy infant who is highly responsive to internal signals will create many more demands on the mother than the child who is relatively insensitive to internal signals. Some of these may be signals to which the mother is unable to respond because of other demands on her time. By the same token, the child who is relatively active and responsive will give more information to the mother about the appropriateness of her actions than the child who is relatively unresponsive, thus making it easier to judge the appropriateness of her responses. The sensitivity of the mother to the responses and demands of her baby, her preferred modes of interacting with the child, her values and beliefs about child rearing, and the other demands of her life situation will also influence the extent to which her actions are appropriate for the needs of her child. The mother who believes in schedule feeding and in not spoiling her child by picking it up right away when it cries will act in ways which are less responsive than the mother who believes in ad lib feeding and in picking up the baby when it demands interaction.

Reality will also intervene, no matter what the preferred practices and values of the mother are. The mother who has many other demands on her time because she has other small children who demand attention, or because she has been ill, etc., will find it less possible to respond promptly and appropriately to the demands of her infant than will the mother who is free to devote all of her time to her infant.

It is not necessary for the mother—or, more correctly the caretaker or caretakers—to respond instantaneously every time the baby cries or to judge accurately what it is that will soothe the cry. However, the development of attachment and the sense of self-competency depends on an overall level of prompt and appropriate behavior on the part of the mother.

THE DEVELOPMENT OF THE SELF

The early indications of competency which result from appropriate interaction between mother and child are the beginnings of the self. The self, in Cooley's (1909, 1922) terms, is the individual as he is known to himself. The way that we know who we are, at least in social terms, is by the way in which other people respond to us. When Mary's mother responds quickly to her crying, Mary gets a sense that what she does can really affect her fate. When Jane's mother responds in inconsistent ways, Jane does not have any sense that what she does has any effect on what happens to her. She gets only a sense of her own ineffectiveness in influencing her fate.

Although preverbal interaction influences the development of the self, the self itself cannot really develop until the child acquires language. With the development of language, the child is able to understand ideas; and the ideas that others express toward her and toward her behaviors tell her who she is. If her mother is constantly telling her that she cannot do something because she is too little, she will begin to develop the idea that she is both little and inept. Because she views herself as inept, she will stop trying difficult things; that is, she will lower her level of aspiration until it fits with her idea of who she is.

Not everybody has the same influence on the self. If everyone had the same amount of influence, the self would be constantly changing, confused, and merely responding to the immediacies of the social situation. People who can influence the self in significant ways are called significant others. Because the child is attached to family members, is dependent on them for many things, and has few if any alternative sources of information about himself, they have a great deal of influence over his sense of who he is. As children develop language and interact over time with a small group of people, they have a better ability to understand the true meaning of the others' gestures toward them. A child may learn, for example, that when his sister comes home from school and says something mean to him, it is not because of anything he has done but because sister doesn't like school and usually acts that way. When a stranger acts angry toward him, however, he is more likely to wonder what he has done to make that stranger angry, because he does not know the stranger well enough to interpret the meaning of the other's behavior toward him except at face value.

One of the major branch points in the development of the self comes when the child first encounters the wider world in a meaningful way, when he must deal consistently and over time with a group other than his immediate family. For most children, this point comes when they first enter the educational system, either in a preschool nursery, a kindergarten, or first grade. At this point, both the teacher and other children in the classroom become significant others.

Elmer was always a quiet and passive child. As an infant he had a relatively low activity level and a low level of reactivity. His mother was rather phlegmatic, and while she generally responded appropriately to Elmer's demands, she was mostly content to let him demand attention rather than stimulating him. Thus, when he first got to nursery school, he was rather quiet and passive, given more to watching than to participating. His nursery school teacher, however, began to demand that he participate more in group play and had a tendency to tell him that he was uncooperative when he preferred to watch or to play by himself. Because the teacher was a significant other—during the school day she was the major adult in his life, and he knew he was supposed to do what she wanted—he began to get a sense that he was not a very good person, that there was something about him that made the teacher angry toward him. Thus, part of his self-concept began to incorporate the idea that he was not a very good person in school. By the time he got to the first grade, he was beginning to reject the whole idea of learning because the feedback he had received told him he was not a person who could learn things, and hence the concept of himself as a learner was not consistent with his growing concept of who he was.

Martha, on the other hand, was the youngest of five children. She liked to try to do the same things that her older siblings did, but because she was younger she could not do them well. Her brothers and sisters often made fun of her when she could not keep up with them. When she first entered kindergarten, she had a relatively poor perception of her own capabilities. However, with encouragement from the teacher she soon found that she could do all the things that kindergarten children are expected to do, and do them very well. Her efforts to keep up with her siblings had given her both role models and skills which were advanced for her age. With positive feedback from the teacher and admiration from her peers, she quickly developed a sense that she was a capable person and became eager to try new things. As her sense of competence developed in school and became integrated into her conception of who she was, she began to understand that her failures at home were not because she was incapable as a person, but because she was younger and not as skilled as her siblings. Thus, she was able to view what she did with her siblings in a more positive light and take pride in what she did, rather than feel ashamed and inept because of what she was unable to do.

Thus, the school experience, and particularly the early years of schooling, can have a major effect upon the development of the self. It can reinforce the feedback that has been received at home, and thus confirm the view that the child has of who he is and what he is capable of, or it can modify the child's view, either positively or negatively.

It is not clear when the self is fully developed, but it is probably not until young adulthood at the earliest. The extent to which the self will undergo major changes is dependent, in part, upon the number and nature of new experiences the person undergoes. When the person encounters only similar situations and consistent feedback about who he is, there is little opportunity or need for the self to change. When the person experiences a wide variety of situations and various different responses to his actions, the self is more complex and differentiated and is more likely to undergo significant modification. Certainly, not all experiences and not all people have the same impact on the self. One incongruous feedback experience is not likely to have a significant effect on the self. By the same token, when all the feedback the person gets is significantly different from the feedback received earlier, the self is more likely to change to reflect accurately the new image received from others. Because the self is still in the process of formation during the early school years, the responses of teachers and peers in the school room are important influences on it.

EFFECTS OF SOCIAL CLASS, ATTRACTIVENESS, AND TEACHER EXPECTATIONS IN SCHOOL

Myrtle is small for her age. She has a pinched-looking face, with small eyes that are set too close together, and a very prominent chin. When she knocked over the paints in nursery school, the assistant teacher became very angry at her and told her she was a very careless child. The assistant teacher later remarked to the head teacher that she thought Myrtle had probably knocked over the paints on purpose. Joanne is a very attractive little girl. Of average height, she has a well-formed, slightly oval face, big blue eyes, and long straight blond hair. When Joanne spilled a dishpan full of soapy water she was carrying, the teacher simply told her that she should learn not to carry things that were too full, and helped her clean up the mess.

Physical appearance is one of the characteristics of an individual which is immediately apparent to others. To some extent, it may reflect a person's self-concept. The external presentation of self in terms of habitual muscle patterns, modes of body posture and gesture, dress, and so on will reflect the person's self-concept. But attractiveness is also dependent upon heredity and nutrition. There are general standards in the United States about physical attractiveness. Beginning at about age three-and-a-half and on through adulthood, people can independently rate others in terms of their physical attractiveness with a high degree of agreement. Work done by Berscheid, Walster, and Dion (Dion, 1973, 1972; Dion, Berscheid, and Walster, 1972) suggests that this physical attractiveness is a primary form of evaluation of the person, and that attractiveness has a significant effect on the responses of both teachers and peers to the person.

When young children see a peer as attractive, they are more likely to want that peer as a friend than when they perceive the person as unattractive. Part of the explanation for this greater choosing of attractive children as friends by these preschoolers may be because they also saw the unattractive children as more likely to show a variety of behaviors which young children do not like—fighting, hitting, saying angry things—while the attractive children were more likely to be seen as friendly, helping, and not hitting others. The interesting thing is that these judgments were made on the basis of photographs of children who were not known to the children making the ratings. While personal knowledge of the children may modify the results somewhat, it seems likely that the initial perception of attractiveness will have a major influence on the expectations of behaviors and the interpretation of the behaviors from attractive and unattractive children, and this will condition, to some extent, the ways in which they actually interact with peers and teachers. These expectations and evaluations are particularly important in understanding how peers react to the child with obvious physical handicaps. Facial deformities are particularly rejected by young children, although all handicaps appear to detract from the attractiveness of the child.

The perception of attractiveness also influences teachers' evaluations of the children's behavior. Attractive children are generally given the benefit of the doubt when they do something wrong. The wrong action is seen as less willful and less harmful when done by an attractive rather than an unattractive child. In fact, misbehavior by an unattractive child is more likely to be seen as a reflection of an enduring and characteristic way of behaving for that child.

It seems likely, then, that physical attractiveness is one of the bases of the expectations which teachers have of the ways in which children will perform in their classroom. Rosenthal and Jacobsen (1968) and others have shown that teachers' expectations have a significant impact on the actual achievement of the child in the classroom. When the teacher expects the child to do well, a variety of messages are given which tend to reinforce positive performance, and negative performance tends to be overlooked. The teacher is apt to give the child for whom he has high expectations extra attention and more opportunities for learning, while systematically excluding the child for whom he has low expectations from learning opportunities. When a child for whom the teacher has low expectations performs well in the classroom, the teacher is apt to respond relatively negatively, both through not recognizing the child's achievement and through devaluing what the child does achieve.

Physical attractiveness is one source of teachers' expectations about the behavior and achievement of the child; social class of the child is an extremely important additional source. Teachers tend to be upwardly mobile people who themselves came from lower-middle-class backgrounds, and they tend to reinforce middle-class standards and values. Lower-class children are perceived to be less motivated toward school work and to be less able. They may arrive at their first school experience with a different set of values and behaviors than those valued by the teacher. Hence, their initial experience in the classroom may reflect the expectation the teacher has: i.e., that the lower-class children will bring less to school and gain less from school. The teacher may then provide fewer opportunities for the lower-class children to learn, thereby ensuring that the teacher's prediction of differences in performance will come true. Rist (1970) has shown, for example, how one teacher almost never called on the lower-class children in her first grade and placed them in a position in the classroom where they had less eye contact with her and were less able to see the blackboard. Not surprisingly, by the end of the first grade they had not learned as much as the middle-class children in the classroom, and continued to perform poorly in school for the next two years at least.

Part of the difficulty, of course, arises from the fact that some of the initial stereotypes may have some basis in fact. Additional difficulties stem from the effect that the implementation of self-fulfilling prophecies has on actual learning, on self-perceptions, and on levels of aspiration. Children do not arrive in school at the same level of development, with the same skills, or even the same values. To some extent, lower-class parents are less sure about what is necessary for success in school and tend to emphasize the child's obedience, while middle-class parents are more apt to emphasize the child's learning. The middle-class child may be more used to picture books, to listening to stories being read, and so on. The child who arrives at school hungry because there was nothing to eat for breakfast that morning will pay less attention during the day. When, in addition to these realities, the experiences that lower-class children have in school demonstrate to them that they are inept, their level of aspiration will be lowered until it is in keeping with their actual level of performance. Because children can know themselves only in terms of how others respond to them, consistent feedback from the teacher that they are poor students will lead to the concept of *I am a poor student* being integrated into their perceptions of themselves. This in turn will lead them to behaviors which confirm that image of themselves and to a rejection of success experiences in school as accidental, not in keeping with who they really are, and therefore not a true reflection of the self (Kallen, 1972).

PART III

(What do they do all day? The role of play and other everyday activities in the child's development, and how we can influence it.)

PLAY IS THE CHILD'S WORK

Observant adults know that the play of children is serious business. Watch the toddler trying to learn how to open the cupboard door, the three-year-old intently "reading" a book, and the fours in fantasy play riding on an imaginary bus or train. They are rehearsing for life, learning how the physical and social world around them works, and testing hypotheses they would not be able to articulate. It is easy for adults—especially busy parents—to feel that when children are playing they are "just having fun" or even "wasting time." Nursery and preschools can perform a very important function not only by providing appropriate play settings and materials for children, but by educating parents about the importance of play in their child's development. Let us look in more detail at some of the functions of play in the development of young children.

1. *Exploratory play: cognitive and motor development.* Manipulation of the physical environment is one of the outstanding aspects of play from infancy through adulthood. Even the newborn (Brazelton, Scholl, and Robey, 1966) is equipped with the sensory capacity to look intently at what is interesting (Fantz, 1963), following and tracking visually within the first few hours of life. Sound and tactile stimulation are also important for young infants, and these needs increase in complexity with age. Watch a young baby playing with its hands, holding them in front of the eyes, then away, in the mouth, then out again, and how he smiles in pure delight as he discovers his toes! He is exploring the physical reality most easily accessible: his own body. In the process, something very important is happening: the discovery of body boundaries. What is "me" is what I feel being touched as I touch it. What is "not-me" is what I touch but do not feel being touched at the same time. It is a very complicated concept and one that a baby lacks the capacity to express at this point, yet it is the beginning of the sense of "self" (Sullivan, 1953).

Janet was the youngest of three children under the age of four. Her mother, a single parent, was overwhelmed by the financial responsibilities and the physical effort involved in taking care of three small children, two of whom were still in diapers. When Janet began to creep and explore the house at seven months of age, she constantly got into danger. She pulled on the lamp cords and tore the telephone book. Her mother spanked her and put her to bed more and more often. After awhile Janet learned to gain mother's approval by sitting quietly in one spot and turning a toy over and over in her hand. By the time Janet entered nursery school at age three, she was both timid about trying new physical activities and somewhat clumsy from lack of previous practice.

John, at fifteen months, wandered into the kitchen and began to try to climb a step stool. He worked very hard, but without success, at getting to the top. When his mother came into the kitchen and tried to help him, he screamed in violent protest. To John the important thing was not being at the top of the stool, but getting there himself. At the same time he was learning both how to get his body to do what he wanted it to do and the present limits of his own capabilities. His mother realized her mistake in assuming that he was trying only to *be* at the top and instead of putting him there, she stood close by to prevent him from falling, but let him continue the exploration on his own. By the time he was three, John was actively exploratory, with good large motor coordination and skill in climbing.

Children learning to do the things they have chosen on their own to learn are as intent as any adult with a challenging task. They do not know that they are learning, and this is important, especially as children become older and wary of things that are "good for them." Sara, age three, received a set of puzzles for her birthday. She was fascinated by the challenge they presented. With her mother's help, she worked them over and over until she was tired. The next morning Sara's mother discovered her up early working on them before breakfast. She didn't know that she was practicing a complex set of tasks including the recognition of shapes and eye-hand coordination skills. It is hard to imagine that she would have worked anywhere nearly so long and devotedly on anything externally imposed, whether for a grade or any other external reward. It is this natural love of mastering the environment and gaining control over their bodies, their surroundings, learning what consequences follow what antecedents, that many children bring with them to the preschool setting. They are more likely to bring this interest if their caretakers have given them opportunities to explore the environment on their own terms while protecting them from things which are physically dangerous to them. The more we can recognize this and aid it by providing appropriate materials and then staying out of their way, and by finding games and tasks that will be fun for children and meet our learning goals for them at the same time, the more we will aid rather than interfere with the natural thirst for mastery that children bring with them.

2. *Developing motor skills.* It is difficult to separate play into artificial categories. Most children's play combines several or all of the components we discuss as separate components. The motor aspect of play is perhaps the most obvious example. Almost any kind of play, even if it is extremely

stationary, will involve motor skills to some extent. The infant crawling after a toy is practicing crawling; the toddler watching a pull toy bob up and down is learning to walk sideways and backwards; the preschooler catching and throwing a ball, jumping rope, skipping, and playing tag is developing large motor strength and coordination. The same is true of the fine motor area. Looking at books involves not only cognitive skills of recognition, comprehension, and increasing vocabulary, but equally important the prereading skills of eye movement and learning to turn pages without tearing them. Building with blocks, painting and coloring, dressing and undressing dolls, cutting with scissors, and moulding clay are all play activities that children enjoy immensely, engage in spontaneously if materials are made available, and contribute to mastery of their own bodies and objects in the world around them.

Individual differences in motor development of children of the same age may be great, not only because of biological differences in rate of development, which in normal children will tend to even out over time, but also because of differences in sex and in individual experiences. During the preschool and early primary school years, girls have a tendency to have better developed fine motor skills than boys of the same age. We do not know whether this is due to some inherent biological difference or whether it is due to the differences in the way boys and girls have been treated earlier in life. Differences in the experiences which particular children have had can also account for very great differences in where they start when they enter the preschool setting. Jenny came from a family that loved to play ball. Everyone in the family loved ball games of all sorts. They watched ball games on television; they played Ping-Pong, baseball, and football in their backyard. Daddy went golfing every weekend, and the children were regularly taken to the bowling alley where both parents bowled in leagues every week. One of Jenny's first presents was a ball. By the time she was two, she could catch and throw a ball as well as most four-year-olds. At three, she was scornful of children who did not identify balls by their correct names: tennis ball, golf ball, football, and so on. Other children may have similar experiences in different areas. Henry, the son of an artist, painted and drew from very early in life. Although there may have been a genetic component to his talent, it probably could be explained just as easily on the basis of practice in a family setting in which art was important. Children basically want to be like the adults they love, and so they imitate the behavior of their parents and other important adults.

3. *Play as anticipatory socialization.* The idea that children model adults is not new, and yet it is an idea that can make us, as adults, very uncomfortable. Listen to children playing house: "Johnny, you've been bad, you're a disgrace to this family, go to bed immediately!" "Do I sound

like that?" mothers ask themselves. Maybe, maybe not. Children also imitate and try out things they hear from people other than their parents. It is an oversimplification, then, to assume that all social behavior we see in children is "what they learned at home." Just as they imitate language and motor activities, children are eager to try different social behaviors on for size and see what happens. The end product of this experimentation is likely to be determined by a complex combination of modeling and interpersonal consequences, both of which we can change, incidentally, with resulting impact on the child's behavior. We will talk more about this later.

The playing of different roles is part of anticipatory socialization. When Mary and Greg play house, not only are they reflecting what they have learned from their own parents and from others about what mothers and fathers do, but they are also trying out ways that they might behave when they become parents. When a group of children in the classroom play bus, they are exploring the roles of passengers, bus driver, and conductor and thus anticipating how they might behave on an actual bus trip. At the same time, the role of the conductor enables them to learn something about the world of work. In play, of course, it is safe to make mistakes, to explore different alternatives for how a role can be played, and to pick different role models at different times in an attempt to see how they fit the developing concept of who I am and how I relate to others.

On whom, then, do children try these social experiments? The answer is on all of us, adults and children, in the child's world. This experimentation with different behaviors is extremely important. The child is laying the foundation for interactions with people later in life. It is good for children to experiment here as it is in other areas of play. The child who is too restricted by a rigid environment will have lost some very important learning. We see such children occasionally, so restricted in their behavior that they do not seem like children at all, sitting stiffly in a chair, afraid to move lest they be spanked. Without intervention, such children will grow up to be socially impoverished human beings. Awkward, fearful, hostile, or just uncomfortable, they will be unable to interact spontaneously (Maurer, 1973, 1974). The early childhood years, before the demands for at least minimal compliance and conformity that school imposes, are the best years for this social experimentation. In the sections on the development of values and social skills, we will talk more about how the adult may most effectively guide these experiments in the directions that we wish them to take.

A word about the development of sex-appropriate social roles is needed here. Children have a natural tendency to identify with their parents. First, usually, they identify with mother, the parent who is apt to spend more time with them in the earliest years of their development. Then, gradually, around ages three to five, they identify more strongly with, that is, imitate more behaviors of, the parent of the same sex as the child. It used to be that this was accepted uncritically as part of the natural order of things; indeed, it was fostered by parents who feared that they might raise a sex-inappropriate child. Sanctions against boys who acted like girls were generally heavier than against girls who acted like boys; the "tomboy" was a familiar figure and parents were generally reassured by the idea that she would "grow out of it." In contrast to this attitude toward girls is the story of an eighteen-month-old boy who was playing with an old pocket-book which, it happened, contained a brick. He was delightedly lugging it around, enjoying his strength, when some teenage boys came along. "Look at him, he looks like a girl," they ridiculed. He never touched the pocket-book again.

Definitions of gender-appropriate behaviors are in the process of change in American society. As we depend more and more on mechanical energy for labor, as it becomes necessary to keep a large proportion of young people out of the labor force by sending them to college, as equality between the sexes becomes an increasingly important part of our legal system, the old distinctions in socialization of males and females appear to be less appropriate to many. Is there really any reason a boy shouldn't play with dolls? Perhaps this early rehearsal might make him a more comfortable father someday. Is it really detrimental to girls to let them play with trucks in the sand box? Maybe they might feel more comfortable around mechanical equipment later in life, rather than seeing competence in this area as "unfeminine." Because we really don't know which of the differences we now see in behavior between boys and girls are biologically linked and which are a result of differential socialization, it seems best to treat children as children with their individual needs and behaviors, without making unnecessary distinctions between the sexes in activities or responsibilities. Our differential treatment of children by sex starts early in life, from infancy onward (Moss, 1967). Because of this it will probably be a very long time before we know the answers to our questions about differences in behavior according to sex.

4. *Interpersonal consequences of behavior.* One of the most important things a child can learn from social play involving other children or adults is "what happens when I do this?" In play involving the physical manipulation of objects, consequences follow naturally from what the child does. Put a ball at the top of an inclined plane, it rolls down, every time. Throw a block straight up in the air and it goes up, then down, and if it lands on your head it hurts. Pour water on your playsuit and it will be wet. Pretty soon, children learn these things because they always follow the initiating act in the same way. Interpersonal relationships are much more complicated because different consequences follow the same initiating behavior

with different people as well as with the same people at different times. This is a much more interesting experiment, and it can make life difficult for parents and teachers while it is making life interesting for the child.

Call Mommy by her first name the way Daddy does, and people may laugh at first at how cute it is. Later, Mommy may get mad and tell you *no*, rather sternly, but if you try it again when she is in an especially good mood, she may laugh again. Even better, try repeating a word you heard an angry driver yell at the car in front of him. Anything could happen. Some people will laugh, there will be shocked silences other times, almost certainly all adult conversation will stop and all attention will focus on you. That's a pretty powerful word! You may get spanked for saying it, or sent to your room, or your little brother may pick it up and you may have the fun of seeing him get into trouble. All in all, it's a lot more interesting than putting water on your playsuit.

Similar experiments go on all the time between children. What happens when you push somebody or refuse to share a toy? You may find yourself playing alone and that's not much fun, so you gradually learn to co-operate. It may work, however, and you may always get the other kids to do what you want to do—at nursery school; but at home in your neighborhood, you may get punched for the same behavior. These are the kinds of social experiments we carry on all our lives. The consequences we have experienced before will shape what we try the next time and, ultimately, what kind of social human beings we become.

5. *Play as a symbolic language for the expression of feelings.* One of the most important functions of play, and perhaps the one most overlooked by adults, is its symbolic meaning. Play is an extremely important way for the child to express feelings indirectly. Just as children act out in fantasy play the things they have seen and heard around them, so do they act out the feelings inside them, particularly those feelings which would be unacceptable to them or to us if expressed directly (Fraiberg, 1959).

When Jeannie's mother brought her new baby sister home, she was delighted. After the new baby had been home about a week, Jeannie said, "When are we going to take her back to the hospital?" The child was expressing a perfectly normal sentiment. Baby sisters and brothers are not very interesting for very long, especially if, in anticipation of the new arrival, the child has been picturing someone a little bit younger but still old enough to play with. The reality of how long it's going to take before this new addition is big enough to *do* anything with can be quite discouraging.

Let us suppose that her parents had said, "Why, Jeannie, you must love your little sister. She's going to be with us always, we certainly aren't going to take her back. Now, give her a kiss to show you didn't mean it and run off and play." If we peeked in on Jeannie alone with her dolls a few minutes later, we should not be surprised to hear her acting out the story of a family in which the new baby dies, only a week after it comes home from the hospital. Such feelings are perfectly normal, and we should not become overly concerned when these sentiments are expressed in play. The world of play is an appropriate, safe place for children to work out these and other feelings, and rather than interrupting such play we can listen and learn from it what the child may be feeling and what issues the child may be struggling with. Later on we may use this information to understand the child better and offer appropriate help. Let us say that mother overheard Jeannie's play and realized that denying her negative feelings may not have been helpful to her daughter. At bedtime Jeannie goes in to check on her sister "to make sure she's all right," since children, and to some extent adults too, fear that their wishes are powerful and may come true. When mother goes to tuck her in, Jeannie may say, "I really didn't mean what I said about taking her back, she's really a good baby."

This is mother's chance to intervene. "Yes, she is, but it must be hard for you sometimes to have her in the house now. Lots of times I'm busy with her and it must be difficult to have to wait for my attention when you're not used to it. I guess a part of you does wish she would go away."

"Oh no, Mommy, I don't feel that way!"

"Well, most children do feel that way about a new baby in the house, even though they love her too. It's funny sometimes you can feel two ways at the same time." Mother, by giving voice to the negative half of the child's ambivalent feelings toward her baby sister, is helping Jeannie to understand and accept her own feelings, both positive and negative. By bringing the "unacceptable" feelings out in the open, she defuses them and makes it easier for Jeannie to talk about, rather than act on the feelings (Ginott, 1969).

The symbolic aspect of play, then, may be helpful in two ways. First, it may be helpful to the child directly to be able to cope with and master in fantasy what is a problem in reality. Second, it may provide us, as helping adults—parents, teachers, and others—a glimpse into what may be bothering a child so that we can be alert for those occasions when we may be able to intervene to give some help to the child on significant issues. It is this latter method on which play therapy is based. As the child plays, the therapist may comment on the meaning of the play, may participate with the child in bringing the play to some new conclusion, or may gain insights from observing the play that will provide help to parents and teachers in understanding and helping the child. Although teachers may not feel comfortable or appropriate in doing the first two play therapy functions, the last may be very helpful in alerting staff to issues which are important to a given child, and, when appropriate, discussing these with parents. Issues which come up with one child can then be dealt with in the curriculum as well as individually, since most issues will be things many of the children will have to learn to cope with at some time: the arrival of a new baby; going to the doctor or the hospital for tests or surgery; the divorce of parents; the death of a pet, a friend, or a family member; moving to a new home; racial, ethnic, or gender prejudice; and, for children with special handicaps, learning to get along with "normal" children and adults in the world outside a protected environment. Handicapped children may have many special worries not only about how they measure up in terms of what they can do (particularly in competition with normal siblings) but in terms of how others will react to them: staring, laughing, or treating them awkwardly or perhaps too politely. All of these are important issues which young children will play out and which they can discuss for short periods of time in groups with the aid of an understanding teacher and perhaps a carefully selected storybook (e.g. Stein, 1974).

"Childhood is playhood" (p. 63) said A. S. Neill (1960). With the many functions of play as outlined above, we can see why. Play truly is the work of the child in all areas of development: motor, cognitive, social, and emotional. We can foster this development simply by providing a setting in which children can safely give free rein to their natural inquisitiveness.

One of the loveliest aspects of natural play, which applies across all areas mentioned above, is that play provides a safe setting in which to make mistakes. It is "safe" in both the physical and emotional senses. Play environments for young children should include equipment which is appropriate for their size and age, and toys should include such features as extreme sturdiness, absence of rough or sharp edges, and absence of small detailing which may restrict imaginative use of the toy and may be easily broken. Good toys invite the active participation of the child rather than making the child a passive observer as so many of today's expensive mechanical toys do. In the emotional sense, play provides a safe place for making mistakes because, in spite of the earnest realism with which children participate in play, they know that it is not real. The scary ghost with the sheet over his head was Tommy just a minute ago, and will be Tommy again, so the child can be somewhat in charge of how much fear he can handle. The grand lady who invited you to tea won't really be angry if you spill the sugar all over her new tablecloth and eat all the cookies, because the cookies, tablecloth, and sugar are all "pretend" and the grand lady is your best friend, Sally. If you put the pieces of the puzzle together the wrong way, it won't really make any difference, the puzzle will just look funny, and if it's really too hard for you to enjoy you can simply put it away and come back to it three months later when it looks interesting again. In some ways, we adults who take our work so seriously may find this the hardest aspect of play to accept: if you do it "wrong" it doesn't matter. We want so much for children to master new skills and meet new challenges that it is easy for us to lose sight of the fact that although we know that play is good for the child, the child doesn't know it and is doing it for sheer fun. If we begin to demand that things done in play be done "right"—the dog colored brown and not purple, the broom used to sweep the floor, not ridden as a pony—we will make the child self-conscious and achievement-oriented, and end by interfering with the learning we wish to foster. By letting children alone to make their own mistakes and learn from them in their own way, and by providing help to a minimal degree and when requested, we will allow them to find their own creative solutions which will be much more useful than any that we could teach them.

VALUES AND HOW TO SHAPE THEM

The title of this section may come as a bit of a shock. We generally think of values as something to be taught in the home, and rightly so, as parents differ in their personal beliefs of right and wrong. What we often overlook, however, is that it simply is not possible to avoid teaching children values if we are going to interact with them at all. Through modeling as adults those behaviors that children will invariably copy, and through all the rules we set for them, which ones we enforce, and the very way we look at a child—smiling, frowning, or quizzical—we teach and shape values. Even a completely laissez-faire setting, such as certain communes have attempted, teaches values: it teaches children to value an unstructured way of doing things. Try as we might, we cannot avoid teaching children values.

If this is so, then, what values do we wish to teach? This is a fundamental question which all parents and professionals in charge of educational and care settings for young children should ask themselves. To fail to examine the question is to teach without knowing what we are teaching, and we may be disappointed with the consequences when it is too late to have an impact on them.

Perhaps we could start by examining some of the values that have been taught in recent years past to children in grade school. They have been a very middle-class set of values both in the sense that they tend to be valued by people in the middle class and that they tend to be exhibited more by middle-class children, whom the school would then reward for good behavior. Such values include neatness, punctuality, hard work, competitiveness, respect for authority, conformity, and achievement orientation. These values have been under fire in recent years and we may wish to keep some, downplay others, and modify still others. By modification, we mean that it is possible to teach children a *relativistic* set of values in which the amount of importance assigned to a given behavior may vary with the situation. For example, in a fire drill, conformity and respect for authority are extremely important values, and the emphasis given them could make the difference between safety and harm in the event of a real fire. It would make sense, therefore, to impress upon children the importance of conforming and following directions from authority figures such as teachers and fire fighters during fire drills. On the other hand, conformity is the value least to be desired during a lesson in creative art. The child who has no sense of what to do except copy the work of someone else has failed to gain the most from this activity. Similarly, respect for authority can be carried too far and can interfere with values which may be more desirable in a given situation, such as care for the safety of others (Nazi Germany provided the world with a fine example of this). (See also Milgram, 1974.)

As the above examples illustrate, we do have relativistic sets of values as adults. All ot us weigh all the time whether we should, in a given situation, value respect for authority or forthrightness; honesty or care not to hurt the feelings of others; the rights of ourselves or the rights of others. So why do we not teach to children what we do ourselves? We believe it is for a very realistic reason: that as adults we realize that children lack the same capacity for reasoned judgment that we, hopefully, possess. Young children, especially, simply lack the capacity for abstract thinking that makes many value decisions possible.

If, then, we want to teach young children relativistic values but at the same time we recognize that they are cognitively unable to handle complex value decisions, what do we do? First, we can weigh our own values carefully; then we can make a deliberate attempt to teach children our value hierarchy rather than to teach each value as an absolute. Most importantly, we can teach them that not all adults agree on what is important in life, just as our beliefs differ with respect to political issues or what religion we practice. Recognizing that there is seldom any absolutely one right way will be a large step toward teaching children tolerance for the beliefs of others, a value that, hopefully, we can agree we would like to instill in young children.

Many adults think that this is too complicated for young children, that it will only confuse them or make them think there is no sense in trying to do what is right since what is right may change with the situation, time, or place. But if we think about it, we are already teaching young children to make such discriminations regarding their behavior: you urinate in the toilet, not on the furniture; you eat food, not dishwasher detergent; you climb up into Daddy's lap and wrinkle his evening paper when he's in a good mood, not when he's scowling over the stock market; you can bang on pots and pans at home but not at Grandma's. Children can and do learn these things at a very early age because they are a natural part of our lives and we don't have to stop and consciously think of them. If we try to become more aware of our value decisions, we can be more deliberate in helping the child to become sensitized to them too. As the child grows older, he can take additional responsibility for making more difficult value decisions.

The most powerful and effective tools we have for teaching our own values to children are *modeling* and *differential reinforcement. Modeling* takes advantage of the natural tendency that children have to copy what they see the important adults in their lives doing. If we wish to teach children to value honesty, for example, it is important that we model honesty for them by being honest ourselves with other adults and with them. This includes sometimes having to say to a child "I am sorry, I made a mistake," or "I don't know the answer to that question." Adults sometimes fear that this will make children lose respect for their elders, but in fact it works in just the opposite way. Children learn to trust and respect adults who can matter of factly admit their own limits. Likewise, we can model our value hierarchy regarding honesty by admiring Aunt Betty's new sofa and then confiding later to the child, "I really wasn't fond of that sofa, but didn't see any point in hurting Aunt Betty's feelings about it."

Adults sometimes feel stymied by the idea that modeling is so important when they want to do things that they would not approve of their children doing. This can be a sore point between spouses in some cases. Here again, though, the relative value hierarchy can be explained. "Mommy and Daddy can stay up late because they are grown-ups. Children have to go to bed earlier because they need more rest. When you are grown up you can decide how late to stay up too." Explanations like this which are honest and simple are understood by young children. The nursery school can handle differences in practice between school and home in the same way. "When you are at home, your family does it that way. Here we do it this way." No judgment need be made about one way being better than the other. They are simply different. Children can accept this sort of explanation matter of factly if we can give it matter of factly. Of course, parents need to be in on the planning of values to be taught in the preschool so that major conflicts between school and home do not develop.

Differential reinforcement refers to the consequences which follow a particular behavior. When the child says "please," do we compliment and smile or ignore this politeness? Do we follow "thank you" with "you are welcome," or is it only when the child fails to be polite that we notice? Positive rewards have a much more effective and lasting influence than negative reinforcement. This means that we ought to notice and reward with a smile or a word of appreciation or a hug whenever we see children behaving in ways of which we approve. When the child fails to do what we expect, it is better to ignore this failing and wait for the next opportunity for praise than to criticize the child. One only needs to observe how uncomfortably little children squirm—when parents are constantly saying, "Say thank you. Did he say thank you? Say thank you to the nice lady"—to understand that the major effect of this interaction is to make the child feel embarrassed about saying thank you and the parents to feel that they have shown to the world that they are "good parents." Recalling the value of modeling should also make us aware that using primarily positive reinforcement will tend to set a more positive, pleasant model for the child to follow in interacting with other human beings, as opposed to being constantly critical of others.

There are times, of course, when some harm to people or property (more often the latter) may occur if the child's behavior is ignored rather than stopped. The preschool has the advantage over the home here in that most of the physical setting has been designed to be "childproof": sturdy and not easily destroyed. In situations where some intervention from an adult is necessary, it is important to have a consistent way of handling the situation which is applied in the same way over time and which emphasizes redirecting the behavior rather than merely scolding. In this way, the child will come to learn that certain consequences will follow his behavior each time, and that the particular behavior is unacceptable, but that there are alternative, acceptable ways of solving the problem. Using *prescriptive* (telling the child what to do) rather than *proscriptive* (telling the child what not to do) language helps the child to see more clearly what it is that he is supposed to do.

As an example, let us suppose that you see Timmy with a large maple block in his hand, about to bring it down on the head of Joey, who has a toy he wants. As you move swiftly toward them you say, "Timmy, put the block down" (prescriptive), reaching his side in time to follow through and enforce this limit by "helping" him put it down, if necessary. If he is not very angry and upset, you may be able to redirect his activity, e.g. "Come and see what we are painting," without further ado. If there is more emotion involved than that, some resolution of the conflict at hand may need to take place before the activity can be successfully redirected. "It looks as though you are angry at Joey" (labeling the child's feelings). "Here when we are angry with people we tell them" (your value statement). At this point, you can have the child practice this by telling Joey he is angry (giving him an acceptable, alternative way to solve his problem). You can then briefly help the children negotiate how they are going to share the toy, or they may do it with a little help from you, or one of them may easily accept a substitute. It is important to recognize, of course, that very young children have a hard time sharing but that they also are easily distracted to another activity because of their relatively short attention span. Fours and fives can usually share pretty well with occasional help. Twos can be easily distracted, but don't share well. The threes may give the most trouble on this issue while they are in transition from one to the other.

Consistency in handling children's behavior is another issue that worries adults. It is not possible for an entire staff to be consistent in every instance with every child. We are not superhuman. Sometimes three fights are going on at once or you have a headache, or it's Friday at four o'clock, and you just aren't up to it. This is not going to irreparably damage the child. What we mean by consistency is that the preschool should have policies for handling common situations, that the staff should know and understand these policies, and that they should try to follow them as much as possible in the situations to which they apply. Staff members can provide valuable feedback to each other in this regard by routinely observing each other, as it is very easy to become fixed in a pattern of reinforcing a child for particular behaviors (positively or negatively) without being aware of the pattern. In giving feedback to each other, we can follow the same rules that we use with the children—modeling, positive reinforcement, and prescriptive statements are more effective in changing behavior than negative sanctions.

In closing this section on values it is only fair that we, the authors, share some of our values. We believe that the most important thing for children to learn in the preschool years is that they are good, worthwhile people who know how to get along with and enjoy the company of others. In other words, in our value hierarchy, a good self-concept and good interpersonal skills have higher priority than such school-related skills as reading readiness and number concepts. The foregoing discussion and examples are based on this value hierarchy, but the same methods, modeling and differential reinforcement, can be used in the service of other values. We hope that whatever value hierarchy you choose to model and reinforce in your school, the decision will be a conscious one.

DEVELOPMENT OF SOCIAL SKILLS

It makes sense for a discussion of the development of social skills to follow the discussion of value development in young children, as many of the values we hope to teach children during these years have to do with how to get along with other people in the context of our culture. Self-care in toileting and cleanliness, manners, sharing, taking turns, and following directions are all social skills that you probably have on your list of valued tasks for children to master sometime between the ages of two and five. As in other areas of development, children's previous experiences have much to do with where they are in the development of social skills. George's mother had waited years to become pregnant. When she finally had her long-awaited son, she couldn't do enough for him. She loved to feed and dress and play with him. As he advanced from the first to the second year of life, she continued to do everything for him as she had when he was a younger baby. Because she talked to him all the time, he exhibited accelerated language development, but because she did not realize the importance of letting him learn how to care for himself, he arrived at nursery school at age three lacking the skill to partially dress himself, put things away, or take care of himself at the toilet.

Geraldine, on the other hand, was the youngest child of a busy mother of four. Although her mother was sometimes too impatient to wait for her to try to dress herself when the family was in a hurry to go somewhere, most often she was interrupted partway through feeding or dressing Geraldine by another child who needed her to find a missing mitten or school lunch. Consequently, Geraldine had many opportunities to experiment with putting on her shirt (or taking it off!) and trying her hand at using a spoon. As soon as she was able to help, her siblings encouraged her to pick up toys because it made less work for them. By the time she was three, she could do a pretty good job of dressing herself (except for buttons and laces) and would pitch right in to help clean up scattered toys.

With children of the same age starting preschool with such different skills, then, it is helpful to have some general time perspective in mind. Children do not learn all of these things overnight. Sometimes they seem to be making progress in one area but standing still in another. There may be growth spurts of improvement in all areas at once and periods where none at all is seen. This can be frustrating for the staff, whose curriculum may be based on smooth progression from one stage to the next. It may be helpful to plot the progress of individual children as a reminder of where they are and how far they have come over time. This is not only useful to help staff remember the level of a particular child, but can also be used as an incentive for the (older) children themselves, if they can earn stars or check marks for successes in an area where they need work. You will recognize this method from the previous section, of course, as one form of positive reinforcement, and here again, coupled with modeling, you have powerful tools with which to work.

It is most helpful if as many of the skills you are working with as possible can be practiced in the form of a game. The stars, then, if used, should not become deadly serious or competitive, but interesting and fun. It is also important that they should not become the main focus for the activity, but rather used as a way of making progress concrete, so the child can "see" the achievement. If the only reason for doing the activity is to earn an extrinsic reward, such as a star, the activity itself will come to have no value to the child and will be stopped very soon after the use of stars is discontinued (Levine and Fasnacht, 1974). Similarly, manners can be practiced by "dressing up" as adults (an activity children love) and play-acting going to a tea party or a wedding or whatever the children choose. Putting toys away can become a game of parking all the cars in the garage, or bedding down the dolls for the night. "Let's put the blocks away," is more fun than, "You put the blocks away." Pictures of the toys pasted to the shelf or cupboard where they belong, accompanied by handprinted signs, "dolls," "blocks," and so on, not only make it easier for the children to remember where things belong but help them to associate two- and three-dimensional objects with printed words. Your staff will be able in brainstorming sessions to think of many more creative ideas to turn learning socially important skills into interesting games which are appropriate to the needs of the particular children you serve.

It is also helpful to have certain routines which happen the same way every day, as these can be the beginnings of building desirable habit patterns in young children. For example, every day after outdoor play we come inside, use the toilet, wash our hands, and go to the story corner until lunchtime. The content can be whatever you want it to be, but the use of a certain routine that the child can depend on every day can give him or her the feeling of learning how to do something really well, so well it becomes easy. This is called "overlearning," and things which are "over-learned" are especially well remembered and retained in years to come. If you think back you may be able to remember some routine or song or nursery rhyme that you repeated so often that you can recall it easily, even as an adult. For the same reason, we wish to break up repetitious undesirable habit patterns because they can be overlearned in the same way if they are allowed to continue without interference (smoking is a good example of this in adults). A skill that a child has overlearned is usually one which he will take pride in teaching to a newer or younger member of the group, and this adds to the feeling of mastery.

CONTROL OF UNMANAGEABLE FEELINGS AND THE DEVELOPMENT OF LANGUAGE

One of the most important developmental changes which we see taking place in human beings from infancy to adulthood is the ability to control, handle, or manage feelings which earlier were overwhelming. The young infant is totally given over to the internal body state of the moment. Hunger, pain, unpleasant extremes of temperature, wetness, all are given the full expression of a lusty cry. This is adaptive for the infant who cannot move about to open or shut the window, go to the refrigerator, or successfully roll away from the infamous diaper pin. Gradually, the infant learns that the appearance of the caretaker is soon followed by relief from the overwhelmingly unpleasant feeling which was the cause of the crying. When the child stops crying at the very sight of mother, having learned that the nipple in the mouth will soon follow, is a very important step. This is the beginning of mastery of the feeling, when the infant can imagine, or fantasize, even for a brief period of time, that the present state of feeling can possibly change or disappear, that "I *will* feel better. This torture *will* cease."

The infant whose care has consistently resulted in this kind of relief from unpleasant feelings gradually learns to delay the gratification of the immediate need for longer and longer periods of time. We don't know, of course, exactly how the world seems to the infant, but we can guess that early in this process there is only a vague sort of feeling that mother will make everything all right, without any real understanding of how her appearance is followed by increasing feelings of well-being. We can see this sort of blind trust and faith in toddler-aged children who feel so much better when the parent is present during painful medical treatments, such as inoculations. We can also, perhaps, guess at their terror when this magic does not always work and sometimes unpleasant things are not relieved or prevented by the presence of the caretaking parent. Luckily, the next step in this process gives the child even more ability to manage and control feelings, partly by gaining greater control over the environment and partly by providing a better way for fantasy and imagining to work. This step is the development of language.

In homes where the cooings and babblings of infants are encouraged and responded to with attention such as smiling, looking, and talking back to the infant, parents are shaping the development of language in their child without being aware of it. This is how we all learn to talk, some sooner, some later, by a combination of listening and copying the sounds we hear and experimentation with the various noises we can produce. Studies of the babbling of infants reared in different cultures have shown that very early in life all babies babble in pretty much the same way, but after a few months of exposure to the particular language of their culture they are selectively using more and more of the sounds of their own language and fewer of the sounds which do not appear in the language they hear spoken around them. That is, the babbling of the six-month-old Chinese baby sounds different from that of the French baby. One fine day, simply by chance, the infant will produce a sound which has meaning in the language of its parents, "mamma." What an uproar of delight there is then, if someone (especially mother) happens to be listening! If there is a very interesting, positive response whenever this chance event occurs, the infant will gradually come to associate his sound production with all the attention and will produce that sound more and more. One magic day the infant will say "mamma" and cause her to appear! This is the beginning of the realization that things have names and that one can produce them, seemingly out of nowhere, simply by pronouncing that magical name.

(The fairy tale of Rumpelstiltskin is based upon this primitive idea [Clodd, 1889; Fenichel, 1945].) Gradually, as more words are learned, this magical control is extended to include more and more objects, and hence, greater mastery of the environment. Now the child can ask for milk, pudding, or cookie rather than simply crying with hunger and then frustration when the wrong food is presented.

Partly because increased motor skills are leading to increasing mobility on the part of the child at about the same time as language is beginning to be established, one particularly powerful word soon gains a prominent place of importance, "no." When the caretaker says that magic word, wishes are not granted, desires are frustrated, and sometimes even a bodily insult—a slap or a spank—is received. This is a most upsetting development and continues to be so throughout life, but the blow is softened when the next discovery is made, "I can say 'no' too!" This is a tremendous discovery. The child can use this most powerful magic and it works, too. Not all the time. Not always in the way one had hoped, but still, things happen differently. Sometimes choices are presented, alternatives worked out. The child has learned an important first lesson in the handling of negative feelings: to express them clearly and directly and have them understood. Crying, of course, is not given up easily or immediately, especially as long as it continues to be effective in obtaining results. But the two-year-old who can say a two-word sentence cries less than the two-month-old, and the four-year-old who can really put feelings and thoughts into words cries a good deal less than either of them. In encouraging children to put their feelings into words so we can understand them better instead of just crying, however, we must remember that there is a certain value in the regressive experience of crying for people of all ages under stress. As one little girl put it, when told there was really nothing to cry about, "I know, but I just have a feeling of crying."

By the time most children enter nursery school, then, they have the most important basic tools for the handling of overwhelming feelings already at their disposal, though yet in unrefined fashion. They have begun to learn to wait for needs to be satisfied, and they have begun to use language to help in this process of mastery. Most of this process goes on internally, but an adult is sometimes let in on it when a child is overheard in private conversation with the self. "First we wash our hands, then we have lunch." "Bobby didn't mean to hurt me, it was an accident."

To hear the words we say to children being repeated and internalized in this fashion should make us more keenly aware of how we speak to children so that our phrases will be most useful to them when they become integrated. We will have more to say about this in the next section on the development of internal controls.

Psychologists who have studied the relationship between language and perception have found that when people have verbal labels for things, it is much easier for them to recognize those things. For example, in a study in which a figure flashed onto a screen was called a "design," it was less perceptually stable than when the same figure was called a "letter." Having a verbal label helped the children to see the image more clearly, even when it was out of focus (McKinney, 1966). Similarly, the child who has learned "goat," "cow," "pig," and "deer" also learns to recognize the differences between these animals and can distinguish them in nonverbal test situations, such as matching tasks; while to the child who has not learned these words, they are all "doggie," or "horsie." Naming, indeed, does give us more power over our environment, just as in the fairy tales.

What this means for helping the child with feelings is that the more words we can teach children that they can use in communicating their feelings to another person, the more control they will have. They will learn to recognize more clearly that not all "feeling bad" is the same and that not all bad feelings have the same remedy. The more clearly they can express and understand what is happening to them, the easier it will be to get help from an adult. This, in turn, will eventually lead to learning how adults solve such a problem and enable the child, gradually, to do more and more problem-solving on his own. In addition to all these advantages, the child who can say in words how he feels and who can receive in turn understanding listening from adults does not have to "act out" the feelings nonverbally through temper tantrums, hitting others, or other nonverbal behavior. Again, it is important to recognize that this is a slow process which takes place over time, and which is, in fact, a lifelong task. Many adults have never learned really adequate ways of identifying and expressing what they feel, both negative and positive. Such people may have a variety of difficulties, from feeling vaguely dissatisfied or out of touch with others all the way to very unhappy love relationships or aggressive acting out. Children with special needs either in the form of deprived family backgrounds (emotionally or economically) or physical handicaps have particular reason to learn to identify and express feelings because these children are least likely to be easily understood by the rest of us, since we see them as different from ourselves.

Probably the feelings which we most want to help the child learn to handle, because they seem to be the most overwhelming, are variations of anger, fear, or sadness. Some specific examples are given below of useful ways to help children deal with these particularly unpleasant feelings.

Anger: Anger is perhaps the feeling which adults are most interested in bringing under control in children. It is most disruptive to other ongoing activities because it may result in damage to property or injury to others and it also frightens most of us, somewhat, even as adults. Most people in our culture are at some level frightened not only of the anger of others, but of their own anger. In dealing with the anger of children, then, it is useful for us to identify our own feelings about the expression of anger and try to sort out which are our personal reactions due to our own rearing and life experiences, and which have more to do with concern for the safety and development of the child. This should help us to learn not to overreact, but to stay as calm and task-oriented as if we were dealing with a problem of a different sort. This is important because it reassures the child that his anger, which feels so overwhelming, uncontrollable, and frightening, does not scare the adults.

An important first step is to *reflect the feeling*. This is so helpful that we should learn to do it routinely both as a way of telling the child, "I understand what you feel, your message has gotten through," as well as giving the child a label for the feeling, as discussed above. The message should be kept simple and direct, "You're angry!" or "You really look mad!" This will usually lead the child to confirm and elaborate on what you have said (if you were correct in your identification of the feeling). "Tommy took my truck." "That made you feel angry." "Yes, he's mean and rotten and I hate him." "You're really mad at him." "Yeah."

On many occasions an exchange such as this is enough to make the child feel better and defuse the anger. He can then be gently directed toward another activity, after his anger seems to have been dispelled by being understood. Sometimes this labeling alone is not enough and the adult can help Tommy and Joey negotiate a way of sharing or taking turns. Children can also be taught to express their anger directly to the child they are angry with as an alternative to hitting. At first, you may have to give them the words, "You can say to Tommy, 'I'm angry that you took my truck'." The other child can be helped to respond by apologizing, if appropriate, or by offering to let Joey have it when he is through with his turn, or whatever makes sense in the given situation. Remember not to have standards for the children that are too high. It takes time to learn these skills, and they will often forget and need to be reminded, "We tell each other when we are angry. We don't hit."

Having toys which can be appropriately used to act out aggression is also a useful practice. Inflatable punching dolls, pegboards for pounding, and aggressive animal puppets like alligators and lions with teeth provide an acceptable fantasy outlet for anger and can be used very directly in situations where a child is not able to cool down through having the feeling reflected. "If you feel like you've just got to hit someone, come over here and give Bo Bo (the inflatable toy) a good sock. You can even pretend it's Tommy if you want to." Sometimes the child may enjoy drawing a picture of the person they feel angry at and ripping it up. This is normally not necessary, however, nor is it as useful to Joey as teaching him to deal directly with the person with whom he is angry. It might be used when the target of the anger is not present, like the sibling or neighborhood bully the child had a row with before he came to school that morning. In general what will help the child most is learning to recognize and label the feeling, having it understood, and then learning ways to solve the problem that brought on the feeling. These are skills which are adaptive throughout life.

Fear: There are two major situations in which we are likely to need to know how to deal with fear in young children. One is the situation where something happens that makes all the children feel frightened, such as a child having a seizure in the classroom, or a fire in the school. In situations of this sort, the children need to be reassured as soon as possible that (1) the adults have everything under control and (2) they (the children) didn't cause the event to happen (if true, which it usually is). The child who was playing with the child who had the seizure, for example, or other children who were nearby, will need special reassurance about this. Young children still have an underdeveloped sense of cause and effect and often feel responsible for things which it would not occur to the adults present that they would feel badly about. This is especially true if they have been having negative feelings about the hurt person, since the line between magic and reality is not quite clear. A child can think he caused the distress of the other by thinking bad thoughts. (Many times adults, who know better, feel this way too.)

After the immediate situation is taken care of, it is important for all of the children to be gathered together for a discussion of what happened. Again, mastery of the feeling comes from understanding. The teacher can begin by reflecting the feeling of the group. "We all felt scared when Susie had a seizure. We will feel better if we talk about it." Teacher can then go on to explain, as simply as possible, what a seizure is and that they can expect Susie to feel better after she has had a nap or whatever applies to the given situation. Children should then be encouraged to ask questions or share their thoughts and feelings about what happened. "I was real scared." "I thought she was dying." "I thought Janet pushed her and hurt her." Other children in the group who have a seizure disorder may be able to use this as an opportunity to share what it feels like. Not only can this be a relief for the child if this has previously been a secret, but it may relieve the other children as well to see that another intact member of the group had the same thing happen to him and looks all right. With open discussion and frank answers to questions, the feelings of fearfulness will be dispelled rather quickly, and the children will be ready to go back to their regular activities. Certain children will need to bring up the topic again from time to time in the next few days which can be handled again by reflecting the feeling, "I guess maybe you're wondering if that could happen to you," and giving information, "Susie's doctor gave her medicine to help keep her from having seizures." Handled in this way if the same or another child should have another seizure, the children will be much less frightened and recover much more quickly. This is evidence of mastery.

The second general type of situation which requires our skills in helping children with their fears is the situation in which an individual child is fearful of something which does not frighten the group as a whole. All children have fears of this sort from time to time; some children have many more than others. Examples would be a child who is afraid of animals or of swinging on the swing. In these cases it is probably most useful to comment on the fear without making it a major focus of attention which could tend to be reinforcing for the child. If Bobby squeals and moves away the first day a rabbit is brought into the classroom, the teacher can comment, "I guess it's a little scary for you, Bobby," and go on with the general explanation to the class. Such a child should not be forced to pet the rabbit nor shamed for being frightened by being told he's a big boy who shouldn't be scared or a "fraidy cat." If the adults are rather matter of fact in their response to this type of fear, the other children will pick up this attitude too and be less likely to make fun of the fearful child. If they do tease or call names they can simply be reminded, "We don't do that here. I wonder if you're angry with Bobby about something else." If children ask about why a child has a fear, they can be answered honestly, "I don't know why Bobby is afraid of the rabbit. Lots of children are afraid of different things."

The unpressured communication of expectations that things will change can also be shared with the child. "I guess you will get used to the rabbit after a while. Then you won't feel so scared." This is, indeed, the case. Most fears of this sort will disappear after the child has been exposed to the feared object over time *without being pressured*. Simply the presence of the rabbit sitting quietly in its cage in the classroom nature corner each day will serve to desensitize the child to what had somehow become a frightening stimulus. On his own, Bobby will begin to approach the rabbit more freely and take more chances by playing close to its cage, until he finally gets up the courage to pet it just a little. Many times it is hard for us as adults to leave children alone to do this work at their own pace. When we feel tempted to pressure the child to swing on the swing or pet the rabbit "just this once" because the fear seems so silly to us and we feel so impatient with it, we would do well to ask ourselves, "What difference does it really make if Bobby doesn't pet the rabbit or Carol won't swing?" We may find that our feelings of competence as helpful adults are being threatened by this child's seeming refusal to make progress. If we can smile at ourselves for feeling this way and realistically accept that if this child *never* feels comfortable with rabbits it really won't matter, the child will be able to relax more easily about this problem too.

We have been speaking, of course, of the "normal" fears that all children have to a greater or lesser degree, especially during the preschool years. If you have a child whose fears are so overwhelming that they interfere with his ability to function in major ways, then you need to discuss this with the parents and together decide on what should be done, probably with consultation from other professionals.

Sadness: We adults like to think of childhood as a happy time, and wish it were not necessary to help children with sadness. We wish they never felt it. Unfortunately, they do. Most instances in which children feel sad or hurt are rather transient: a bruised knee, exclusion by others from a game, or disappointment over an expected treat. Again, in these instances, reflecting feelings is very helpful so the child feels understood. "That hurt. You really fell hard. Yes, it hurt." It is surprising how much less crying there is after a fall when the adult present reflects the feeling. Many times the child just picks up and goes on playing from there. If a cut is bleeding, some soothing washing and the application of a Band-Aid to mark the battle scar can go far toward helping the child feel better. One of the things adults sometimes wonder is whether to hug or hold a child who is upset, or whether this will only encourage the behavior by rewarding it. We believe that there is nothing wrong with hugging or holding an upset child to soothe him; indeed, it seems humane: (1) if it's not overdone to the point that the adults are making a big fuss over every little problem the child encounters, and (2) if hugging and lap sitting can also take place when the child is feeling happy and good. It is only when the *only* physical contact a child can get from an adult is by being sad or hurt that one begins to see a child who continually falls out of trees and cries brokenheartedly at the drop of a hat.

In addition to reflecting the child's feeling and giving a soothing hug to the upset child, it is helpful to give the child an opportunity to talk about the feeling. Let the child tell you what happened that was so upsetting, and continue to reflect the feelings you hear to let the child know you are listening. When the child seems to have finished and is feeling better, you can then suggest an activity, perhaps a quiet one such as painting or drawing, and the hurt will heal itself. Many times children are ready to resume what they were doing before at this point, with considerable good cheer. As easily as hurts come, many of them are forgotten.

You may occasionally run into a more difficult situation in which there is a child in the group who is experiencing chronic sadness, that goes on over time, rather than the more usual transient sort we have discussed above. In this instance, after talking with the child, you will probably want to contact the parents to discuss with them what is going on in the family. When a child of this age displays chronic sadness it usually means there is some situation at home which is responsible, such as the death of a relative, divorce of parents, or some other important separation such as mother becoming very ill and going away to the hospital for an extended period of time. In such a family crisis situation it is easy for its effect upon the child to be overlooked because the parents are preoccupied with their own feelings of sadness or fear as well as practical details, such as finances. The preschool can be of tremendous help to such a family in turmoil by continuing to provide a stable environment for the child while the family is upset and by providing the child with caring, listening adults at a time when important adults in the family may be temporarily emotionally unavailable to the child while they are trying to cope with their own feelings.

THE DEVELOPMENT OF INTERNAL CONTROLS

Developing control of oneself from within is one of the things that growing up is all about. Although not all adults achieve optimal levels of self-control, most must develop at least a minimum of self-control in order to avoid the severe sanctions of our society: social ostracism or removal to jails or mental institutions. In the preceding sections we have alluded to many of the kinds of things which may happen to different children to foster or hinder this ultimate expression of social and emotional development. A summary review of the most important factors is given below:

1. *A reasonably predictable environment.* As described in the preceding section, this enables the child to begin to wait for short periods and, gradually, longer periods of time for gratification of needs and desires. If the environment is very unpredictable, that is, if the child cannot trust what will happen, he will not learn to wait for things. This was shown very clearly in an experiment in which an adult told a group of children they could have "one candy bar now, or two later." The following week, the experimenter returned and broke his promise to half of the children who had chosen to wait for the two candy bars, telling them he had run out. Again, they were given a choice of "one candy bar now, or two later." The children to whom the adult had previously broken his promise now chose "one candy bar now." They had learned not to trust the environment. This effect held regardless of the sex, race, or social class of the child. It was not safe to wait (Seagull, 1964).

It is because of this that we spoke of the importance of consistency in the section on the development of values. The preschool teacher can help the child to learn to wait for things by providing a trustworthy, that is, reasonably consistent, predictable interpersonal environment.

2. *Clear, enforced limits or rules.* A child, or anyone, can only follow rules if he knows what they are. If it is all right to hit another child one

day but not the next, pretty soon it may seem hopelessly confusing to know what is acceptable. If the rules are not clear, they can never become internalized as the child's own. This is one reason why we stressed talking with children in the section on values. Making our values for the child's behavior explicit as rules (e.g., "We hang up our coats before we start to play. We wash our hands after we use the toilet.") enables the child to adopt or internalize them as his own.

We can see, then, why global statements like, "Be a good girl," are not really helpful to the child because they are vague. Saying exactly what we mean is more likely to get results and provides the child with a sentence to say to remind himself, "We don't hit other people. We put our toys away."

One sometimes hears children saying such rules to themselves during the stage when they are in transition between being externally controlled (by the adult's rule, enforced by the adult) and internally controlled (by internalized rules felt as conscience, enforced by feelings of doing well, or of guilt when transgressed).

This brings us to the important question of enforcement. If the adult states the rule clearly, and then fails to enforce it when transgressed, this presents a confusing message to the child. "Daddy said I had to go to bed, but when I didn't go, nothing happened." What could this mean?

In such a situation the child soon learns that verbalized adult rules are not "real" rules, since they do not have to be obeyed. If as adults, therefore, we do not feel up to enforcing a rule, we should not give the child that rule. The same is true if we are unable to provide enforcement. We should only verbalize rules we can enforce. This means removing the child from the situation or the situation from the child. "Now it's bedtime" needs to be accompanied by walking with the child to bed and tucking him in. If a child hits another child with a block after being told the rule about not hitting, the blocks should be put away, or the child should be moved to a different activity, away from the blocks.

It is important to keep in mind that the purpose of this is to help the child learn and internally adopt the rule as his own, rather than to punish him for wrongdoing. This distinction is not always apparent, but it is meaningful. Punishment, per se, may be a way of venting our own anger at the child and may be unrelated in content to the event. If we can be clear that the reason for enforcing rules is to help the child learn to follow them even when an authority is not present, we will be able to stay away from the kinds of punishment (such as physical punishment) which may make us feel better, but which do not help the child achieve internal control of impulses.

3. *Proximal timing of enforcement.* A logical extension of the concept of enforcing a clearly stated rule by removing the child from the activity or the activity from the child is that this must happen in close time prox-

imity to the transgression. This is especially important with very young children whose time concept is very different from ours, as adults (Goldstein, Freud, and Solmit, 1973). To a two-year-old, a day can seem as long as a week does to an adult. A disciplinary action which lags several minutes or hours behind the transgression which it was supposed to affect, then, will seem totally unrelated to the child. Indeed, it can be seen by the child as a kind of willful "meanness" on the part of the adult. If, for some reason, then, we cannot intervene quickly to enforce a rule, we ought simply to let it go until the next time when our action can be understood by the child to relate to the relevant behavior.

4. *Prescriptive teaching.* As we explained in the section on the development of values, giving rules *prescriptively* (thou shalt) rather than *proscriptively* (thou shalt not) helps to make the rules clearer and more understandable to the child. The clearer a rule is, the more easily it is internalized. Prescriptive rule-giving, then, aids in the development of an internalized locus of control, which leads, in turn, to greater value clarity and relevance (McKinney, 1975). Two studies have uncovered some interesting side effects of prescriptive rule-giving by parents: (1) children reared prescriptively see their mothers more positively (more rewarding and less punishing) than those reared proscriptively (McKinney, 1971); and (2) children reared with an emphasis on prescriptive rules are more generous than children reared with an emphasis on proscriptive rules (Olejnik and McKinney, 1973). As the authors of the latter study explained: "It appears that emphasis on prescriptive values by parents teaches children what they ought to do, while emphasis on proscriptive values merely indicates to children what not to do without specific instructions on how they ought to behave" (p. 311).

5. *Intrinsic rewards.* It should be obvious that if we wish a child to develop control from within, that is, a conscience, we need to build a system of rewards from within: that is, based on feeling good about oneself when doing what is right and not feeling good about oneself when doing the wrong thing. As pointed out in the section on the development of social skills, the use of external rewards and punishments (e.g., giving candy, tokens, or money, or withholding such treats) which have no actual connection with the activity involved tends to lead to external control of behavior. When the rewards stop, the rewarded behavior stops. When the punishing authority figure is not present, forbidden behavior is resumed. An intrinsic reward system, on the other hand, leads to approved behaviors being done for their own sake, because they are fun, pleasurable, interesting, or lead to increased self-esteem or other good feelings while doing them. For example, rewarding children with tokens (an extrinsic reward) for reading will increase the amount of reading they do as long as the

tokens are given and have value to the children. Soon after the use of tokens is discontinued, however, time spent reading drops considerably. A short-term gain without lasting results is the effect over time. Choosing books that are very interesting (an intrinsic reward) to the children, however, results in increased time spent reading as long as the books continue to hold the children's interest—which can be a very long time indeed. Thus, the development of an interesting, exciting curriculum that involves the children in learning for pleasure will have a much more lasting effect than giving external rewards for doing basically uninteresting work.

Keeping this in mind, then, we can help children to feel good about controlling their actions themselves by paying attention to the good things they do and commenting, prescriptively and close in time to the behavior, on how good they must feel or how proud they must be of themselves. "Johnny, that was very grown-up of you to let Mary have a turn on the swing. You are getting to be such a big boy."

"Jane, you climbed to the top of the tall slide even though you were scared. That was hard to do, but you did it. You must feel very proud of yourself."

"George, I see you helped Billy with the fingerpaints. It feels good to be able to help someone else, doesn't it?"

"Children you all pitched in and helped put away the toys so quickly today. The room looks so nice now. That was a job well done, a job to be proud of."

In addition, we can point out those connected events which intrinsically follow each other. "Now that we've cleaned up the paints, there is room on the table for drawing."

"If you dump the snow out of your boots they will be dry when it is time to put them on to go home."

"When you learn to write your name, you will be able to apply for your own library card."

All of these prescriptions represent a challenge. None of us can be perfect in our dealings with children. There will be difficult times, and mistakes will inevitably be made. At such times, perhaps it will help to remember that children are basically very forgiving and that they have an innate interest in life and the desire to please adults. If we care about them and try to foster their development as best we can, they will do the rest.

BIBLIOGRAPHY

Bell, S.M., and Ainsworth, M.D.S. "Infant Crying and Maternal Responsiveness." *Child Development* 43(1972):1171-1190.

Brazelton, T.B., Scholl, M.L., and Robey, J.S. "Visual Responses in the Newborn." *Pediatrics* 37(1966):284-290.

Bronfenbrenner, U. "Socialization and Social Class Through Time and Space." In Maccoby, E., Newcomb, T., and Hartley, E. (eds.), *Readings in Social Psychology* (Third Edition). New York: Henry Holt and Co., 1958.

Clodd, E. "The Philosophy of Rumpelstiltskin." *The Folklore Journal* 7, part 2, (1889):135-163.

Cooley, C.H. *Human Natures and the Social Order.* New York: Charles Scribner and Sons, 1922.

Cooley, C.H. *Social Organization.* New York: Charles Scribner and Sons, 1909.

Dion, K. "Physical Attractiveness and Evaluation of Childrens' Transgressions." *Journal of Personality and Social Psychology* 24(1972):207-213.

Dion, K. "Young Childrens' Stereotyping of Facial Attractiveness." *Developmental Psychology* 9(1973):183-188.

Dion, K., Berscheid, E., and Walster, E. "What is Beautiful is Good." *Journal of Personality and Social Psychology* 24(1972):285-290.

Escalona, S.K. *The Roots of Individuality.* Chicago: Adline Publishing Co., 1968.

Fantz, R.L. "Pattern Vision in Newborn Infants." *Science* 140(1963): 296-297.

Fenichel, O. *Psychoanalytic Theory of Neurosis.* New York: Norton, 1945.

Fraiberg, S.H. *The Magic Years.* New York: Scribner, 1959.

Ginott, H.G. *Between Parent and Child: New Solutions to Old Problems.* New York: Avon Books, 1969.

Goldstein, J., Freud, A., and Solmit, A.J. *Beyond the Best Interests of the Child.* New York: The Free Press, 1973.

Kallen, D. "Nutrition and the Community." In Kallen, D. (ed.), *Nutrition, Development and Social Behavior.* Washington, D.C.: U.S. Government Printing Office, 1972.

Levine, F.M., and Fasnacht, G. "Token Rewards May Lead to Token Learning." *American Psychologist* 29(1974):816-820.

Lewin, K. *Field Theory in Social Science.* New York: Harper and Bros., 1951.

Lewis, M., and Rosenblum, L.A. *The Effect of the Infant on its Caregiver.* New York: Wiley, 1974.

Maurer, A. "Violence Against Children." *Journal of Clinical Child Psychology* 2(1973):2-58.

Maurer, A. "Corporal Punishment." *American Psychologist* 29(1974):614-626.

McKinney, J.P. "Verbal Meaning and Perceptual Stability." *Canadian Journal of Psychology* 20(1966):237-242.

McKinney, J.P. "The Development of Values—Prescriptive or Proscriptive?" *Human Development* 14(1971):71-80.

McKinney, J.P. "The Development of Values: A Perceptual Interpretation." *Journal of Personality and Social Psychology* 31(1975):801-807.

Milgram, S. *Obedience to Authority: An Experimental View.* New York: Harper & Row, 1974.

Moss, H.A. "Sex, Age and State as Determinants of Mother Infant Interaction." *Merrill-Palmer Quarterly* 13(1967):19-36.

Neill, A.S. *Summerhill.* New York: Hart Publishing Company, 1960.

Olejnik, A.B., and McKinney, J.P. "Parental Value Orientation and Generosity in Children." *Developmental Psychology* 8(1973):311.

Rist, R. "Student Social Class and Teacher Expectations: The Self Fulfilling Prophecy in Ghetto Education." *Harvard Educational Review* 40(1970):411-451.

Rosenthal, R., and Jacobsen, L. *Pygmalion in the Classroom, Teacher Expectation and Pupils' Intellectual Ability.* New York: Holt, Rinehart and Winston, 1968.

Seagull, A.A. The Ability to Delay Gratification: Special Class Versus Situation Variables. Unpublished doctoral dissertation, Syracuse University, 1964.

Stayton, D., and Ainsworth, M.D.S. "Individual Differences in Infant Responses to Brief, Everyday Separations as Related to Other Infant and Maternal Behaviors." *Development Psychology* 9(1973):226-235.

Stayton, D., Ainsworth, M.D.S., and Main, M. "Development of Separation Behavior in the First Year of Life." *Developmental Psychology* 9(1973):213-225.

Stein, S.G. The Open Family Books: *About Dying. About Handicaps. A Hospital Story. Making Babies. That New Baby.* New York: Walker and Co., 1974.

Sullivan, H.S. *The Interpersonal Theory of Psychiatry.* New York: Norton & Co., 1953.

Thomas, A., Birch, H., Chess, S., Hertzig, M., and Korn, S. *Behavioral Individuality in Early Childhood.* New York: New York University Press, 1963.

Thomas, A., Chess, S., and Birch, H.G. *Temperament and Behavior Disorders in Children.* New York: New York University Press, 1968.

Yarrow, L. "Separation from Parents in Early Childhood." In Hoffman, M. and Hoffman, L. (eds.), *Review of Child Development Research.* New York: Russell Sage Foundation, 1965.

CHAPTER 2

Psychopathology in the Preschool Child and Its Assessment

Randolph T. Harper

INTRODUCTION

It is not unusual, even at this point in time, to be met with reactions of incredulity, cynicism, astonishment, or even hostility when one begins to speak of significant disturbances in the psychological development of preschool children. When, at the turn of the century, Freud postulated the significance of early childhood experiences for adult psychopathology and the intricate complexity of the child's individual psychological makeup, many reacted similarly. Some went beyond these initial reactions to pursue their own studies of the child's psychological development in its normal and pathological aspects. Since that time, for those who have been willing to observe and wonder, children and particularly their inner world have proven to be so rich and complex that after approximately seventy-five years of extensive work by many, we may be little more than faltering toddlers ourselves.

The child continues to have an enormous potential for intriguing, delighting, surprising, enlightening, puzzling, frustrating, and frightening us while confronting us with many challenges as child scientists and practitioners. Adults have always had difficulty in truly seeing, hearing, and being emotionally open to children. Even though we currently have the advantage of many prior workers making it easier for us by directing our attention to various aspects of the child's development and functioning, each of us must still in our own way rediscover childhood. The problems in understanding the experience of the child are increased as we move closer to preverbal periods of functioning and also as we deal with dis-

RANDOLPH T. HARPER has a private practice in New Orleans, and he is the Co-ordinator of Professional Training and Education at the Developmental Disabilities Center for Children at the Louisiana State University Medical Center. His primary interest is child and adult psychoanalysis.

turbances in development which are further from the norm. The more severe and debilitating disturbances are more easily recognized and accepted as existing even if they are not very easily understood or corrected. There are many other disturbances manifesting themselves in the preschool child which can become quite subtle as we approach the norm and, consequently, might remain unrecognized and neglected. The remainder of this chapter will attempt to outline briefly some principles and points of view regarding assessment of childhood disturbances as well as to survey briefly some patterns of psychopathology which occur in the preschool child. Such principles, viewpoints, and descriptions can serve to facilitate our identifying children in need and planning how to help them. They can also serve as conceptual guides to observing and thinking about children. Obviously, each of us is still left with the task of discovery which leads to actually seeing and knowing our children.

METHODOLOGICAL ISSUES

There are many methodological issues of relevance to our topic. I will select and briefly note a few of these issues, primarily to establish a frame of reference for our central topic. It is best that they are made explicit.

First, and quite fundamentally, the primary tool for doing our work is the same as the object of our studies and efforts in many ways. When we study a child's physical, sensory, perceptual, cognitive, linguistic, social, and emotional development, we do it primarily through an instrument, our own selves, which has traveled the same road of development and still carries the effects and some residuals of the periods of development which we are studying at the moment. When we observe a child, attempt to conceptualize his development, or plan to influence that development, our primary instrument in this endeavor of seeing, thinking, and creative planning is our own self. The various behavioral sciences have this peculiar methodological situation, wherein the object of study has significant identities with the instruments conducting the study. This offers us the opportunity for empathy with our subject matter, but also opens us up to particular blind spots, prejudices, and biases considerably more intimate and powerful than those faced by some of our colleagues in other sciences. The gains in empathy are balanced by limitations in objectivity.

Another closely related issue is our position as participant-observer. When we work with children, we are sometimes relatively more one than the other, but we must respect the fact that even when we are attempting to adopt a neutral, objective, unobtrusive stance in the extreme degree we are still influencing what we are observing. This phenomena we share closely with our colleagues in other fields.

There are three other methodological issues which are quite intricately related to each other. These are the utilization of theory; the specific variables one selects for observation, assessment, and intervention; and finally, the level of abstraction at which one is functioning at any given point in time.

Any particular scientific theory has only limited relevance and utility. If at all valid, it will have explanatory, predictive, and utilitarian power with a particular specific frame of reference only. Moreover, it will carry with it costs of various assumptions and biases that will interfere with the possibility of seeing things differently and acting differently. The best one can do is to know the particular focus of convenience for the specific theory which is being used at the moment, and to do one's best beyond that to avoid orthodox rigidities, while staying open to the challange of seeing things anew. Regarding knowledge of the specific focus of convenience for the theoretical point of view being employed at any given time, one should know what realm of phenomena for which it has the greatest explanatory, predictive, and utilitarian yield. One should attempt to be as clear as possible regarding these limitations and boundaries with respect to any particular theory.

The particular variables we observe, assess, and attempt to influence with interventions are also clearly reflective of choice. One should be explicit and quite aware that a good deal of selectivity is operative in this process. We essentially undertake a sampling of many possible variables and work with a very few of the total possible universe from which we might select the variables. If one has some conceptual basis influencing the selection of these variables, then it is possible to utilize observations about the various information developed through observation of specific variables to refine the underlying conceptual position. In any event, it is best to confront oneself regarding the factors which influence our choices in this realm.

Next, it is important to be aware of the level of abstraction or the level of inference upon which we are operating at any given point. When we speak of a particular child at any given moment, are we dealing with reports of material which is relatively close to the event level—that is, concrete observations of individual behaviors—or have we moved up the levels of abstraction to first-, second-, or third-order inferences about a child, his development, and his functioning? It is relatively close to the primary event level, for example, to have a frequency count of the number of different words a child used in a unit of time under specific conditions. It is a higher order inference to make a normative statement about his language development and still more inferential to comment upon aspects of linguistic structure and organization.

Each of these methodological issues has reciprocal influences upon the other; that is, the particular theoretical stance, the variables selected, and the level of inference provide important reciprocal influences on our conceptualization and practical approach to any child. It is, again, important to recognize this because of the complexity of our subject matter. In order to understand any child adequately, multiple variables have to be utilized. Further, one must work carefully at the various levels of basic observation, inference, and finally integration of these multiple functions. Moreover, no one theoretical approach or method is yet adequate to accomplish the overall task and many must be utilized. This utlization should not rest on a random eclecticism but should be based on as much critical awareness and rational selectivity regarding the comparative utility of one theory, set of variables, method of study, or intervention as is possible at this stage in the development of our sciences and technologies.

We can now leave the more general comments regarding a methodological frame of reference and turn to the specific realm of psychopathology and its assessment in the preschool child.

PARADOXES

As we work with children we function in ways that must often deal with dialectics which at times seem radically paradoxical, and at other times, the poles of these dialectics seem more capable of compatibility and integration. How often we find ourselves relatively more at one pole and then at the other. How often we may become so convinced of the validity of one pole or the other as to neglect utterly the opposite point of view or the interesting range of possibilities in between these polarities. We often range from moment to moment as scientist then practitioner; theoretician then pragmatist; observer then participant or intervenor; objective then subjective; analytical then intuitive. We can each easily add to this list from our own daily experiences. At the moment, as I approach the issue of discussing various disturbances, another polarity presents itself: that of the individual and of the class, the unique and the common.

The further we proceed with the detailed intensive study of any individual, we come to see more and more evidence which simultaneously demonstrates the true uniqueness of that individual and his similarities to others of his fellows. The individual stands out with increasing clarity as an individual and we also see his relationship to and membership in a class of individuals. Psychology has never resolved this dialectic, and, indeed, has never lived with it very comfortably.

For the purposes of our topic, this dialectic presents itself in the following form. If we pay exquisite detailed attention to the individual, we may pay dearly in many ways by not recognizing his relationship to any class of individuals; e.g., he may have a particular disturbance which has been observed, detailed, and recognized by others. On the other hand, we know that despite the demonstrated circumscribed validity of some of our classifications, we seldom find the "classic" case which fits all details related to a particular syndrome or disturbance. Moreover, the personality in the preschool period is quite fluid and faces many developmental phases or environmentally induced challenges and opportunities in the future during which there are major reworkings of personality organization. Adolescence is the most clear example of this phenomenon. In attempting to assess any individual and subsequently plan an intervention approach, one can learn much and avoid repeating unnecessary errors or fruitless endeavors by attending to previous efforts with others who share certain critical similarities with this individual. Issues of differential treatment planning and prognosis are in the forefront here. Yet, a particular individual, no matter how much he may resemble a particular class, never is totally identical in all features with all members of the class. He may possess certain critical assets which others lack and may well surprise us with his use of assistance which failed others. The opposite possibility is also to be expected. The famed pigeonhole is not such a simple creature after all. It needs to be resisted but not totally ignored.

The approach here deals with the problem in a pragmatic but, I believe, theoretically and scientifically sound way. The degree to which you may find the approach presented reasonable, applicable, and useful may ease but certainly not eradicate these dilemmas based on the polarities and paradoxes inherent in human functioning and development which face us in our work with children. The practical solution is to develop a way of observing, assessing, and conceptualizing the individual as an individual on the one hand, and on the other, to have a detailed knowledge of working and discriminating characteristics of various classifications of relevance. It is only by developing ourselves in both directions that we can best come to understand the specific individual with whom we might be working at the moment and learn from him, so as to refine our understanding of children in general. In this way, our work with this individual can contribute to his progress and to our work with others.

Here, too, an additional methodological point may be helpful. In our work we continually shift from inductive to deductive approaches. We deal with hypothetical understandings which we constantly revise in the light of new developments with any given child. We formulate an understanding of a child and this becomes our hypothetical basis and our starting point. From this we make certain predictions which our further work with the child serves to prove or disprove. In the light of these new data, we revise our hypotheses and the cycle begins anew. In this way, we can best deal with the many dilemmas and perplexities which are the warp and woof of our work with children. This open-ended cycle of *observe, hypothesize, predict, intervene, observe, reformulate* is the best guarantee against the danger of rigidly forcing a child into some procrustean category or going along on some aimless, uncritical, "intuitive" wandering with him. Any practitioner dealing with children is at his best as this kind of applied scientist or action researcher who accepts the creative challenges of dealing simultaneously with issues of investigation and influence.

Some of the groundwork regarding the specifics of assessing psychopathology in the preschool child has been covered in the other chapters of this volume. A thorough knowledge of normal, sound development is necessary in order to begin to recognize, evaluate and understand deviations from the norm. Obviously, in developing any plan of intervention, knowledge of normal development is essential to establish goals, evaluate progress, and determine outcome. Issues related to assessment of normal development as addressed in Chapter Three are again critical and applicable. The procedures and methodological issues related to assessing normal development come into play here also. The fourth chapter recognizes the significance of dealing with the individual child in a holistic and integrated way. No matter how we might dissect and trace various specific individual aspects of development, we should never lose sight of their interrelationships and of the artificial nature of these conceptual and operational distinctions. Some of these interrelationships between various aspects of functioning and development can find no more dramatic and convincing illustrations than will be seen in the chapters dealing with the emotional and social life of the mentally subnormal, neurologically impaired, or sensorily handicapped child. In such instances, the adaptational struggle of the child is quite vivid and the reverberating interinfluences of neurological, motor, sensory, perceptual, cognitive, linguistic, motivational, emotional, social, and cultural factors are often striking and, indeed, unmistakable. The same concern with the whole child needs to be respected since adequate development of any child requires so much more than the precise interface which any of our various interventions can provide.

THE INDIVIDUAL

With respect to the need for a means of observing, assessing, and conceptualizing the individual as an individual, the particular model to be discussed here is based primarily upon psychoanalytic ego psychology in terms of the general theoretical position and more particularly upon the extensive work of Anna Freud and her colleagues in the area of assessment of both normality and psychopathology in child development. This work is best represented in her volume titled *Normality and Pathology in Childhood: Assessments of Development* (1965). While psychoanalytic ego psychology is the primary model for this discussion, the reader will readily see that a general model of clinical problem-solving provides the background and context both conceptually and practically. A number of principles, concepts, and procedures which are not specifically psychoanalytic contribute to the approach. Perhaps the best single reference for the broader model of clinical problem-solving related to evaluating psychopathology in children would be Report No. 62 of the Group for the Advancement of Psychiatry entitled *Psychopathological Disorders in Childhood: Theoretical Considerations and a Proposed Classification* (1966). These models are used in a complementary, mutually enhancing fashion.

While the focus of convenience of a psychoanalytic model has historically concentrated upon and demonstrated significant power in elucidating the development and organization of the child's inner world, that is, his intrapsychic functioning, it has never lost sight of the significant relationships to both the biological substratum of the organism and its interaction with the environment from the levels of the interpersonal to the social and cultural. Taking the point of view of individual psychology and specifically one's inner world as the starting point and central focus, an effort is made to understand the individual's development and functioning in interaction with biological and environmental determinants and influences. The individual is viewed in no way as a passive recipient of these influences but as a full partner in shaping his own destiny within the context of biological and environmental givens and determinants. The individual is viewed as an active influencer and organizer of his experience. Any assessment must therefore be a multidimensional one including an understanding of the child's functioning at the physiological, psychological, and social levels of organization. Moreover, these various factors are not viewed in isolation from each other but are seen as having a complex interplay and as dynamically interacting with each other. Further, they should be understood not only in terms of their current functioning but also in their origins and historical development to the current level and mode of functioning. They are, of course, not evaluated in any absolute terms and the data and their assessment are constantly viewed in a developmental frame as to their phase appropriateness and adequacy. Thus the Group for the Advancement of Psychiatry report emphasizes evaluation as multidimensional, relativistic, and dynamic dealing with complex considerations at the physiological, psychological, and social levels of organization and proceeding beyond a simple descriptive understanding of behavior to include a genetic and dynamic understanding within a developmental frame of reference (G.A.P., 1966). No single facet of a child's functioning can be adequately understood when viewed in isolation. Adequate understanding is developed only when a particular facet of a child's functioning is placed in this more comprehensive frame of reference and viewed in an integrated, holistic developmental scheme as one attempts to make judgments regarding normality or pathology which then lead to the design of interventions.

For these and additional reasons Anna Freud has proposed that the child's developmental functioning as an ongoing process be utilized as the essential criterion in reaching any judgments regarding the presence and degree of severity of psychopathology. To exemplify briefly some of her rationale, we might refer to her own discussion regarding the inapplicability to children of several clinical criteria which are frequently utilized in determining the presence and degree of severity of psychopathology with adults. These include the presence of symptoms, the presence or absence of subjective suffering, and the impairment of functioning. With children, symptoms can represent quite transient normal responses to expected stresses which are intrinsic to development. Further, with children it is often their family members or other adult figures such as teachers who experience some significant degree of subjective discomfort rather than the child. The child himself is often quite oblivious to any subjective distress. Impairment of functioning is also questioned as a determining criterion because regressions are to be expected as normal variations in development and indeed contribute to positive adaptations. All assessments which stop at the descriptive level are inadequate and fraught with the possibility of significant misunderstanding of the child. To know that an individual child manifests a particular kind of behavior or cluster of behaviors is only a beginning point in the assessment and provides no basis for understanding the roles of these specific behaviors in his overall development and functioning. Any specific behavior can have a variety of either favorable or unfavorable effects on current and future development and functioning as well as a variety of internal or external causes. These considerations are critical in determining whether or not any intervention should be attempted and obviously the specific nature of the intervention. The role of the behavior in the child's overall functioning and development must be understood prior to any diagnosis and its related treatment plan. To achieve this, the child's development understood as a multidimensional, dynamic process is utilized as the superinordinate and organizing criterion regarding the presence and nature of psychopathology, while an assessment of the multiple specific aspects of this development provide the basis for determining the precise nature of the kind of treatment which might be undertaken.

Anna Freud makes the following comprehensive summary of her position in this regard:

> It is obvious, in the light of the foregoing, that child analysts have to free themselves from those diagnostic categories which are rigid, static, descriptive, or for

other reasons alien to their field. Only when they have done this, will they be able to look at the clinical pictures before them with new eyes and assess them according to their significance for the process of development. This implies redirecting their attention from the symptomatology of the patient to his position on the developmental scale with regard to drive, ego and superego development, to the structuralization of the personality (stable borders between id, ego, and superego), and to modes of functioning (progression from primary to secondary thought processes, from pleasure to reality principle), etc. It implies asking themselves whether the child under examination has reached developmental levels which are adequate for his age, whether and in what respects he has either gone beyond or remained behind them; whether maturation and development are ongoing processes or to what degree they are affected as a result of the child's disturbance; whether regressions or arrests have intervened, and, if so, to which depth and on what level.

To find the answers to such questions, a scheme of average developmental norms for all aspects of the personality is needed. . . . The more complete the scheme becomes, the more successfully will the individual patient be measured against it with regard to the evenness or unevenness of progression rate, harmony or disharmony between developmental lines, and temporariness or permanency of regressions (p. 123-124, 1965).

Viewing development and problems of assessment in this way, Anna Freud and her colleagues have put forward the concept of developmental lines (A. Freud, 1963 and 1965) and have devised a conceptual and practical tool of assessment known as the metapsychological profile (A. Freud, 1963 and 1965; Nagera, 1963). The metapsychological profile in its original form is a psychoanalytic tool designed for use in the clinical psychoanalytic setting by persons sophisticated in terms of both the theory and the technique of psychoanalysis. However, the principles and methodology which inform the metapsychological profile can serve as a model for assessment in situations other than the clinical psychoanalytic one and for utilization by developmental specialists other than child psychoanalysts. Its potential in other situations is especially maximized by utilizing complementary principles from the more general model of clinical problem-solving already referred to above. The metapsychological profile recognizes that an adequate understanding of any specific behavior cannot be attained from any single point of view. The profile itself provides a means of organizing these multiple points of view into a composite understanding of an individual child. In this chapter a very brief overview will be presented and some considerable liberties will be taken with respect to adding features and altering some of the conceptual language to render the material more readily applicable to the nonanalytic setting and reader. For an accurate understanding and presentation of the profile itself, the original references should be consulted (A. Freud, 1963 and 1965). Moreover, if one wishes to see an example of its application to children from the ages under consideration in this volume, one might wish to consult the description of the profile applied to infants (W. Freud, 1967 and 1972) and to the preschool child (R. Furman and A. Katan, 1969).

The first step is the descriptive level. This involves a detailed description of the specific phenomena which have become the object of concern. It may involve such things as symptoms in the technical sense, questionable behaviors, or the failure of certain functions to develop at expected times. These issues should be described in terms of their manifest features, intensity, frequency, circumstances under which they occur, and the history of their first becoming manifest up to the present time.

One then broadens out the descriptive and historical understanding of the child beyond the parameters of problem behaviors in the narrow sense. At this point the child is described at his current functional level with respect to aspects ranging from his personal appearance to his general personality functioning.

Next, the child's personal history and family history are reviewed. These several topics taken together provide the opportunity first of all to review factors of potential relevance to understanding the identified problem behaviors at the level of the biological substratum or the physiological level. That is, with respect to both the child's general development and the problem behaviors the physiological factors are reviewed. One also looks to the functioning and history of other members of the family at this level. In this way potential hereditary, constitutional, and temperamental factors are included as well as possible disturbances or deficits in normal physiological functioning. This obviously becomes the place in which factors at the other end of the spectrum, the social and cultural, are also included. Sufficient understanding of the personality of each significant person in the child's experience is developed in order to understand their potential impact on the child and vice versa. An effort is made to understand the key interactions at different phases of development with respect to their nature and mutual impact. Beyond this interpersonal level factors of social and cultural significance are also enumerated. One also seeks to delineate any other potentially significant environmental influences and to understand them in relationship to the particular time in the child's development at which they had their influences.

The next level of assessment concentrates on the variables which have to do with the child's individual psychology, and a study of the structure of the child's personality is undertaken. In psychoanalytic terms this means an assessment of the phase adequacy and distribution of drive development. Ego and superego functions are next reviewed regarding their intactness, phase adequacy, organization, and integration, and the presence of any interferences with functioning is noted. To state the same issues in nonpsychoanalytic terms and to utilize more general terms related to personality theory, the phase adequacy and functional adequacies of personality variables dealing with motivation, coping and control mechanisms, socialization, and values are examined separately and in relationship to each other as emerging structural components of the individual child's personality.

This detailed structural understanding is then utilized to examine questions regarding the presence or absence of specific fixations and regressions. It further serves to answer questions regarding the presence of conflicts, whether of an internal or external nature, and the specific nature and determinants of these conflicts. Some general characteristics regarding the child's frustration tolerance, sublimation potential, manner of dealing with anxiety, and the overall balance of progressive versus regressive developmental forces are also assessed.

In the section which concentrates on the analysis of the personality structure from the point of view of drives, ego, and superego functioning or in more general terms on the development of various primary motivational variables, coping mechanisms, socialization, and values, a number of specific issues are emphasized. The specific primary motivational variables of interest from a psychoanalytic and ego psychological point of view are grouped under the development of the libidinal drive and the aggressive drive. Both of these are examined as to their developing in phase and as to whether or not they function in a relatively stabilized and consistent manner. Both are also examined in terms of the direction of their expression and investment either within the self or toward people or things in the external world. In this respect particular attention is paid to the libidinal investment in the self to see if it is sufficient enough to ensure an appropriate level of self-esteem without undue distortions either in the direction of the underestimation or the overestimation of the self. The level of libidinal investment in others is also examined for its phase appropriateness. Here the developmental line which Anna Freud proposes that traces the child's development from dependency to eventual emotional self-reliance and adult object relations is most applicable. The child's development is traced from its early biological unity with the mother and the eventual differentiation process which occurs from the normal autistic and symbiotic phases through the separation-individuation phase leading to the establishment of object constancy in the young preschool child (p. 65, Anna Freud, 1965). As one examines ego functioning or in more general terms the child's coping functions, particular attention is first of all paid to the presence or absence of any primary organically based delays or deficits within the range of ego functions such as motor development, perceptual and sensory development, etc. The adequacy of major ego functions is assessed and one notes the evenness or unevenness of progression of various ego functions. The child's particular defenses are also noted as is their relationship to his developmental phase and the overall balance and effectiveness among the various defenses.

This represents the very briefest and most cursory overview of what is a quite demanding, detailed effort to understand any aspect of a child's overt manifest behavior and functioning. With such a detailed, individualized understanding of the child ranging across the levels of the biological, psychological, and social, we can now proceed to issues of classification and treatment planning.

THE GROUP

A number and at times indeed a perplexing number of classifications for childhood psychopathology have been developed. For example, the Group for the Advancement of Psychiatry report provides an appendix listing and outlining some twenty-four such classification schemes (pp. 297-325, G.A.P., 1966). Obviously, the issue regarding the classification of childhood psychopathology is not a settled one. In this section a comprehensive review and the presentation of a full classification system will not be presented. Selectivity will be exercised particularly by presenting groupings of responses and disorders which are relatively more frequent and more crucial for understanding the child in the first five or six years of life. The selections made here rely on more comprehensive presentations of classifications of psychopathology and more specifically upon classification systems and related conceptualizations developed by A. Freud (p. 147, 1965; 1970), the Group for the Advancement of Psychiatry (1966), Settlage (1964), and Nagera (1966). Before proceeding further, as an example of the areas included in such a more comprehensive approach the following major categories are offered in the classification system of the Group for the Advancement of Psychiatry. We might note that most of these major categories include a number of subcategories. The categories include: Healthy Responses, Reactive Disorders, Developmental Deviations, Psychoneurotic Disorders, Personality Disorders, Psychotic Disorders, Psychophysiologic Disorders, Brain Syndromes, Mental Retardation, and a miscellaneous category entitled Other Disorders (p. 217, G.A.P., 1966).

The first grouping to consider would be that concerned with normal or healthy responses. While some specific aspect of behavior has become of sufficient concern to become the object of assessment, the determination is made based upon the assessment that the response falls well within the normal range of variations in development. There is stage appropriateness of functioning as well as an adequate balance of progressive versus regressive forces. If any interventions are needed they are likely to be in the nature of some follow-up to ensure the accuracy of such a determination or some counseling or education of the concerned adults regarding the normal nature and meaning of the child's behavior. Should the adults remain concerned despite adequate communication regarding such information, some exploration and working through of the causes of their concern would then be indicated.

The next groupings to consider cover a wide range of phenomena and generally might be termed reactive disturbances. In these instances the child's response takes on some degree of maladaptiveness but can be traced to some specific precipitating environmental event or situation. The interaction between the child's own resources determined by his endowment and developmental progress with the environmentally stressful event or situation is of particular interest. These disorders are particularly frequent in the infant or preschool child both because of the relative instability of internal psychological mechanisms for dealing with stress and because of the relatively more complete dependence of the young child on his environment to maintain adequate internal functioning. The objective severity of the stressful event or situation is not the determining factor but rather the nature of the child's response. One is concerned with the external events in reaching determinations regarding interventions but obviously one child might develop a maladaptive response to a relatively mild external stress while another could handle a significantly more stressful event adaptively. From a preventive point of view attention can also be paid to such stresses. That is, one can anticipate that one or another event or situation would place a particular child under stress and take measures to try to minimize the impact of these events or situations in advance. The maladaptive responses of the child can range from relatively transient ones to responses which become more entrenched, difficult to alter, and precursors of other maladaptive patterns of personality functioning. The child's range of responses to environmentally induced stresses extends across the full gamut of physiological and psychological reactions. One could see sleeping or eating disturbances, gross signs of emotional distress in various discharge mechanisms, behavioral disorders, or the development of multiple symptoms. The specific intervention plan should address itself to the child's individual responses as well as to the specific environmental stress. Often the stress cannot be totally eradicated but measures can usually be taken to reduce their impact upon the child. Supportive measures can be introduced to aid the child in the reinstitutionalization of his equilibrium and specific steps should be taken to remediate the disturbances in his developmental progression.

Lying somewhat between normal responses and disorders of a reactive nature are developmental crises. Here the child's response demonstrates some degree of maladaptiveness but the precipitating stress is not of an external or environmentally induced nature. The child's behavior is in response to some stress due to the normal progression of development and the various internal demands which it makes upon the child. An example would be a debilitating degree of anxiety in reaction to some of the expected stresses in the separation phase of development. It might include maladaptive efforts to manage the anxiety. Here again, the maladaptive behavior could be of a relatively transient nature or could indeed be the early organizing elements contributing to the development of more crystalized and longer lasting maladaptive behaviors in subsequent phases of development. Interventions here might again focus on the education of key environmental figures as to the nature of the child's distress in relationship to the developmental issues which he is facing so that the child's caretakers can facilitate his experience of stress and facilitate the development of more positively adaptive responses.

Psychophysiological disorders, brain syndromes, and developmental deviations each demonstrate the intricate nature of the interaction between the physiological, psychological, and social dimensions of functioning. They are being treated collectively here in part because there is no specific type of personality functioning circumscribed to each disorder. Rather psychological manifestations in these groupings can extend across the range of conduct disturbances, neurotic patterns, and psychosis as well as effects in various manifestations of affective and cognitive functioning. The psychophysiological disorders represent some significant somatic dysfunctioning, usually of organ systems related to the autonomic nervous system. Psychological and environmental factors play a contributing role but definitely in interaction with physiological ones. In the brain syndromes some either focused or diffuse brain dysfunctioning is either documented or inferred and connected with either acute or more chronic interferences with psychological functioning, particularly in affective, perceptual, cognitive, and behavioral spheres. Developmental deviations may refer to a relatively more global departure from expected maturational progression or to a departure with respect to a specific line or lines of development such as one or another area of sensory development, cognitive development, or language development. Causative factors can be more purely environmental than in the psychophysiological disorders or brain syndromes, but they are often contributed to substantially by biological factors affecting maturational processes.

In all of these disorders the organic or physiological component must be carefully evaluated and in most instances will have substantial etiological influence. What is also important to note is the developmental level of the child and personality development up to the point of onset. This would include attention to the current developmental stresses which the child is facing as a normal expected stress and his current life situation. This evaluation of developmental level and personality development addresses the meaning which the particular psychophysiological, neurological, or maturational issue might take on to the child and his parents.

Obviously some of these problems are manifest at birth or in early infancy and all of these issues become quite critical in the child's early life and development. Weil (1970) has presented an excellent discussion regarding the interaction between the child's basic organismic equipment and state of functioning in early life with specific structural aspects of personality development dealing especially with individual variations with respect to the organismic substrate and its influence on a variety of structural personality variables such as tolerance for anxiety, perceptual sensitivity, activity level, discrimination, memory, and capacity to integrate experience effectively. The interaction of these factors and their influence on the eventual organizing and regulating functions of the personality are well demonstrated. A child manifesting one or another of the psychophysiologic, brain, or maturational disturbances is particularly likely to have one or another of the structural aspects of his personality development significantly compromised or threatened by the disturbance at the physiological level. While we have been emphasizing these several areas which have substantial causative influence from the physiological level, it is also worth noting another set of problems which can have similar effects in that they can create major structural deficits in the realm of personality development. These are primary deficiencies which originally have an environmental basis and may or may not lead to one or another organic deficit in addition to major structural deficits in the personality organization. Here the reference is made to one or another substantial environmental failure such as varying degrees of stimulus deprivation often related to certain economic and sociological factors. Such deficiencies and environmental failures can lead to permanent organic damage of one kind or another and to deficits in personality organization which might result in substantial ego dysfunction, mental subnormality, or an atypical behavioral syndrome. Interventions with problems in these several areas can at times, depending upon the nature of the problem, be rather circumscribed and brief. With many of these disorders the interventions require a complex interdisciplinary approach and often extend through major portions of the developmental cycle with appropriate revisions of the treatment plan being undertaken at different points in time. These include specific medical treatments, various habilitative therapies, special education, family or environmental intervention, and one or another of the psychological interventions ranging from specific behavioral therapies to psychotherapy.

There are four remaining major classifications of disorder to consider with some reason to introduce them as a group. These include the psychoneurotic disorders, personality disorders, borderline syndromes, and psychoses.

One issue centers around the presence or absence of these disorders in the first six years of life. It is clear that there are some specific forms of childhood psychoses, such as early infantile autism and symbiotic psychosis, which appear in infancy and the preschool period, while it is generally held that schizophrenic disorders do not. Some authors feel that an organized psychoneurosis can be present toward the latter years of this period while others feel more strongly that a fully organized psychoneurosis is not present until the school-age period. There is generally more agreement that personality disorders and crystalized, organized borderline syndromes are not present until the school-age period. However, it is clear that the developmental antecedents of psychoneurosis, personality disorders, borderline syndromes, and later versions of psychosis can often be observed in the first five or six years of life. Indeed, many of the critically determining underpinnings are established in these early stages and while the more complex neurotic or psychotic overall organization is not crystalized in this period, the developmental antecedents of the later organization can well be outlined and followed.

A continuum regarding severity of disturbance can well be assumed ranging from neurosis through personality disorder to borderline syndromes and psychoses. It is also possible to conceptualize the personality disorders as falling closer to the neuroses with respect to certain critical developmental antecedents including the assumption of a more adequate physiological substratum to underlie development and more adequate mastery of the various developmental tasks in early life. Continuing along the same line of thinking, the borderline syndromes and psychoses can be seen as being somewhat closer to each other than to the personality disorders and neuroses. It is hypothesized that in these more severe disturbances there is a greater likelihood that the initial physiological substratum provided a less adequate organismic base for development and that the early life experiences lead to some significant failures in mastery and development.

Relying in part on the theoretical and empirical work of Mahler (1968; 1976), Settlage (1964) makes just such distinctions, employing the terms *neurotic character* and *psychotic character* instead of the terms *personality disorder* and *borderline syndromes*. Significant distinctions regarding the psychopathological basis of neurotic character disorders or personality disorders in contradistinction to psychotic character disorders or borderline syndromes are drawn by Settlage. Referring to the work of Mahler he sees the psychopathological basis for psychotic character disturbances and the psychoses as rooted in some adaptive failure in one or another of the phases of development which precede the establishment of object constancy in the third to fourth years of life. Thus he sees the potential for some failure in the early autistic phase (zero-three to four months), the normal symbiotic phase (three-four months to eight-twelve months), or the early steps of the separation-individuation phase (eight-twelve months to three-four years) as providing the psychopathological basis which might lead to the eventual formation of a psychotic character disorder or provide the basis for the development of psychosis itself. The kinds of failures which are referred to would lead to major disturbances in the development of significant ego functions and major failures in the development of adequate object relationships. The neurotic character and the neuroses themselves on the other hand are hypothesized to proceed through these early developmental phases with sufficient adequacy and mastery to ensure relatively sound ego development and to lead to the establishment of object constancy. This kind of object constancy presupposes the adequate perceptual and cognitive achievements which allow the child to maintain an internal representation of the primary caretaking object even in its absence. Then the emotional relationship to the object can organize itself around this internal representation in the absence of the object also. In this way there is a gradual internalization of an increasingly constant and positively emotionally valued and invested inner image of the care-taking object. This allows the child to function with increasing separate-ness from the actual direct presence of the caretakers and with increasing individuality. Because of the relatively positive emotional investment, the child is able to maintain feelings of security and safety away from the object and is able to utilize his own coping mechanisms or ego functions with increasing independence. The child is significantly less dependent directly on the object's presence for the adequacy and stability of his own emotional and adaptive functioning.

With this general background we can proceed to a discussion of the psychoneuroses, personality disorders, borderline syndromes, and psychoses as they or their developmental antecedents manifest themselves in infant and preschool periods.

To begin with the psychoneuroses, it was mentioned earlier that psychoneuroses in the most formal sense are not likely to occur until the end of the preschool period and perhaps in their more complex and fully organized forms not until early school age. A fully organized psychoneurosis is many-faceted and multidimensional. It is an extremely economical effort of the individual to resolve and integrate many prior and current developmental lines and conflicts in one complex organized psychological structure and inner adaptation. In many senses it presupposes relatively normal positive and constructive development and represents a more circumscribed focused compromise within this context of relatively positive developmental progress. Perceptual and cognitive development have proceeded without any major deficits or arrests being manifested which would be caused by some psychodynamically determined mal-adaptive effort. In particular the establishment of secondary process thinking and reality testing are rather sound. The child has further progressed through the normal autistic, symbiotic, and separation-individuation stages in a positive manner and has established emotional object constancy. This allows for age appropriate degrees of individuation, sexual identification, and social integration. Substantial progress has been made in terms of the internalization of parental and societal standards and values. Cognitive and emotional development now allow for the internal representation of current and past psychological conflicts and struggles as well as efforts to resolve these conflicts on an internal basis. To some degree this inner adaptive effort becomes unsuccessful. It requires some compromises in adaptation which affect the adequacy and fullness of future development. Generally some regression is employed as part of the adaptive effort. Circumscribed and focused distortions of elements of reality related to the core conflicts are involved. The adaptive efforts fail to deal fully with the threatening nature of the core conflicts which creates the experience of some anxiety. This in turn can lead to the formation of psychological symptoms which attempt to deal with the conflict at a symbolic level. Further, a repetitive patterned response is developed reflecting the neurotic organization. This patterned response achieves some degree of containment over the core conflicts and anxiety but also has self-defeating, self-perpetuating maladaptive features to it. In some form while it partially contains and manages the threatening conflicts it also interferes with more effective, fuller resolution of them. It repetitively involves the individual in some significant frustration and essentially in this sense provides a block to the fuller realization of the individual's potential in future development.

While this fuller form of the psychoneurosis is again not generally observable in the preschool period, one does see some of its precursors and early formation. Nagera (1966) has an excellent discussion of the developmental progression through the preschool years toward the establishment of a psychoneurosis. He makes an interesting distinction between neurotic conflicts themselves and the fully organized neurotic pattern. Neurotic conflicts are conceptualized as relatively simple units which do however represent an internal psychological struggle. Thus a child in the preschool period could well be struggling with more circumscribed, focused inner conflicts that have not yet reached the level of complexity and been integrated into the overall personality structure in the manner of a formal neurosis.

We can now move to the furthest side of the continuum and examine the psychoses themselves. In general the psychoses are disorders which show very significant distortions in the realm of major ego functions, object relationships and affect. The disorder may manifest itself with dysfunctions in one or all of these areas. More particularly, children with psychotic functioning demonstrate major difficulties in their relationships with other people; problems in the development of basic psychological processes such as perception, motility, speech, and language; bizarre, stereotyped, or unusual behaviors; strong resistance to change; a proneness to panic reactions and uncontrolled emotionality; major problems with their sense of identity; disordered thinking; and at times blunted intellectual development.

In terms of what has already been said about their progress through the developmental spectrum, they are likely to show some major failure to progress satisfactorily either through the normal autistic phase or the normal symbiotic phase. These early failures leave them quite vulnerable and interfere with the successful development of a smooth transition to secondary process thinking and reality testing; an adequate negotiation of the later separation-individuation phase; and therefore a failure to establish the emotional investment in the internal representation of the caretaking object in a stable, reliable way. Early differentiations of the self from the other are not adequately developed and the child fails to separate adequately. He remains quite dependent on the caretaker in terms of the need for more actual supplementing of his own functioning to feel emotionally stable and for his basic ego functions to work adequately. Indeed, it is as if the child did not develop such that he were in possession of his own self and inner world but that these remain quite incomplete and therefore quite dependent upon another person's self and mind to complement and fulfill. These children are therefore quite vulnerable to overwhelming senses of anxiety and panic.

Two very clear-cut forms of psychotic functioning appear in early life. The first, early infantile autism, is readily acknowledged as such. This centers on an extremely early onset within the first few months of life, usually and certainly within the first year. There is a basic failure of attachment to the caretaking figure and the manifest picture includes such by now familiar observations as the child's interest in maintaining a highly predictable degree of sameness in his environment; stereotyped and sometimes bizarre motor behavior and emotional aloofness; preoccupation with inanimate objects and self-stimulation; delays in speech development or in mechanical nonlinguistic use of speech; and major problems in the perception of reality.

Another form of psychosis which appears in early life is the symbiotic psychosis. Here a successful attachment is made to the mothering figure within the first year of life and by most criteria the early development appears to go well. The first signs of difficulty center around the need to maintain the symbiotic tie to the caretaking figure and resistances to and problems in entering into the early phases of the separation-individuation phase of development. Indeed, the precipitating stress for the outbreak of more dramatic manifestations of a psychotic process may well be some actual or imagined threat to the symbiotic relationship. The manifest picture usually includes some degree of emotional aloofness or withdrawal, autisticlike behavior, panic reactions, intense clinging, and distortions in the perception of reality.

The G.A.P. report also makes mention of another category where there is definitely psychotic degree and kind of functioning in the first several years of life, but wherein the child does not clearly fit either the picture of early child autism nor the symbiotic pattern.

With this understanding of the two ends of the continuum, the psycho-neuroses and the psychoses, we can briefly make note of the place of personality disorders (neurotic character structure) and the borderline syndromes (psychotic character structure). Essentially, utilizing a character trait or personality trait as a major adaptive effort to resolve internal conflicts and to deal with threat or anxiety is an alternative coping device to the development of psychoneurotic defenses and symptoms on the one hand or psychotic mechanisms on the other. Character traits or personality traits refer to relatively habitual modes of behavior usually coupled with such inner determinants as rather habitual attitudes, values, feelings, and beliefs. Such habitual modalities are then utilized in order to attempt to resolve conflicts that arise within one's self and to allow the person the maximum degree of adaptive functioning and satisfaction at the same time. Following Settlage one can distinguish a developmental process wherein the sequence of development in early life is much like that preceding the formation of a psychoneurosis versus a developmental progression in early life which is more similar to that leading to the development of a psychosis. However, what eventuates at a certain point is the utilization of these characterological mechanisms rather than neurotic or psychotic ones.

Thus in the picture of a personality disorder which might emerge in the school-age child eventually, at the preschool level we would find a reasonably adequate progression through the normal phases of autism, symbiosis, and separation-individuation with the clear establishment of emotional object constancy and reasonably adequate ego development. One might observe however a relative absence of the periodic formation of neurotic conflicts and the development of transient symptoms relating to these conflicts through the preschool years. Rather the child may show a preference to utilize these characterological mechanisms to deal with their own conflicts. For example, a child may attempt to deal with conflicts over his own aggression by behaving in an overly self-controlled manner. Still another child might choose to deal with these conflicts through behavioral outbursts and disturbed conduct. It would be very difficult to say definitely in the preschool period that the primary picture in childhood or adulthood would be a character disorder or personality disorder in contrast to a primarily psychoneurotic picture. But one can definitely see what particular traits or characteristics might be preferred in the preschool years.

Turning to the borderline syndromes, we see in the preschool years the expected difficulties in either the autistic or symbiotic phase leading to further difficulties in the separation-individuation phase. There is the expected problem in the establishment of emotional object constancy with its attendant difficulties in object relations and problems with separation issues. There are definitely developmental disturbances in basic ego or coping mechanisms including intermittent problems in reality testing and the perception of reality and significant problems with attaining more integrated ego functioning. With so many significant basic underlying developmental problems the character traits in this picture are utilized primarily to defend against the possibility of openly developing an active psychotic process rather than defending against more circumscribed neurotic conflicts and their related anxieties. As Settlage points out, the psychopathological basis is a psychotic one, but character traits are utilized to protect against the development of these overt processes. These children are characterized by the manifestation of significant problems in ego functioning such as magical thinking, omnipotent thinking, failures in reality testing, adequate integration and synthetic functioning, and the development of age adequate defenses. Their object relationships are significantly compromised, and they will frequently show intense anxieties over separation or basic security in relationship. As noted already there are problems with respect to object constancy, and they are much more likely to relate to other people as part objects rather than as whole objects. That is, they are likely to perceive others in terms of one or another facet of their potentiality in relationship to their own needs rather than being able eventually to perceive them as separate whole individuals in their own right. They are quite prone to a loss of control over their feelings and to periodic states of internal disorganization and confusion. They are quite prone therefore to regressions and to rather rapid shifts in the level of their ego functioning. Unlike the neurotic child or the neurotic character problems, their malfunctioning does not essentially represent the situation where a child has positively mastered the major developmental challenges and may regress from a more advanced level of functioning under some threat at the advanced level; but in these situations it is hypothesized that there are primary failures to develop in certain critical areas.

The discussion of interventions is rather complicated but to the degree that one is seeking to effect some change in the basic internal mechanisms—such as object constancy, tolerance for anxiety, etc.—psychoanalytic and exploratory psychotherapeutic approaches would be considered. As one approaches the end of the continuum closer to the psychoneurotic and the neurotic character, the prognosis is significantly more favorable than dealing with borderline syndromes or childhood psychoses. However, these methods do have relevance even in these more severe disturbances. The individual decision is a complicated one depending a great deal on the exact specific strengths and vulnerabilities of the particular child being evaluated. Parental treatment is more likely to be relevant with the greater degree of disturbance and with the younger child. When the child is primarily psychoneurotic and close to school age it is often possible to be quite successful without major parental involvement. The more the psychopathology includes basic distortions of ego functioning, other forms of intervention aimed specifically at these problems are indicated. This can include the range of interventions extending from specific behavioral approaches to various educational approaches. At times, very major intervention into the environment may also be indicated.

BIBLIOGRAPHY

Freud, A. "Assessment of Childhood Disturbances." In *Psychoanalytic Study of the Child*, Vol. 17. New York: International Universities Press, 1962, pages 149-158.

Freud, A. "The Concept of Developmental Lines." In *Psychoanalytic Study of the Child*, Vol. 18. New York: International Universities Press, 1963, pages 245-265.

Freud, A. *Normality and Pathology in Childhood: Assessments of Development.* New York: International Universities Press, 1965.

Freud, A. "The Symptomatology of Childhood: A Preliminary Attempt to Classification." In *Psychoanalytic Study of the Child*, Vol. 25. New York: International Universities Press, 1970, pages 19-41.

Freud, W. "Assessment of Early Infancy: Problems and Considerations." In *Psychoanalytic Study of the Child*, Vol. 22. New York: International Universities Press, 1967, pages 216-238.

Freud, W. "The Baby Profile: Part II." In *Psychoanalytic Study of the Child*, Vol. 26. New York: Quadrangle Books, 1972, pages 172-194.

Furman, R., and Katan, A. *The Therapeutic Nursery School: A Contribution to the Study and Treatment of Emotional Disturbances in Young Children.* New York: International Universities Press, 1969.

Group for the Advancement of Psychiatry. *Psychopathological Disorders of Childhood: Theoretical Considerations and a Proposed Classification,* Vol. VI, Report No. 62. New York: Mental Health Materials Center Incorporated, 1966.

Mahler, M. *On Human Symbiosis and the Vicissitudes of Individuation Vol. 1, Infantile Psychosis.* New York: International Universities Press, 1968.

Mahler, M., Pine, S., and Bergman, A. *The Psychological Birth of the Human Infant; Symbiosis and Individuation.* New York: Basic Books, 1975.

Nagera, H. "The Developmental Profile: Notes on Some Practical Considerations Regarding its Use." In *Psychoanalytic Study of the Child*, Vol. 18. New York: International Universities Press, 1963, pages 511-541.

Nagera, H. *Early Childhood Disturbances, the Infantile Neuroses and the Adult Disturbances* (Monograph No. 2). In *Psychoanalytic Study of the Child.* New York: International Universities Press, 1966.

Settlage, C. "Psychoanalytic Theory in Relation to the Nosology of Childhood Psychic Disorders." *Journal of the American Psychoanalytic Association*, 12(1964):776-801.

Weil, A. "The Basic Core." In *Psychoanalytic Study of the Child*, Vol. 25. New York: International Universities Press, 1970, pages 442-460.

CHAPTER **3**

Assessment of Social and Emotional Development in the Preschool Child

Robert H. Bradley and
Bettye M. Caldwell

Assessing the social and emotional development of preschool children is a challenging assignment. It is rather like trying to catch a soap bubble in your hands. The bubble floats before you, delicate and glistening, inviting capture and inspection. Yet, no matter what strategy of entrapment you employ and no matter how cooperative the forces of nature, it is nearly impossible to hold the fragile film in your hand long enough to examine it. Before you have an adequate look, it is gone.

The problems of measuring social competency are better understood now than in the past, but solutions remain largely elusive. In the following pages, we will attempt to synthesize knowledge about measurement and about learning and development in children. Hopefully, our effort will be helpful in pointing the way to the most useful assessment practices.

PERSONALITY THEORY AND ASSESSMENT PROCEDURES

In the field of educational and psychological measurement, there has certainly not been anything approaching a consensus as to what types of measurement techniques are most appropriate for use with young children. In one of the most famous historical attempts to understand emotional functioning in a young child—Freud's analysis of "Little Hans"—the analyst never even saw the child. Instead, all the information considered

ROBERT H. BRADLEY is an Associate Professor in the Center for Child Development and Education at the University of Arkansas, Little Rock. His major interests include child development, early childhood education, and research and evaluation.

BETTYE M. CALDWELL is a Professor in, as well as the Director of, the Center for Child Development and Education at the University of Arkansas, Little Rock. Her major interests include child development, early childhood education, and social policy.

in the analysis was taken from the father. Reliance upon parental report as a technique for securing information about children's social and emotional development has actually appeared to increase in the years intervening between Little Hans and the present. An example can be found in the landmark study of Sears, Maccoby, and Levin (1957) who attempted to relate patterns of child rearing to manifestations of personality in children. Maternal interview served as the only source of data about the social and emotional functioning of the five-year-old children who were the focus of the study. Similarly, the bulk of paper and pencil (Cattell and Coan, 1957) and card-sorting assessment procedures (Ireton and Thwing, 1968) introduced in recent years assumes that the parent, or an equally knowledgeable adult, can give the information necessary for generalities to be drawn about the social and emotional functioning of a child. Others have challenged this undue reliance upon adult report (Caldwell, 1974; and Caldwell, Bradley, and Elardo, 1975) and have urged instead that more and better observational methods for assessing directly the functioning of the children be developed.

Adequate assessment cannot proceed without a sound theoretical underpinning as to what types of behavior are worth assessing. Unfortunately, there is little in the way of systematic theories of personality development for the very young child. The major exception is the theory of attachment to a primary care giver (Ainsworth, 1973) as a foundation for subsequent manifestations of personal social development. When theory is precise, as is the case with attachment theory, methods come forth to help provide the documentation necessary to validate the theory. When the theory is imprecise, fuzzy, or virtually nonexistent, then the development of assessment procedures lags behind.

Success in assessing the development of young children is equally dependent upon our knowledge of how humans develop in the particular area being measured and upon our evaluation of different assessment procedures. Therefore, a critical question is: *What do we know about the social and emotional development of the young child?* Certainly, we know a great deal more than we knew two decades ago. A taxonomy of objectives in the affective domain has been published (Krathwohl, Bloom, and Masia, 1964), methodologies for investigating questions about development have been improved, and some valuable longitudinal data have been gathered. However, in the affective taxonomy as well as in most approaches to synthesizing knowledge about social and emotional development, little thought has been given to its appropriateness for very young children.

A major developmental factor affecting performance on tests is the socialization process. When children come into the world, they are not socialized. That is, children are not born knowing how they are supposed to behave in the wide range of situations in which they will find themselves. This does not mean that they lack a response repertoire. Indeed, each child has certain response tendencies for dealing with persons, objects, and events. Some babies are extremely active in their responses to the world around them; others are quiet and passive (Brazelton, 1972). Until children have had the opportunity to learn how they are expected to act in various situations, it is difficult to interpret how competent or how socially healthy they are compared to other children. For this reason, it is often more meaningful to compare an infant's performance at any given point in time to what is typical for him most of the time. Comparing a child's performance to that of others becomes more meaningful as the child gets older, because some similarity of learning opportunity for most children can be assumed.

One additional characteristic of social-emotional development with clear implications for measurement is the close relationship between affective states in the very young child and the child's behavior. Young children do not try to conceal their affective states. Thus, observations of infants in natural, everyday settings can often provide excellent clues about emotional status. Riccuiti and Poresky (1972) claim that extreme positive and negative emotional reactions (i.e., prolonged crying as an indication of tension) can be identified with considerable confidence. They warn, however, that many of the infant's reactions are not without ambiguity. Children's responses often contain both positive and negative aspects. For example, when a child sees a stranger, he may both smile (indicating interest) and turn away (indicating fear). Another example is a child who upon receiving a new toy says he likes it but then quickly puts it down. In such instances, it takes very careful observation to gauge the child's true emotional state.

Another problem which complicates any assessment procedure is the inability to separate clearly a young child's behavior into components such as cognitive, affective, and psychomotor. There is a strong interdependency among areas of development; and, in a very real sense, any assessment of the young child is assessment of the total child. To make this point more concrete, we might consider the following test item: *Child follows teacher's directions.* Does this item measure affect or cognition? Intriguingly, while much attention has been given to the close relation between affective and cognitive behavior (e.g., Kamii, 1971), relatively little attention has been paid to the association between affective and psychomotor behavior. Yet movement and feeling are closely linked in the infant. What better index of an eight-month-old child's interest in an object than how rapidly that child crawls toward the object? Or what better clue can a sensitive parent find of incipient illness than a sudden change in activity level?

One of the implications of the infant's unified development is that handicaps cannot always be identified as belonging to one domain versus another. Suppose, for example, we find a child who is very slow to interact with things around him. Would it be accurate to say that the child is socially backward, emotionally disturbed, motorically retarded, or cognitively impaired? Such distinctions are almost impossible to make. Furthermore, even when the type of impairment is clear, handicaps in the cognitive and psychomotor domains will often result in poor performance on socioemotional measures. Thus, it is necessary to be cautious when interpreting the performance of young handicapped children on these measures. Of course as the child grows older, it is easier to distinguish among the various areas of development. The inability to make such distinctions in the development of a very young child no doubt accounts for some of the poor predictive accuracy of infant scales in regard to performance in later childhood and for the apparent failure of remedial experiences to improve the situation.

As children grow older, their emotional reactions tend to cluster into identifiable personality traits. Each trait involves a large number of specific, discrete behaviors. The trait of enthusiasm, for example, might involve such behaviors as looking about the room with wide eyes, smiling and laughing while playing with toys, and running quickly to see new people or events. However, though a trait involves many behaviors, no one behavior is valid (by itself) as an indicator of the trait. To be more specific, suppose a child was observed running to greet a person. Would it be likely that he would be called enthusiastic on the basis of that behavior alone? Certainly not. For older children, therefore, elaborate observation schemes or other measurement procedures (e.g., paper-and-pencil tests) are required to assess social and emotional development adequately.

SPECIAL CONSIDERATIONS
IN ASSESSING YOUNG CHILDREN

ASSESSMENT PROBLEMS
ASSOCIATED WITH IMMATURITY

The very young child is not easy to work with in an assessment situation—to offer the understatement of this chapter. In fact, most persons would agree that greater skill and more training are required for sensitive assessment of the very young child than are needed for persons carrying out this function with older children. The developmental characteristics associated with extreme youth or immaturity produce difficulties, and extra cleverness on the part of the instrument developer or the person conducting the assessment is necessary if any degree of accuracy is to be achieved.

A first deterrent is simply the extremely short attention span of the very young child. The attentive state of the infant during an assessment session must be reported in order for the information to be properly interpreted. An infant who is alert and attentive can be expected to achieve a much higher rating of developmental maturity than one who is drowsy and inattentive. In proposing that this condition of receptivity to stimulation be regarded in interpreting test scores, and in calling it "state," Wolff actually introduced a new concept to the field of infant assessment. Although it is perhaps most applicable when assessing very young infants, the "state" of the young child during any type of assessment, especially one concerned with social or emotional functioning, must be considered. Most assessment procedures have some sort of cover sheet on which the person making the assessment can record any unusual events which might shorten the young child's attention span (such as loud noises coming from an adjoining room, or a turned-on TV set in the corner) or heighten irritability (such as receiving an injection or a sharp scolding from a parent). The assessor will always take such states of the child into consideration in interpreting results.

By definition, an assessment involves some interaction between at least two people—the child being assessed and the adult carrying out the task. Very young children often do not have sufficient experience with older persons to participate in such interactions without some anxiety or discomfort. While there are obviously individual differences in degree of shyness in strange situations, most young children experience shyness to some extent. Because of the almost universal appearance of such behavior and because of the extent to which it can distort the characteristic behavior of the child, social and emotional assessment is especially likely to reflect this limitation (shyness).

The absence or limitation of language functioning in young children of necessity limits the range of assessment procedures that can be used with them. In spite of the distortions that are possible when verbal report is relied upon to learn how someone feels about a particular situation, the possibility of such a report greatly increases the range of responses possible for any individual. Further, even though verbal report may still leave the assessor with the task of trying to interpret what the person "really meant" by what he said, the absence of any such verbal report can create an even greater burden of interpretation.

The fact that very young children are often nonverbal or minimally verbal is responsible for the greater reliance upon parental report as a means of understanding the child's social and emotional functioning and of identifying any problems that might be present in the situation. Although no one—including the most sophisticated interviewers or therapists—can hope to know and understand the nuances of a child's emotional functioning better than the parents, that understanding can also be biased and misleading. Parents who desperately want to deny the presence of any problems in the child, or who are so overcome by chronic problems of interaction with a different child that they exaggerate every slight atypical tendency, can provide misleading information. Thus, while parental report is an important source of information about social and emotional functioning of young children, it should rarely be the only source of information. This point will be amplified in the subsequent discussion of decisions made on the basis of assessment.

ASSESSMENT PROBLEMS OF HANDICAPPED AND MINORITY GROUP CHILDREN

It is quite possible that all the assessment difficulties associated with immaturity will be even more striking in handicapped children. Distortions of attention are one manifestation of central nervous system damage, so short attention spans should certainly be expected. Furthermore, young handicapped children have often not had the exposure to other adults that non-handicapped children might have had, thus predisposing them to stranger anxiety or shyness. Verbal functioning through which the child could communicate important feelings might be either delayed or distorted. Parental report will be influenced by the dynamics of the parents' attempts to cope with the child's handicap, and the child's own style of responding to any given assessment procedure will reflect his gain or pain associated with previous contacts. Thus, whatever the assessment problems associated with general immaturity, they are likely to be magnified when the young child has some sort of developmental or social handicap.

Evidence was found by Golden and Birns (1968) that infants and toddlers from lower socioeconomic backgrounds were "more difficult" to examine than infants from middle-class families. In the study, they were interested in determining whether there was a statistically significant difference between the mean developmental quotients of eighteen-month-old and twenty-four-month-old infants with different social histories. They found no average difference in terms of the numerical score; however, in order to get a complete score on the lower-class infants they had to work harder and spend more time, often scheduling a second session in order to complete the procedure. The investigators felt that this early class difference in general receptivity to the assessment procedure might help explain some of the differences in results so often reported as a function of social class. Hertzig, Birch, et al. (1968) also reported that cultural and ethnic patterns affected children's responses to test procedures. Even when they controlled for overall IQ level, significant differences in test-taking "style" were found in children from different ethnic backgrounds. These stylistic differences will, unless the assessor is aware of the possible bias they can create, influence the scores made by these children.

The history of test development in the socioemotional area for handicapped and minority children is basically one of neglect. These children are usually administered tests designed for the "normal" Anglo child. Such a practice is analogous to giving "hand-me-down" clothes to younger siblings. The same garments which make the elder child sartorially resplendent are frequently tattered and ill fitting when worn by the younger. To put the matter more technically: to the extent that a child differs from the Anglo normal in any way which affects test performance, the validity of many tests is open to question. Interpreting the performance of these children is subject to error, often unknown error.

Research provides some clues to typical response patterns for certain handicapped and minority groups; but additional normative data are badly needed for accurate interpretation of scores made by such children. More broadly, further development of concepts about the "mental health" or "adaptiveness" of various subgroups is required. Mercer (1974) has raised several substantive issues with respect to the intellectual assessment of minority group children. Similar issues should be raised with respect to the socioemotional assessment of both handicapped and minority group children. In brief, Mercer contends that children have certain rights which must be considered. The rights, briefly stated, are:

1. *The Right To Be Assessed As a Multidimensional Human Being.* Many children are judged as maladjusted on the basis of a single test, though that test assesses only a fraction of the total number of human dispositions. For some children, maladjustment is situation- or domain-specific. Their adjustment in other situations is quite adequate.

2. *The Right To Be Fully Educated.* For many children, educational assessment is a prelude to being stuck in a special class or treatment which in no way meets their individual developmental needs.

3. *The Right To Be Free of Stigmatizing Labels.* The problems associated with being labeled as retarded, speech-impaired, emotionally disturbed, learning-disabled, behaviorally disordered, and so forth are clearly documented. Mercer argues that the educational environment must be carefully structured so as to avoid the negative stereotyping which accompanies such labels.

4. *The Right To Individual Identity and Respect.* As a general rule, standardized tests in the affective domain assess those competencies considered "normal" in Anglo-centric societies while ignoring many of the competencies indicative of mental health in various handicapped groups or other cultures.

5. *The Right To Be Evaluated Within An Appropriate Normative Framework.* Many assessment procedures employ a single normative framework for interpreting the scores of all children. Those tests ignore the fact that the experiences of many handicapped and minority group children differ widely from those of the dominant group. Thus, for these students, comparison to the norm can be misleading.

In sum, it is preferable to design new tests or adapt old tests to meet the special needs of minority groups and handicapped children. Further, when evaluating handicapped or minority group children with instruments designed for and normed on "normal" Anglo children, extreme caution in interpreting the results must be exercised by the assessor.

SELECTION OF AN APPROPRIATE INSTRUMENT FOR ASSESSING THE YOUNG CHILD'S DEVELOPMENT

When selecting an instrument to measure social and emotional development in young children, it is essential to consider the decision one wants to make on the basis of the resultant score. By and large, there are four different types of decisions that are made using such information: screening, diagnosis, formative evaluation, and summative evaluation. The first two of these involve gathering information about *individuals*. The information is then used to make decisions about those individuals. The last two types involve collecting data about *programs*. On the basis of this information, modifications are made in existing programs and decisions are made as to whether a given type of program should be abandoned or made available to comparable individuals or groups.

SCREENING AND DIAGNOSIS

Screening tests are generally used to determine if children have a particular set of characteristics which make them appropriate candidates for a special program. The purpose of a screening test is to select those children who will benefit from a special program. Gallagher and Bradley (1972) point out that selection decisions are fundamentally dichotomous ones—a child either goes into a program or he does not. Therefore, the best screening instrument is the one which does the best job of balancing errors in deciding whether a particular set of characteristics (most often a handicapping condition) is present or absent in the individual child. A good screening instrument is one which has both a low percentage of false positives (those identified as having the condition who, in fact, do not have it) and a low percentage of false negatives (those identified as not having a condition who, in fact, do have it).

The second major type of decision is diagnostic. Diagnostic instruments involve a detailed examination of the child in order to match the child with an appropriate program. The purpose of a diagnostic test is to classify children according to the specific type of program they need. The distinction between selecting and classifying is an important one. For example, a test which does an excellent job of screening children for adjustment problems (that is, it does a good job of selecting children who are sufficiently maladjusted to warrant placement in a program) may be ineffective in pointing out what specific type of program that child needs. The good diagnostic test must discriminate, for instance, between those children whose adjustment difficulties stem from a family relations problem and those whose adjustment difficulties stem from poor achievement, because the underlying reasons for the problems imply different directions for remediation. Since a diagnostic test is used as a basis for choosing between different programs or treatments, the differential validity of the test must be demonstrated.

The third basic type of testing decision is called a formative evaluation decision. Once a child has entered a program matched to his individual needs and capabilities, it is important to monitor the child's progress during the program and to check for errors in the program. Essentially, a formative evaluation is designed to allow one to decide whether modification is needed in the program in order for the child to develop in a satisfactory manner. In general, the instrument that determines whether the child possesses certain prerequisite characteristics which make him a good candidate for a particular program is different from the instrument which locates where in the program a child is experiencing difficulty. In many instances, diagnostic tests are concerned with individual differences which predispose an individual to receive a certain kind of treatment. Formative measures, by comparison, are primarily concerned with changes within an individual in skills, attitudes, and so on, resulting from the selected program. Since the purpose of most educational or therapeutic programs is individual improvement, it is often useful for formative evaluations to contain items which are maximally sensitive to individual growth. Therefore, the best items for formative evaluation are not those that approximately 50 percent of the students "pass" and for which there is an approximately normal distribution. The best items are those which almost nobody passes prior to participation in the program and which, it is hoped, almost everybody will pass at the end of the program (see Carver, 1974, for a discusssion of edumetric tests).

The fourth and final type of decision is what Gronlund (1973) calls a summative evaluation decision. At the end of a program it is often necessary to make decisions related to the final performance of participants. Should the program be continued? Should an individual be certified as having certain skills and attitudes? Should a participant enter the next level of the program? Did the program accomplish its objectives? In formative evaluation, the focus is on a procedure which measures improvement in each of the specific competencies achieved during the program. In summative evaluation, the focus is more general—one wishes to obtain a representative sample of performance on program objectives and related variables. Since individuals are likely to differ in terms of how much they have benefited from a program, it is often useful to include items which assess a fairly wide range of performance for each content area. That is, one would want to include items that almost everyone would pass, items that some of the participants would pass, and items that almost no one would pass. Including items which have a wide range of difficulty is useful regardless of whether the individual's performance is compared to norms or to more specific performance criteria.

ASSESSMENT TECHNIQUES

Assessment in all its varied forms involves some type of observation. It may involve observing a written response to a question. It may involve observing behavior in a specially designed, highly controlled situation. It may involve observing reactions which occur during routine activities. Each kind of observation has its own advantages and disadvantages which will be a function of the type of information needed to make a certain decision. In this section we will survey assessment techniques. As part of the survey, we will offer suggestions about the usefulness of these different methods for making the four types of program decisions described in the previous section.

NATURALISTIC OBSERVATIONS

A large proportion of the decisions made about children require the decision maker to know how a child is likely to behave in a particular kind of situation. Unfortunately, it is very difficult to predict accurately the behavior of children. Young children's moods change rapidly; and, since they do not have well-established personality traits, their responses are likely to be different from one kind of situation to another. For this reason, a child's performance on a paper-and-pencil test of "aggressiveness" will probably not be a good indicator of how aggressively the child will act in a classroom. A more accurate prediction is likely to be obtained by observing the child as he "naturally" behaves in a classroom situation.

Systematic observations of behavior in natural or typical settings are termed naturalistic observations. Many schemes for making naturalistic observations have been developed [many of these can be found in *Mirrors for Behavior* (1970) and *Measures of Maturation* (1973)]. By and large, each system is designed to be used in one particular type of setting (e.g., a self-contained classroom). Naturalistic observation systems require the designation of categories for the particular types of behavior in which one is interested. For example, suppose someone is interested in aggressive behaviors of four-year-olds in kindergarten. One might start categorizing in terms of various types of physically aggressive acts and various types of verbally aggressive acts. One then observes and records children's behavior using the categories developed. Observations are typically made at several points in time in order that they might more accurately represent a person's typical behavior.

Naturalistic observations have several advantages over other types of measures. First, since children's behavior is simply recorded as it occurs during the course of ordinary events, there is less chance that the behavior will be changed by the introduction of an "irrelevant cue." By comparison, a formal test instrument or an unusual new activity often signals to the child that he should alter his behavior in accordance with the new situation. Using naturalistic observations also does not entail introducing an "irrelevant difficulty." The reading level of some paper-and-pencil tests is too hard for many children to understand, thus causing the children to give an invalid response (see Messick and Anderson, 1970, for a discussion of this issue). In sum, behavior observed in appropriate natural settings tends to be fairly representative of the child's typical behavior; and as Whitla (1968) has stated, the greater the similarity between the measurement environment and the criterion environment (i.e., the situation one is really interested in), the greater the chance that one can predict a child's behavior with accuracy.

Systems for making naturalistic observations vary considerably in the number of behaviors examined and the complexity of the categories used to examine these behaviors. Allen, Rieke, Dmitriev, and Hayden (1972) have demonstrated that useful information may be obtained by simply counting particular behaviors in a given time span or by noting how long children engage in certain activities. In some cases, a more elaborate system may be required. Gordon (1966) notes, for example, that one sometimes wants to know the specific conditions under which an individual is likely to behave in a particular manner. One easy to use observational system which gives moderately detailed information about children's social behavior can be found in the CIRCUS Preschool Inventory published by Educational Testing Service. This instrument not only provides information about how frequently children engage in certain types of activities, but also whether they prefer to do so alone, in a group, or whether they attempt to enlist the teacher's involvement in the activity.

Naturalistic observations have the advantage of being relatively objective as compared with teacher or parent ratings of a child's behavior. Ratings done by teachers and/or parents are usually retrospective. Hence, they are only as good as the parent's or teacher's memory. All ratings, even when done by an "objective" observer, are affected by the biases of the rater. They are also influenced by the rater's sensitivity and insight with regard to behavior of the child being rated. Moreover, the validity of ratings depends on how systematically the rater has observed a child, how suitable the situations were in which the child was observed, and how clearly the behavioral categories were defined. Of course, schemes for categorizing natural behaviors also reflect the personal biases and values of the person who designed the system for observing. Therefore, great care must be taken when choosing a system so as to reduce the effect of bias as much as possible. To this end, there are several requirements which must be met in order to assure that reasonably valid information is obtained for naturalistic observations: (1) a sufficient number of suitable observations must be made, (2) the observations must not alter the behavior of the one observed, and (3) the behavior observed must be sufficiently concrete and thus permit substantial agreement by different observers on the behavior being categorized.

Naturalistic observations are especially useful for diagnostic evaluation where the major intent is to plan beneficial experiences for children. Naturalistic observations can also be useful for formative and summative evaluation purposes if the objectives of the program include improvement of specific social competencies or changes in certain behavior patterns. However, naturalistic observations are often not useful for screening purposes since they tend to require a considerable amount of time to collect. In fact, one of the major disadvantages of naturalistic observations is that it is burdensome to gather the kind of meticulous information required of all but the simplest observational systems.

Finally, because naturalistic observations involve recordings of discrete behaviors in particular settings, the information obtained is often not particularly useful for making inferences about underlying social traits. Persons employing this technique should, therefore, be cautious in extrapolating from the specific data obtained to much broader categories of socioemotional development.

BEHAVIORAL AND SITUATION TESTS

On occasions when it is not feasible to observe children in real-life settings, it is often useful to observe them in situations which are designed to simulate real life. There are two principal ways of setting up contrived situations for the purpose of observing the reactions of children: situational tests and behavioral tests. In a situational test, the child is placed in a "pretend" or "play like" situation and is then given instruction about the part he is to play. The behavior of the child in the play situation is then recorded and taken as an index of his attitude toward certain things or as an example of how the child would behave in the real situation. One area of development where a situational test might afford a very useful type of measurement is role-taking. For example, the tester could present the following situation to a child: "Suppose someone came up and hit you. Show me what you would do." The answer could then be evaluated in terms of how much the child would consider the feelings of others in his actions. Many types of social competencies could be assessed using similar kinds of situational tests. Such tests might contribute valuable formative and summative evaluation data for programs aimed at the development of social skills.

In a behavioral test, the individual is not asked to pretend that he is involved in a particular situation. Rather, the individual is observed in a real situation. However, it is a situation which has been set up by the tester to reveal a certain underlying trait or behavior pattern. Hartshorne and May (1928-1930) designed behavioral tests to measure such traits as honesty, cooperativeness, and truthfulness. In their research, honesty was measured by allowing students to grade their own papers, after which a check was made to see how correctly each student scored his own paper. Behavioral tests in many instances can be introduced into a situation so unobtrusively as to appear a natural part of the ongoing events. Observations done under such conditions are very much like naturalistic observations.

A major problem with situational and behavioral tests is that they represent a rather limited view of the child's total behavior. Moreover, the situations are so contrived in some cases, especially some situational tests, that the generalizability of the observations to real life is very doubtful. However, observations done in contrived situations can be particularly helpful when there is insufficient time or resources for detailed observations in natural settings and when only a small amount of information is needed in order to make a decision. For these reasons, situational and behavioral tests probably have considerable potential as screening and evaluation instruments. In cases where relatively detailed observations are done via situational and behavioral tests, the information may also be useful for diagnostic purposes. However, detailed tests of these types can sometimes be unwieldly and time-consuming.

One final point to consider regarding situational and behavioral tests is that tests of this type have been developed only for a few social and emotional characteristics. Indeed, it is hard to imagine how one might develop such a test for certain areas of social development (e.g., self-concept or confidence). In sum, it would appear that observations in contrived situations might provide valuable information about certain aspects of affective development, but only limited information about others.

OBSERVATION IN CLINICS

Valuable information about the emotional health of young children may be obtained by observing them in clinic settings. Observations done in clinics may range from naturalistic observations to behavioral and situational tests. Observations may also involve such activities as "doll play" situations. In these situations, a child is given one or more dolls and told that they represent family members. The child is then observed as he plays with the dolls. His behavior is taken as an index of the child's attitude toward his own family. "Doll play" methods are similar to projective techniques discussed in a later section.

The more prolonged and detailed clinical observations are, the more likely they are to provide useful information for diagnostic purposes. One of the primary obstacles to overcome in these observations is the fact that children are unlikely to act in a clinic the way they do in common situations. The clinic is strange to most children and serves to alter their normal reactions. Careful planning can reduce the effect of "strangeness" and allow accurate information to be gathered about a child.

SELF-INVENTORY MEASURES

Observations of behavior in naturalistic settings and contrived situations are useful primarily as indices of relatively discrete, simple behaviors or behavior patterns. Such observations, unless they are extremely extensive, do not provide a good index of general personality traits, dispositions, or attitudes. To assess personality characteristics and generalized behavior patterns, psychologists have relied heavily on various types of self inventories such as attitude scales, personality inventories, interest inventories, and self-concept scales. The most commonly used self inventories involve presenting the child with some type of stimulus (question, statement, and nonverbal) and then asking the child to react to the stimulus by choosing an alternative from among those that are provided. The following are examples of self-inventory items: (1) What do you like to do most? A. Go to the zoo. B. Read a book. C. Play football. (2) You should share your toys with other children. A. Yes. B. No. (3) Point to the picture that is most like you.

Most self inventories contain a series of stimuli or test items. There are two major reasons for using several items rather than just one or two. First, if a child responds similarly to several related items, the tester can be more confident that the information obtained is reliable. Second, a series of items allows the tester to make relatively accurate judgments about the "intensity" of a child's feelings about a particular thing. Using a series of items, it is possible to determine the range of conditions under which the child will react in a particular way. For example, a child's responses to a series of items about preferred activities might show that Johnny likes roller skating better than visiting the zoo or reading a book, but not better than going to a movie or watching TV. With a series of items, it is also possible to obtain information with regard to the areas of activity in which a particular belief, disposition, or expectancy is held. That is, it permits the tester to make relatively accurate judgments about the "extensity" or generalizability of a child's feelings about a particular thing. For example, a child's responses to a series of questions about personal control may indicate that the child perceives that he has lots of control in social situations, but very little control in academic situations.

Structured inventories and scales have a distinct advantage over most other types of measurement when the object is to obtain information quickly about the intensity or extensity of a particular attitude, disposition, or characteristic. However, structured inventories present several problems which are difficult to solve when assessing young children: (1) social desirability, (2) semantics, and (3) response set (Nunnally, 1967).

Social desirability. When responding to items on self inventories, individuals sometimes choose the response which they think is most socially acceptable rather than the response which most accurately conveys the way they feel. Fortunately, this threat to the validity of measurement, termed social desirability, is probably not as much a problem with little children as with adults. Children tend not to be as aware of what is socially desirable. In fact, some young children are so familiar with taking tests or reacting to strange adults that they may not understand what they are supposed to do in a test situation. Rather than reacting to the test situation as it is intended, a child may be caught up in relating to the adult tester or may treat the situation as a game or may feel that he is involved in an irrelevant exercise. Thus, while social desirability may be less of a problem with young children, there are numerous other typical reactions which result equally in an invalid result (see Riegel, 1975, for an especially interesting discussion of alienation in the testing situation).

Language problems. Of all types of tests, self-inventory tests present probably the greatest number of problems with respect to language. The most basic issue involves whether a child understands the test item as it is intended by the test developer. It is highly improbable that all children will interpret self inventories as they are meant. Children are limited both in terms of their vocabulary and in their use of grammar. For culturally different children, the problem is even more acute. Interpreting which items are problematic for young children is difficult not only because of language limitation but also because interpretation depends on the psychological meaning the child attaches to an item. How closely a child's psychological interpretation of an item agrees with the test developer's psychological interpretation of an item is largely known. However, it is probably safe to say that the large majority of children's tests still tend to be adultomorphic. Piaget and other developmentalists have provided great leads regarding a child's concept of self and the world, leads that will be useful in improving most instruments for children. Related to this issue is an intriguing rhetorical question posed by Sigel (1974): "When do we know what a child knows?" He contends that for young children especially all knowledge is context bound. That is, a child will indicate that he understands something in one context but not in another. For example, a child may show that he understands the concept of two by taking two cookies from a plate during "snack time," but not show that he understands the same concept when asked to give the tester two blocks from an array of eight presented on part of a psychometric test. It is hard to imagine a context more alien to most children than being asked a series of questions about how they feel by a stranger who is sitting beside them writing things on a piece of paper. More fundamentally, it is hard to interpret a child's responses when they vary from one context to another. To paraphrase Sigel, when do we know what a child feels? The form of an item may be as critical as its content.

In sum, great care must be taken in writing items for children. The vocabulary must be simple. The items must contain a very limited number of phrases or clauses. Items which have two or more clauses in the stem plus several clauses to choose among in responding to the stem are incomprehensible to all but the very brightest children. It is particularly difficult for young children since most items have to be read to them, thus making it necessary that they recall and organize all pertinent information from the items without benefit of referring to the items in written form. The language problems inherent in self-inventory scales are probably a principal cause for the low reliability of most of these measures for young children.

Response set. Since self inventories typically involve making a choice from among several alternatives, it is easy for young children to develop a set when responding to items. Among the more common response sets is saying "yes" to every question. Another common response set is choosing the first alternative when responding to an item. In general, children's personal behavioral style is more likely to affect their performance on self inventories than on other types of assessment procedures. As a case in point, consider the child who characteristically responds impulsively in situations. This child is likely to blurt out an answer from among alternatives in a test rather than carefully considering how he really feels about a certain issue. By comparison, an impulsive response style would probably have little effect on inferences made on the basis of naturalistic observations or projective measures. This threat to the validity of information obtained by self inventories can be reduced by devoting careful attention to the construction of the inventory in terms of the format for items and the directions provided.

PROJECTIVE TECHNIQUES

In situations where valid information is hard to obtain due to the limitations of children's language, some psychologists and educators have relied on projective techniques when assessing social and emotional development. Projective techniques usually involve presenting a verbal or pictorial stimulus to a child and then directing the child to create a response of his own. Familiar projective devices include the Rorschach and Holtzman inkblots, TAT pictures, the House-Tree-Person and Goodenough Draw-a-Man tests, and various incomplete sentence instruments. Coding systems, sometimes very elaborate, are developed to score an individual's response. Some projectives, such as incomplete sentence tests, are relatively structured in that they provide at least some information about the kind of response that is desired. Other projectives, such as inkblot tests, are almost completely unstructured in that they provide almost no guidance about how to respond. The principal intent of projectives is that they allow a person to reveal certain latent or unconscious aspects of personality. One of the limitations of projectives, however, is that they generally focus on evaluating the total personality rather than separate traits (Walker, 1973).

While projectives are less dependent on a child's ability to interpret the intent of an item than are self inventories, projectives like inkblots and incomplete sentences are more dependent on a child's ability to produce a verbal response. Since young children often have poor verbal facility, their responses to projectives are frequently unscorable. By the same token, there are projectives which do not require a verbal response. Nonverbal projective procedures such as Draw-a-Man and House-Tree-Person require the child to draw a person or other objects freehand. The figures produced by a child are scored according to various coding schemes, and inferences are made about such things as the child's self-concept, level of anxiety, degree of intimacy, and attitude toward others. Sometimes children are allowed to paint or draw anything they wish. Their paintings are then analyzed using various scoring criteria and inferences are made about certain personality characteristics and attitudes.

Projective techniques have been extensively used in clinical settings as a means of diagnosing underlying psychological problems. Their use outside of clinical settings has been more limited, although a considerable amount of attention has been devoted to measuring such characteristics as locus of control and achievement motivation with projectives. Part of the popularity of these tests lies in their potential to reveal underlying motives, motives which may not be revealed through observing behavior in natural settings or in recording responses to self inventories. In the sense that hidden motives are more likely to manifest themselves in new or unstructured situations, projective tests have a kind of "face validity." Unfortunately there is but a meager amount of empirical validity for these instruments. Children who show aggressive responses to inkblots often do not behave aggressively in real life. Likewise, children whose responses to TAT pictures contain a lot of achievement imagery do not always act in an achievement-oriented manner in real life. Furthermore, projectives have rarely shown sufficient discriminant validity in terms of pointing out children who will be good candidates for a certain type of treatment and those who will not. Thus, while on the surface they appear to be useful for screening and diagnosis, it seems fair to conclude that their usefulness has not been demonstrated. Perhaps most fundamentally, there is serious doubt as to whether children's responses to projectives actually represent a portrait of their underlying personality. As Walker (1973) has noted, "projection with children is not the same as with adults, for children perceive the world quite differently. The reality and fantasy production of the child should be understood more thoroughly before personality interpretations are placed on children" (p. 25).

One final comment with respect to projectives: while rather elaborate coding systems have been developed for scoring responses to some projectives, coding procedures with adequate theoretical and/or research bases are lacking for almost all social and emotional characteristics.

PARENT AND TEACHER
INTERVIEWS AND QUESTIONNAIRES

While all the measurement procedures discussed to this point have involved some type of direct observation of the child, useful information about children can also be obtained indirectly via interviews with parents and teachers or questionnaires filled out by parents and teachers. These procedures have two principal advantages over direct assessment of the child: (1) it is often more convenient, and (2) adults have superior language skills and thus can provide certain types of information which children cannot. Depending on the parent's (or teacher's) insight and candor about their children, interviews can afford extremely valuable information. Unfortunately, not all parents are sensitive observers, nor are they all entirely honest.

Interviews and questionnaires are probably most reliable when they involve discussions of recent events. Time has a way of clouding the memory of even the most astute observers. Reliability is also likely to be enhanced if the trait examined is clearly defined and if the adult is provided rather specific choices to make among alternatives. For example, a question like "How would you rate your child's aggressiveness?" leaves itself open to a variety of interpretations. A question like "How many times a day does your child hit other children? a. Less than once. b. 1-3 times. c. 4 or more times" is better. For this reason, written questionnaires are often more reliable than verbal interviews. Rightly handled, however, a verbal interview can be as reliable as written questionnaires. Furthermore, they have an element of flexibility that written questionnaires typically do not have.

Information obtained from parents and teachers lends itself most readily to screening, somewhat less readily to diagnostic evaluation. After all, even the most observant parent provides only secondhand information about a child. Interviews and questionnaires are generally less well suited as the sole index of program effectiveness (formative and summative evaluation). In some cases, they would afford helpful information about a child's achievement in a program. However, it would be rare that they would provide adequate assessment of a child's progress on specific program objectives.

The validity of interview and questionnaire procedures has not been established for most areas of social and emotional development. Furthermore, it seems unlikely that these procedures will ever be valid sources of information for some social and emotional variables (e.g., underlying motives, personal expectancies, self-image). However, if properly designed, they may be useful as measures of relatively concrete behavior patterns, interests, and certain attitudes as well as gross indices of severe emotional disturbance and social deviancy.

ASSESSING THE SOCIAL
AND EMOTIONAL ENVIRONMENT

We cannot conclude this chapter without at least a brief discussion of a point of view which the authors consider essential to any sort of valid assessment procedure: i.e., the importance of including an assessment of the quality of the environment in which the traits under study have developed. Debates as to the relative importance of a child's inherent capacity to develop and the power of the environment to influence the development are futile. Both are important, and neither can be ignored. Yet when we conduct an assessment for any of the four types of decisions discussed in this chapter—screening, diagnosis, formative evaluation, and summative evaluation—we often neglect to pay any attention to contributions made by the environments in which the child is developing (home, school, total society, etc.).

Let us take as an example the first type of assessment decision—screening, usually for the presence of some handicapping condition. The target of our screening is usually a young child who, if found within our screening net, will be referred for a more complete diagnosis. Suppose that a child, so located, is developmentally retarded. Obviously the retardation may be due to any of a variety of causes, all of which could be compressed into two categories, or possibly a combination of the two: (1) some type of pre- or perinatally caused condition, or possibly a tissue-damaging illness contracted postnatally; or (2) a pattern of environmental stimulation quantitatively and qualitatively inadequate to facilitate the child's developmental progress. All the etiological factors compressed under (1) occurred in the past. Thus, in most cases, intervention is likely to be ameliorative rather than truly corrective. The etiological factors operating in (2), however, are contemporary and presumably still functioning so as to impair the child's level of functioning. Thus, effective intervention could hopefully signify the possibility of drastically changing the child's level and pattern of functioning. It is important to keep this distinction in mind between historical and contemporary causation of a developmental dysfunction and between amelioration and true correction. Any screening program should also include some concern for identifying environments which are likely to be playing a major contemporary role in the depression or distortion of a child's developmental potential. By and large, however, screening efforts have largely ignored the competence or adequacy of the environment and have looked for deviance in children. It is quite likely that greater benefits would accrue to society if, in our screening programs, we looked for malnourishing environments and sought to remedy their contemporaneous potential to produce a developmental malfunction in the children living in that environment.

For the past several years we have been engaged in the task of producing and standardizing measures of the environment. To date we have published two inventories which we call HOME (Home Observation for Measurement of the Environment), both of which are relevant to the task of assessing the social and emotional development of young children. One of the inventories is designed for use with families whose children are in the birth to three-years age range, and the other (older) is for use with families of children during the traditional preschool years of three to six. Each inventory has been factor-analyzed into several subscales which touch upon the kinds of experiences found in an array of empirical studies (see Cald-well, 1974) to be associated with favorable development of young chil-dren. A quick review of the labels assigned these factors in the birth-to-three version of the inventory will reveal just how appropriate they are for consideration in the assessment of social and emotional functioning: emo-tional and verbal responsivity of the mother, avoidance of restriction and punishment, organization of the physical and temporal environment, pro-vision of appropriate play materials, maternal involvement with the child, and opportunities for variety in daily stimulation. In a series of studies, we have found scores on this inventory to be contemporaneously associated with children's performances on infant scales, and to be predictive of direction of change in intelligence test scores over time. Our current re-search plans call for a greater effort to relate the scores on the HOME In-ventory to patterns of social and emotional functioning in young children.

In this discussion we do not mean to be necessarily advocating the use of our inventory, although we are now convinced that its ease of adminis-tration, high interobserver reliability, and acceptable psychometric char-acteristics make it worthy of consideration. Rather, we are advocating a position—that is, inclusion of an assessment of the environment whenever an individual assessment is conducted—which we believe will vastly im-prove the quality of any assessment of children. It is our hope that the next few years will witness a sharp increase in the development and stan-dardization of procedures which can provide sensitive measures of the environments in which young children are developing. Only when such instrumentation is available will we be able to make a significant concep-tual advance in the process of assessment of social and emotional function-ing in the young child.

SOURCES OF INFORMATION
ABOUT SOCIOEMOTIONAL TESTS

In this chapter we have not attempted to provide detailed information about specific testing instruments. Rather we have attempted to discuss some of the issues which affect the assessment of socioemotional develop-ment in young children. There are numerous sources of information about specific instruments in this area. The ERIC system operates a Clearing-house on Tests, Measurement, and Evaluation at Educational Testing Ser-vice, Princeton, New Jersey. In addition, a number of professional jour-nals, either regularly or periodically, contain information about tests. Among them are: the *Journal of Personality Assessment*, the *Journal of Projective Techniques*, the *Journal of Educational Measurement*, *Educational and Psychological Measurement, the Journal of Applied Psychological Measurement, Test Collection Bulletin, Child Development, the Journal of School Psychology, Psychology in the Schools, the Journal of Consulting and Clinical Psychology, the Journal of Abnormal and Social Psychology, Perceptual and Motor Skills, American Journal of Orthopsychiatry, Exceptional Children, and the Journal of Special Education. Finally, there are several major reference works that provide detailed descriptions and reviews of tests (see Figure I).

FIGURE I

Buros, O. (Ed.) The Seventh Mental Measurement Yearbook. Highland Park, N.J.: Gryphon Press, 1972.

Buros, O. (Ed.) Personality Tests and Reviews. Highland Park, N.J.: Gryphon Press, 1970.

Johnson, O., and Bommarito, J. Tests and Measurements in Child Development: A Handbook. San Francisco: Jossey-Bass, 1971.

Buros, O. (Ed.) Tests in Print. Highland Park, N.J.: Gryphon Press, 1974.

Walker, D. Socioemotional Measures for Preschool & Kindergarten Children: A Handbook. San Francisco: Jossey-Bass, 1973.

Coordinating Office for Regional Resource Centers. Preschool Test Matrix. Lexington, Kentucky, 1976.

Northeast Regional Resource Center. Early Childhood Assessment List. Hightstown, N.J., 1975.

Technical Assistance Delivery System. Evaluation Bibliography: Tadscript No. 2. Chapel Hill, N.C., 1973.

Cross, Lee, and Goin, Kennith W. (Eds.) Identifying Handicapped Children. New York: Walker and Co., 1977.

Haepfner, R., Stern, C., and Nunmedal, S. (Eds.) CSE-ELRC Preschool/Kindergarten Test Evaluations. Los Angeles, California, 1971.

As part of a thorough search for appropriate assessment instruments in the socioemotional area, it is often beneficial to include research publications and project reports within the domain of the search. Highly reliable and useful assessment procedures are frequently developed as part of experimental treatments or intervention efforts. In many instances, these instruments are not cited in the types of sources listed above. Searching through research and project reports for tests buried in them can be a time-consuming process. However, the result is often an excellent instrument and a savings in time as compared with the hours taken to develop a new instrument.

SUMMARY

At the beginning of this chapter, we offered the analogy that trying to assess socioemotional development in a young child is like trying to hold a soap bubble in your hands. Success in this enterprise is enhanced by maintaining a respect for young children, their unique capabilities and their unique ways of interacting with objects, events, and people. These unique characteristics make us question the usefulness of many assessment procedures when employed with children, including those which have proven quite useful with adults. Success also depends on a recognition of the unified yet transitory nature of a child's emotional responses. The emotional states of children change quickly; and their behavior is difficult to separate into cognitive, affective, and psychomotor components. Interpretations of performance on socioemotional measures are often inadequate, moreover, if not made in the light of information about the child's developmental environment. As a final comment we offer what may be an unnecessary observation: improvements in our ability to measure socioemotional development in children depend on developing and validating more complete theories of child development. Until such knowledge is available, caution must be exercised when making decisions about children on the basis of test scores. Testers will have to summon up extra powers of patience, sensitivity, and creativity. In so doing they may yet provide a means of inspecting the elusive bubble that is socioemotional behavior with all its wondrous colors.

BIBLIOGRAPHY

Ainsworth, M. "The Development of Infant-Mother Attachment." In Caldwell, B., and Ricuitti, H. (eds.), *Review of Child Development Research.* Chicago: University of Chicago Press, 1973.

Allen, D., Rieke, J., Dmitriev, V., and Hayden, A. "Early Warning: Observation as a Tool for Recognizing Potential Handicaps in Young Children." *Educational Horizons* 50(1972):43-54.

Anderson, S., Ball, S., Murphy, R., and Associates. *Encyclopedia of Educational Evaluation.* San Francisco: Jossey-Bass, 1975.

Bloom, B., Hastings, J., and Madous, G. *Handbook on Formative and Summative Evaluation of Student Learning.* New York: McGraw-Hill, 1971.

Bradley, R., and Caldwell, B. "Issues and Procedures in Testing Young Children." In *ERIC/TM Report No. 37.* Princeton: Educational Testing Service, 1974.

Brazleton, T.B. *Infants and Mothers: Differences in Development.* New York: Dell, 1972.

Caldwell, B. Home Observation for Measurement of the Environment. Unpublished manuscript, 1974.

Caldwell, B. "The Malnourishing Environment." In *Symposia of the Swedish Nutrition Foundation XII.* Uppsala: Almqvist & Wiksell, 1974.

Caldwell, B., Bradley, R., and Elardo, R. "Early Stimulation." In Wortis, J. (ed.), *Mental Retardation and Developmental Disabilities, VII.* New York: Brunner/Mazel, 1975.

Carver, R. "Two Dimensions of Tests, Psychometric and Edumetric." *American Psychologist* 29(1974):512-518.

Cattell, R., and Coan, R. "Child Personality Structure as Revealed in Teachers' Behavior Ratings." *Child Development* 28(1957):439-458.

Cronbach, L. *Essentials of Psychological Testing.* New York: Harper & Row, 1969.

Ebel, R. *Essentials of Educational Measurement.* Englewood Cliffs, New Jersey: Prentice-Hall, 1972.

Gallagher, T., and Bradley, R. "Early Identification of Developmental Difficulties." In Gordan, I. (ed.), *Early Childhood Education* (Yearbook of the National Society for the Study of Education). Chicago: University of Chicago Press, 1972.

Golden, M., and Birns, B. "Social Class and Cognitive Development in Infancy." *Merrill-Palmer Quarterly* 14(1968):139-149.

Gordon, I. *Studying the Child in the School.* New York: John Wiley & Sons, Inc., 1966.

Gronlund, N. *Preparing Criterion-referenced Tests for Classroom Instruction.* New York: Macmillan, 1973.

Hartshorne, H., and May, M. *Studies in the Nature of Character:* Vol. I; *Studies in Deceit:* Vol. II; *Studies in Self-Control:* Vol. III; *Studies in the Organization of Character.* New York: Macmillan, 1928-1930.

Hertzig, M., Birch, H., Thomas, A., and Mendez, O. "Class and Ethnic Differences in the Responsiveness of Pre-school Children to Cognitive Demands." *Monographs of the Society for Research in Child Development* 33(1968).

Ireton, H., and Thwing, E. *Minnesota Child Development Inventory.* 1968 (publisher unlisted).

Kamii, C. "Evaluation of Learning in Preschool Education: Socio-Emotional, Perceptual-Motor, Cognitive Development." In Bloom, B., Hastings, J., and Madous, G. (eds.), *Handbook on Formative and Summative Evaluation of Student Learning.* New York: McGraw-Hill, 1971.

Krathwohl, D., Bloom, B., and Masia, B. (eds.). *Taxonomy of Educational Objectives Handbook II: Affective Domain.* New York: David McCoy, 1964.

Measures of Maturation. Philadelphia: Research for Better Schools, Inc., 1973.

Mercer, J. "A Policy Statement on Assessment Procedures and the Rights of Children." *Harvard Educational Review* 44(1974):125-141.

Messick, S., and Anderson, S. "Educational Testing, Individual Development, and Social Responsibility." *The Counseling Psychologist* 2(1970): 80-88.

Mirrors for Behavior. Philadelphia: Research for Better Schools, Inc., 1967, 1969, 1970.

Nunnally, J. *Psychometric Theory.* New York: McGraw-Hill, 1967.

Riccuiti, H., and Poresky, R. "Emotional Behavior and Development in the First Year of Life: An Analysis of Arousal, Approach, Withdrawal, and Affective Responses." In Pick, A. (ed.), *Minnesota Symposia on Child Psychology,* Vol. VI. Minneapolis: University of Minnesota Press, 1972.

Riegel, K. "Subject-Object Alienation in Psychological Experiments and Testing." *Human Development* 18(1975):181-193.

Sears, R.; Maccoby, E.; and Levin, H. *Patterns of Child Rearing.* Evanston, Illinois: Row and Peterson, 1957.

Sigel, I. "When Do We Know What a Child Knows?" *Human Development* 17(1974):201-217.

Stufflebeam, D., Foley, W., Gephart, W., Guba, E., Hammond, R., Merriman, H., and Provus, M. *Educational Evaluation and Decision Making.* Itasca, Illinois: Peacock, 1971.

Tyler, R., and Wold, R. (eds.). *Crucial Issues in Testing.* Berkeley, California: McCutchan Publishing Corporation, 1974.

Walker, D. *Socioemotional Measures for Preschool and Kindergarten Children: A Handbook.* San Francisco: Jossey-Bass, 1973.

Whitla, D. (ed.). *Handbook of Measurement and Assessment in Behavioral Sciences.* Reading, Massachusetts: Addison-Wesley, 1968.

CHAPTER *4*

Treatment of Preschool Children: An Overview

Norbert B. Enzer,
Nicholas Abid, Jr., and
Linda Beth Benaderet

The publication of Freud's paper, "Analysis of a Phoebia in a Five-Year Old Boy," in 1909 would seem to be the first clear report of the direct treatment of a preschool-aged child. This case arose apparently from Freud urging his friends and students to collect direct observational data on the lives of young children. In essence, this study was much less an attempt to examine the therapeutic process and the special considerations relevant to the therapeutic approaches with a young child than it was an attempt to further elucidate certain dimensions of child development. By the 1920s, there was a growing awareness that the treatment of disturbed children and adults was indeed different.

ASSESSMENT OF THE PRESCHOOL CHILD

Any therapeutic effort must be based upon a complete evaluation of the child, the home, and perhaps the day-care center or preschool program in which the child functions. Assessment must include not only problematic areas but strengths and assets as well. It is essential to review all aspects of development against the background of appropriate group norms, and each

---

NORBERT B. ENZER is Chairman of the Psychiatry Department at Michigan State University in East Lansing. His primary interests are in families, child development, and the handicapping conditions of childhood.

NICHOLAS ABID, JR. is a Resident In Psychiatry at the University of Washington. His interests include emotional disorders in children and handicapping conditions.

LINDA BETH BENADERET is an Intern at Zieger-Botsford Hospital Corporation in Detroit. Her major interests are psychiatry and internal medicine.

aspect must be assessed in relation to the child's own potential, constitutional factors, and temperament. Furthermore, the relationship between development areas must be evaluated with the knowledge that these areas can and do overlap, progress, and regress independently of each other. This distinctive feature of fluctuation in development can make the diagnostic process quite difficult. As the psychic apparatus solidifies, it is less difficult to rule out maturational and developmental influences as a reason for the problems.

The expectations, attitudes, tolerances, and feelings of parents and other key adults in the child's life are also critical to the evaluation of the preschool child. The importance of parents cannot be overestimated. The preschool child struggles throughout these years with a host of issues which relate directly to his relationship with his parents, and the interactions with parents are critical to the assessment of the child in this period of life. Specific deviations, deficits, or handicaps may elicit concern or rejection and certainly will create affective responses often of disappointment, guilt, and anger. And these in turn will influence the nature of the interaction with the child. However, even more subtle features which may not be universally viewed as significant limitations may create similar though less obvious responses in parents. Even behaviors which might be viewed as assets occasionally produce negative responses in parents. The bright, inquisitive, verbal three-year-old may be seen as overly intrusive and annoying or the parents may fear for his safety. Parents have their own fantasies and wishes for their child. An understanding of the nature and the content of these may aid in understanding parental actions and attitudes. With such an understanding, the therapist is in an excellent position to assist in evaluating the appropriateness of these hopes and in providing guidance.

CHILD DEVELOPMENT

Early in development, the child is moving toward greater individualization, object constancy, and a sense of autonomy, but not without considerable ambivalence. Neubauer (1968) describes the two-year-old, "all in all, the child's emphasis is still on wish fulfillment and on fears and fantasies rather than reality. Fantasies are common, so are distortions of events according to the internal condition of the two-year-old. Fantasy and reality are in continuous interaction. Egocentricity is the basic position, but now there are beginning steps toward objectivity." Mahler (1973) has subdivided separation-individuation into differentiation, practicing, reproachmal, and object constancy. If the child is not progressing through the first three phases satisfactorily, object constancy will not be established. Indeed, Mahler describes a "reproachmal crisis" where the child becomes increasingly aware of his vulnerability in the grown-up world and his inadequacy in dealing with it. This can lead to a regression from a practicing phase to a more dependent one.

The child frequently attempts to control parents with clinging and aggressiveness combined with negativism and defiance; consequently, parents are often perplexed and bewildered. Their expectations and affective responses may encourage or impede further individualization. They may intensify the fears of the child that their love and concern is fragile and might be withdrawn at any time. The fear of loss of the parent's love is of utmost concern to the child and in later development, fear of loss of the parent may precipitate anxiety.

Self-worth may be jeopardized. Parents are viewed as omnipotent; and, as a result, they are seen as a powerful source of security and certainty, but also as very threatening. In a general sense, the preschool child's belief that the parents will not allow harm to come to him is a strong protective device. The very presence of a parent can prevent the development of acute anxiety in the child in threatening situations.

As the child further abandons the pleasure principle as a major source of this attachment to parents, he begins to have a greater willingness to forego immediate gratification in favor of more long-term benefits. Some level of self-control begins, but whether this control is based on pride or on doubt and shame is largely dependent upon the nature of the interactions with parents. Erikson (1959) points out that parental firmness and tolerance are critical, not only in this regard, but also in the child's willingness to be tolerant of others. Once the process of separation and individuation is complete and the child has developed a sense of autonomy—based more on pride than on shame and on some level of self control—the influence of parents is somewhat diminished.

Fantasy. In consideration of the developmental aspects above, fantasies temper the child's relationship to the external environment. It is worthwhile to distinguish, however, between fantasy and misinterpretations of reality due to the immature level of cognitive ability. Fraiberg (1959) presented this example of reality testing delightfully in the story of a two-year-old girl who said to her father, "do it again, daddy" after watching the sun set. The child's belief in such incredible power must be viewed with respect and not with amusement.

At this age children feel their own thoughts and wishes have the power of action. Reality testing is a developmental feature of the ego that inevitably encompasses fantasy. Parents and significant others should avoid destructive manipulation of this development. Such a thought process does not abide by the laws of logic, time, place, and causality; the child's view of the world may be very different from that of the therapist. The difficulty in fully distinguishing reality from fantasy, which is present in the younger preschool child, makes it essential that the therapist continually aid the child in recognizing reality and the limits of thought, fantasy, and wish. Yet, such efforts cannot be based on rationality, for the child cannot be expected to think rationally. Preschool children have different amounts of "fluctuating certainty," which is a temporary inability to differentiate a real from an imaginary danger. The ability to differentiate further is a sign of developmental progress, and continued uncertainty beyond the age of about four years should be viewed as a sign of anxiety interference.

Common fantasies of early childhood include distorted views of the mother-child relationship as well as sexual fantasies regarding the family romance. The roles and capabilities assigned in the child's fantasy differ from time to time. Fraiberg (1959) points out that a mother may be viewed as a "good fairy" at one time and a "witch" at another.

The Family Romance. The family romance provides another later stage upon which the relationship with parents is played out. Fantasies about sexual differences, reproduction, and the relationship between the parents themselves provide a setting for the later development of the child's desires and fantasy toward the parents as differentiated sexual beings. These fantasies and the intended anxieties place the child in considerable jeopardy. Again the actions of the parents, their feelings, and their expectations become critical. While play and fantasy are both used by the young child as a means of overcoming fears and mastering threatening situations, fantasy itself can produce fears. Often, the young child can more easily deal with those fears which arise from fantasy than those which arise from real threats such as parental absence or anger. The content of the expressed fantasy reflects the child's experiences with the real world and the psychological processes which result from and are used to deal with these experiences. Some children have great difficulty in expressing fantasies. Such difficulties in the child who has language should be viewed as evidence of a problem in affective or cognitive development.

Verbalization. Verbalization itself increases the possibility of distinguishing fantasy and wish on one hand and reality on the other. It also evidences an increasing ego control over affects and drives. Verbal expressions of internal feelings follow the ability to describe the outer world. "In short, verbalization leads to the integrating process, which in turn results in reality testing and thus helps to establish the secondary process" (Katan, 1961). Often children referred for treatment have considerable difficulty in verbalization, making it essential that they be approached with great flexibility and that information be obtained from other sources and from behavioral observations rather than spoken words.

COMMUNICATING WITH THE CHILD

Anthony (1964) delightfully describes communication with the preschool child as centering around three different worlds. One is the "bread and butter world" of the child which concerns his typical behavior day: i.e., what he enjoys doing, what he dislikes, how he wastes his time, etc. The second world of the child is the "bedroom world" where inhabitants are his age and are fantasies and dreams with which he is involved. This world, which is more expressive than communicative, is basically in the preconscious. Finally, there is the world of experience, which is the unconscious world that is the reservoir of feelings, urges, and impulses. The key to opening up this world, Anthony states, is a trusting relationship between therapist and the child. He has also utilized in this therapeutic approach with children a number of communication techniques that he has observed between mothers and their children. These techniques include: coping with fearfulness, abreacting aggressive feelings, reversing role, allowing the child to be the comforter, counteracting an emotional storm with "intellectual oil," prolonging the time of contact, responding tangentially, and allowing the child to take the more forward role. Communication can be a disconcerting force in therapy. The therapist must learn to set limits on destructive behavior. This does not mean that the amount of therapeutic material will be limited. However, the therapist must look for "token" motor expression: i.e., that behavior which would subtly exemplify the inner feelings of the patient. Unrestricted action can increase anxiety, give instinctual gratification, and very often serve defense and resistance mechanisms. Therefore, one must become skillfull in techniques which channel destructive means of expression into nondestructive ones.

SYMPTOMS

The evaluation of the preschool child and the therapeutic plan which may emerge from it requires a careful study of the complexities of the development of the child and his environment. But it also requires an equally careful assessment of the symptom patterns and their relationship to the developmental process and to the reactions of others. It is often difficult but essential to separate transient symptoms arising from usual developmental stress from more fixed symptoms. Attention is often focused on the concepts of arrest and regression as an explanation for symptoms or behavioral deviations. Too often the fact that developmental arrest or regression is for all practical purposes never complete, and that when such phenomena do occur they affect only certain dimensions or aspects of development, is overlooked. While some aspects may be affected, development in other areas of the child's life does continue.

Even in situations of severe problems in statuary growth, while there are likely affects on other aspects of development, there may be considerable cognitive development and continuing developmental adaptation. Early infantile autism is likely the most extreme form of "arrest" in development of interpersonal relationships. And yet, these children do continue to develop in other ways—they grow and they develop motorically. At times, the progressive development in other areas can be viewed with hope. Compensations can and do occur. On an experiental basis, this would seem to be particularly true if there is a constitutional or biological problem which may interfere with the overall process of development. Children with difficulties in fine motor movement may avoid such areas and find satisfaction in other activities which demand fewer fine motor skills. At other times, developmental progress in areas not directly related to primary symptoms, may add significantly to the difficulties. The care of the child with severe brain damage may be further complicated by growth in height and weight. The ability of parents to control and protect the child with early infantile autism may become compounded by the development of locomotion and by growth itself. In addition, progress in some areas of development may alter the feelings and tolerances and attitudes of parents. Deficits in one area may become more obvious and increase the anxieties and concerns of parents. Progress may also increase the expectations that the primary symptoms will abate spontaneously and frustration may be elicited if they do not.

It is clear that a symptom or a symptom pattern can affect other aspects of development directly or indirectly, yet development does proceed and that progress may have a positive or negative effect on the functioning of the child and of the other people around him. It also seems clear that the symptom alone, even a rather limited one, can affect the people around the child and thereby influence his developmental progress and adaptation. Thumbsucking in a preschool child may be only a minor symptom, and yet it may be of such concern to some parents that inordinate attention is drawn to it, affecting other aspects of the interaction with parents. Thus, the meaning of the symptom or symptoms to the parents and to the child become a critical point in the evaluation of the preschool child.

Whatever the symptom or symptom pattern or deficit, one must remember that the basic needs of the child are not fundamentally different from other children. While there may be certain differences in time patterns, sequences and perhaps in intensity, it is not the needs of the child that are different but rather the available strategies to meet those needs.

TREATING THE CHILD

Parents. Certain aspects of development take on particular importance in the evaluation and/or treatment of a preschool child with emotional or social problems. These aspects often require flexibility and special considerations in technique. The preschool child is rarely brought for evaluation or for treatment because of his or her own initiative. That decision virtually always rests with parents or other caretakers. A consultant to a day care center or preschool program may be asked to discuss and even perhaps observe a child prior to any direct involvement with parents. This poses special problems at a clinical level and at an ethical level as well. It would appear that a developmental specialist or a therapist acting in such a capacity should probably avoid any direct contact with a child without the clear knowledge and consent of the parents. Should a need appear evident from the initial consultative discussions with the staff in such a setting, the individual should encourage the staff to engage the parents in a dialogue aimed at further defining the problems and bringing parents into the treatment process. Teachers, day care workers, and family physicians often are in a position to refer the parents of a preschool child to an appropriate resource for help. Unfortunately, parents often share with their referred preschool child a significant problem at the outset. Because the decision is not made by the child, he often lacks understanding of why he is being referred, what the problem is, why the particular resource is appropriate, and what to expect. Parents likewise may comply with an expert's suggestion with virtually an equal lack of understanding. Like the child, they may approach the situation with fear, bewilderment, guilt or resentment.

Gordon (1970) states, "Two real dangers must be avoided when parents turn to us—we should not allow ourselves to be drawn into giving advice. Not only should we explain that there is no easy, practical solution, but we should also avoid prescribing remedies and thereby perhaps reinforcing a dependency on authoritative figures. Secondly, acceptance and experience of personal success are essential for satisfactory parenthood, and demonstrations of what parents regard as superior and esoteric knowledge may increase their sense of inadequacy and failure." She further states, "all our efforts should be directed toward mobilizing the parents' inner resources and supporting their self-esteem." Therapists must be willing to approach both child and parents as if neither of them know why they have come for help or what to expect from therapy. With the parents, this lack of understanding may reflect: a lack of knowledge about child development or about the functions of helping persons; their view of the nature of the symptoms; or their values of their own emotional status and defense mechanisms. While in some cases there may be certain similarities in parents and their children regarding the need for consultation and therapy, there are differences as well which must be recognized. The preschool child does not come to evaluation or therapy on his own. Often the child does not experience suffering; the parents do. By and large, it is the parents not the child who make sacrifices for intervention. The expectations may well be different. Parents may expect therapy or intervention to change the child, while the child, even those who experience internal suffering, may expect the external environment to change and thus relieve his discomfort. Such differences in expectations may reflect fundamental issues in the development of the child and in the psychodynamic forces within the parents. Mothers often seem to view children under five essentially as extensions of themselves. Thus, if there are problems in the child, the mother may feel she is responsible or that she herself also has "problems." Such feelings may produce considerable anxiety and guilt along with varying degrees of denial, projection, or repression. Many of the conflicts in the preschool child are between inner drives and instincts and the environment rather than between inner drives and the conscience as is more likely the case with older children and adults. Parents, particularly the mother or other primary care givers, form a crucial part of the environment. On the other hand, the preschool child's dependency, his belief in parental omnipotence, and his own limited capacity for insight are likely to lead him to the conclusion that the disturbances are external rather than internal. While there may be certain stylistic differences between agencies and individual helping professionals, it is usual in the treatment of preschool children for some contact with parents to be made before the child is seen. During this contact, the appropriateness of the referral must be explored and the issues delineated. Laying foundations for a therapeutic alliance with parents is a crucial task in the initial contacts with the parents. It may be very difficult to establish an alliance with a preschool child, and unless parents are committed to intervention, little productive work may be accomplished.

It is essential that parents understand and agree with the goals of therapy so that they can prepare their child for the first contact with the professional. It is often necessary for the parents to receive aid in planning the means by which they will prepare their child. The preparation should be simple and open, and it should include determining the child's level of cognitive function.

The manner in which the parents present their intentions to proceed is crucial. If they are uncertain or ambivalent, such feelings will inevitably be conveyed to the child. Under such circumstances, the child's first contact with the helping person may be fraught with difficulty, and such difficulty may convince ambivalent parents that further evaluation of the troublesome areas is useless.

Virtually all preschool children are fearful during their initial evaluation sessions. Some show aggressive behavior in direct proportion to their level of anxiety. Others may be remarkably inhibited and may have great difficulty in entering the office or the playroom; it is probably much less difficult to form a therapeutic alliance with such a child than with a child who is *successfully* defending himself against a host of anxieties and can more easily resist therapeutic measures. Inadequate or ambivalent preparation of the child may clearly intensify reactions. Parents need to be forewarned and themselves prepared for these possibilities and reassured that the therapist will not hold them responsible for the child's behavior. Both the evaluation and treatment of the preschool child require that the parents recognize that the child may have a limited understanding of the process.

Therapist Relationship with the Child. The therapist must make it clear to the preschool child that while he is neither the parent's "agent" nor their ally, he is also not in opposition to them. He simply shares their concern even though he behaves differently with the child than do they. Because of the child's perception of parental power, his need for security and love, there is a unique kind of "loyalty" which may draw the child toward even a seemingly malevolent parent. Such attachment may make it exceedingly difficult for the troubled preschooler to be open about his feelings or to create new relationships, which though perhaps more positive, threaten ties to the parents. Emotionally healthy youngsters are more likely to be frank and to accept others than are those who are really in great need.

There is at the present time a great deal of controversy regarding the nature of the relationship between a preschool child and the therapist. Some suggest children do not develop a *transference* with their therapist as adults may. Others believe that the capacity for fantasy, the capacity to internalize conflict, and the ability to integrate these conflicts into their personality structure are evidence that transference does occur in young children. At any rate, a therapist must be cognizant of the nature of the relationship with the child and recognize the importance of ongoing experiences both within the therapeutic setting and in the real life world of the child's home. The vulnerability of the young child in interactions with parents and to fantasies about parents, as well as the child's limited defense mechanisms may create therapeutic situations which are difficult for the child. Nonetheless, attachments do develop toward therapists, and these are often remarkably like the attachments that have gone before, or they may reflect certain displacements of phenomena current in the child's life.

Careful study of interpersonal relationships in a child's life may help in understanding the nature of the relationship with the therapist. As therapy progresses, the child may view the therapist as a poorly defined member of the family rather than as a replacement for one or the other parent. Such a relationship may be important even after relief of symptoms has occurred. Because of the dependency of the child on his home and the critical quality of interactions at home, it is of the utmost importance that the family be involved in therapeutic work with a preschool child. At the very least, parents need a reasonable and understandable explanation of the nature of the problem and some ideas of how their interactions can be helpful. They must feel like partners in the effort to assist their child. They further need an understanding of the nature of the goals and the treatment of the child.

Confidentiality. The issue of confidentiality can be as important in the work with a preschool child as with an older child or adolescent. However, the rules may be somewhat different. The young preschool child seems to think his ideas are the only ones possible and if others have any ideas at all, they are surely the same. The older preschool child may not only recognize differences, but may also feel that some of his thoughts and feelings are quite unacceptable to his parents. Nonetheless, from the outset, the child needs to know that it is known to all involved that the subject of the therapy is the child: his feelings, development, behavior, and his relationship to others. He further needs to know that his parents will be involved in discussions with the therapist about him in which there will be a mutual exchange of information. "Secrets" shared in confidence with the therapist can be treated as such and the child can be so assured, unless such assurance would not be in his best interest. The interpretations of the therapist and his other efforts will more likely be accepted if the child recognizes that the parents endorse therapy. In some cases, this requires parental presence.

Therapeutic Approaches. Decisions regarding therapeutic approaches must be based on the specific needs of the child and parents and on their strengths and assets. Approaches cannot be determined on the basis of diagnostic labels. The approach should be flexible enough to allow the child to choose the modes of communication and expression most comfortable for him. A passive role by the therapist is often necessary for this to be accomplished.

Schopler and Reichler (1971) have demonstrated substantive improvement in severely disturbed children with parents carrying the primary responsibility for intervention. While there are a few rules, it does seem apparent, all else being equal, that the younger the child the greater the potential for an indirect approach—with the parent(s) being the primary therapist and the professional serving as a "consultant," "supervisor" or even therapist to the parent(s). Those situations in which therapy with the parent(s) is such that it may interfere with the treatment of the child or in which parents resist therapy require direct contact with the child. If the symptoms in the child seem to have arisen from trauma or conflict which accompanied development with which the parents have had considerable difficulty in the past, it is best that the child be seen directly.

The possibility of significant change through, and benefit from, the therapeutic process is high. Conflicts and behaviors are less likely to be internalized fully and defenses less rigid in the preschool child—who is still in the process of developing and needs help with integrative work, defense development, and adaptation. The young child needs help in handling his excitement, wishes and fantasies, and later needs assistance in internalizing standards and self control. At various times and to varying degrees, therapy involves uncovering, educating, seeking alternatives, clarifying, supporting and reassuring. The child needs the opportunity of a more satisfactory interpersonal experience and the therapist can aid in this by relating to the child as a real person and encouraging the child to relate similarly to the therapist. The therapy should provide a means by which the pathologic reactions of the past can be undone and integrated into new adaptations and behavioral patterns. It should also, with a preschool child, be orientated toward the future to a far more significant degree than in work with older children or adolescents. Therapy should pave the way for future development.

Therapeutic Interpretations. There has been considerable controversy and discussion of the role of therapeutic interpretations with preschool children. While rather extreme positions have been taken in the past, it would appear that there is currently a general view that brief, clear interpretations aimed at further adaptation do have an important function. If interpretations address experiences which were inadequately understood, they may well relieve anxiety in parents. If, however, they focus on the impulses, attitudes, or behaviors which are associated with rebuke or punishment they may intensify anxiety.

Despite the potential for change in the preschool child, the environment and the parents particularly impose limits. The capacity for change in some parents is great and such change may greatly facilitate more healthy development in the child. With others, little change may be possible and though therapy may assist the child in reaching a more optimal adaptation to the environment and a somewhat diminished vulnerability, the goal of healthy emotional and interpersonal development may not be accomplished. The maintenance of a positive relationship between therapists and parents during therapy and particularly during termination may provide a foundation which will allow the parents to seek further help in the future if needed. If a positive relationship with the therapist can be maintained beyond the point of symptom relief, the child may be more willing to accept help in the future. Furthermore, sustaining the relationship permits greater independence to occur through the natural course of development and for other social relationships to develop, thus limiting the force of noxious influences in the home environment.

Group Therapy. Group therapy itself, involving only preschool children and not their parents, has also proved useful with some children—particularly those who seem to have difficulties in interactions with peers, either because of withdrawal or aggressiveness. These groups are formed around play activities and provide an opportunity for supervised free play in which some sensitive environmental controls can be imposed by the therapist.

Groups of children, and groups of parents and children, provide a superb opportunity for a broad range of observations regarding the child's functioning and progress. Many believe that for most preschool children, peer group interaction is virtually essential to the overall therapeutic effort. Whether this occurs in a nursery school, a therapeutic nursery school, or a therapeutic play group would depend on the child's needs and his tolerances.

The setting and the structure of therapy with a preschool child may be quite different from that with an older child. The room in which the work takes place needs to have characteristics with which the child is comfortable. It should not appear fragile or formal, it should convey the message that it is a room for young children, not one for adults in which children are simply guests. Again, there are differences in opinion.

Therapeutic Environment. Some child therapists simply set up their own offices in such a manner that they will accommodate young children, with a play area and some toys readily visible. Others maintain that work with preschool children requires a separate and distinctive playroom with all necessary equipment and materials available in the room. The room itself should be big enough so that if a young child feels a need for moving some distance, it can be accomplished. Crowded quarters may increase the anxiety in the active preschooler.

Toys and other equipment used in the therapy differ greatly, but to some extent the number and variety of "things" with which the child can engage depends on the experience of the therapist. Sometimes therapists prefer a well equipped playroom, often with a rather standardized inventory including a sink with running water, a sandbox, building blocks, dolls, trucks, weapons, eating utensils, a doll house and doll family, games, paints, crayons and paper, modeling clay, and perhaps many other fixtures. It is important to assess the needs of a particular child and the toys or other equipment which will facilitate communication and the specific therapeutic effort. It must be remembered that for some children, particularly those that are quite disturbed, often with some difficulty in reality testing, and those who seem hyperactive, an abundance of toys may be distracting and confusing. There should be an opportunity for children to keep something special from one session to the next in some safe place. But, toys are a distancing device between the therapist and the child which initially decrease anxieties and facilitate communication between the therapist and the child. It is hoped that the sessions progress from those in which toys are the main avenue of expression, to sessions in which the child talks to the therapist and eventually with the therapist.

Therapeutic Sessions. The frequency and timing of therapeutic sessions needs some thought with the preschool child. The younger child may have considerable difficulty with time durations and being able to carry on a theme in therapy. Much material which arose during one session may be lost by the next if there is too much time in between. On the other hand, if a toy or drawing of some importance in one session can be maintained and available for the next, a child's memory and ability to pick up where he or she left off may be amazing. Frequency should not be regulated administratively, and considerable flexibility may be required. Some preschool children do better when seen in specific therapeutic work more than once weekly, while with others it seems to make little difference. The time of day of therapeutic sessions can also be important. A child's natural pattern of activities, including rest periods for some, needs to be considered. Seeing a preschool child during the time he would usually be resting is often unproductive and occasionally devastating for all. The duration of sessions themselves may need to be shortened to accommodate fatigue. While there is a need for flexibility in dealing with the preschool child, there is at least as much need for regularity. The child needs to know what to expect. Patterns should not be changed without the child's knowledge.

Nursery Schools. The preschool child may gain considerably from treatment approaches involving groups of children. Children who are hospitalized with medical problems may be relieved of some anxiety in relating to the hospital through group interactions with other preschool children. The form of such groups is often similar to a nursery school. At times, it may be appropriate for the therapist to recommend a nursery school experience for the young child. This experience may provide an opportunity for positive interaction with healthier peers, a potential for more supportive and understanding interactions with adults, and a respite for parents.

Therapeutic nursery schools have developed which address the needs of emotionally disturbed preschool children specifically. These nursery schools must be able to meet the changing demands of the children of various ages for which they care. While the newborn or very young child may need tactile or visual stimulation, the one-year old needs an environment for walking, talking, and self-learning. The older children need an atmosphere for cooperative play.

Various roles and tasks are assigned to the therapeutic staff of such programs. They may interact directly with the child both in groups and individually. The amount of time devoted to each child during the school day is determined by the needs of the child. The personnel may teach, support, clarify, provide structure and limits, and encourage affective expression through play and verbalization. In some programs, parents, particularly mothers, are directly involved in the activities of the therapeutic nursery school and with the children themselves. In these programs, teachers and therapists assist and guide the interaction of mothers and their children. They serve as role models. This approach offers the advantages of somewhat expanded time in therapeutic activities, a setting which is more usual and "normal," and an opportunity for peer interactions for the children. Mothers may gain greatly from their interactions with the staff. They may develop greater sensitivity to their child's needs, new ways of interacting with the child, and reassurance in being able to share some of the responsibilities. At times, they may find comfort in the realization that a child may be difficult even for a "professional."

Therapeutic nursery schools provide either group or individual therapy for parents in addition to any direct involvement with the children. This work may be conducted by those who directly work with the children or by staff who are unrelated to the children's activities.

Pharmacotherapy. The question of pharmacotherapy in the preschool child raises strongly held but often divergent opinions among child psychiatrists and other physicians. It is vigorously requested by some parents and equally vigorously resisted by others. The preschool child is developing neurophysiologically as well as emotionally and intellectually. Drug actions and drug doses are frequently less well understood in the young child than in the older child or adolescent. At the very least, medications should be considered only as part of an overall therapeutic plan and should be used with specific indications and goals. Frequent evaluation of effectiveness and potential side effects are essential and medications should be discontinued promptly, yet appropriately, if they are ineffective or if signs of important side effects or toxicity appear. No child should be maintained on medication longer than is absolutely necessary.

Institutionalization. Almost inevitably, when the problems of preschool children are discussed, the possibility of removing the child from the home is seen as a solution. While it is inappropriate and in cases unrealistic to view this approach as a "last resort," the approach does require careful consideration and great caution. The importance of parents, even not ideal parents, cannot and must not be dismissed. Even though it may be possible to create a positive rationale for removing a child from the home, the negative consequences and the realistic possibilities of a better solution must also find their way into the decision-making process.

There may be negative consequences of leaving a child in the home, but there are also negatives in removing the child. The actual safety of the child must be considered and weighed against the psychological consequences of either choice. This is perhaps the most serious decision to be made, and it must not be made without complete information and understanding.

Sharing Information with Parents. Some parents require more than periodic information sharing. There are differences of opinion regarding the child's therapist actually working with the parents. There are those who maintain that the model established in the traditional child guidance clinic where the child's therapist did not work with the parents is still most appropriate. Others believe that with the preschool child particularly, it is more important for only one therapist to be involved. At some level, many preschool children seem to expect their therapist, perhaps like their baby sitter or preschool teacher, to interact as well with their parents. It does seem safe to say that both approaches have been useful and perhaps the judgment should be based not so much on abstract rules, but on the specific needs of the child and the parents, the nature of the therapy, and on certain practical considerations. The therapist can never learn too much from the parents. He must use what he learns with great care. As in any other area of therapy, patients or clients tend to color their remarks with their own personal biases and perceptions. Whether or not all of the information is relevant to the therapeutic process must be carefully reviewed by the therapist.

At times, it is appropriate for the parents to be present during the therapeutic sessions. Such sessions may involve individual work with the child or may be part of an ongoing program in a therapeutic nursery school. Aside from such involvement, parents may be included in other ways in the therapeutic process. At one level, the therapy of the preschool child may be conducted via the parents without direct contact with the child beyond evaluation. Because of the unique closeness that exists between a preschool child and the mother, a mother may be able to understand and influence her child more during this period. There are three general methods employed. The first of these is based on education in parenting. In such an effort, the work is focused on the process of development with specific attention to the specific needs of her child and alternative means of responding to those needs. This approach is useful in assisting parents who themselves are well integrated personalities and whose child is basically having difficulty with the usual stress and conflicts of development. At another level, the parent(s) may be involved in their own individual or couple's therapy aimed at resolving internal or interpersonal conflicts, with the expectation that improvement in the relationships with the child will result. Finally, the parent(s) may be involved in a supportive, educative therapy with the intent of supporting, understanding, and directly intervening with the child. Indirect approaches to the treatment of the preschool child are most appropriate when the parents' conflicts have not yet been internalized by the child. While a great many parents may benefit from learning to help their child, some are not likely to be capable of being the primary therapeutic vehicle. Those who are psychotic, those with infantile personalities, those who are involved in hostile-dependent relationships, those who feel the child does not need help, those with defenses or symptoms similar to their child, and those whose child's symptoms unconsciously represent something about themselves are not appropriate candidates for this indirect approach. Parents may also be involved in supportive ongoing educational therapy while their child is involved in his own therapeutic effort. At other times parents, because of their own needs, may require therapy aimed at their own problems.

SUMMARY

Clearly, the early recognition of emotional or social difficulties in the very young child and appropriate intervention hold much appeal. The plasticity of the young child and the effectiveness of environmental change often make such intervention worthwhile. One must recognize, however, that often those problems recognized earliest are also those most severe and those most resistant to change. Therapeutic efforts must be based on an understanding of the uniquenesses of this period of development. Furthermore, therapy must be flexible and be based on a thorough understanding of behavioral patterns and symptoms in the child and of family interactions.

BIBLIOGRAPHY

Anthony, E.J. "Communicating Therapeutically with the Child." *Journal of the American Academy of Child Psychiatry* 3(1964):106-125.

Erikson, E. *Identity and the Life Cycle.* Vol. 1. Psychological Issues. New York: International Universities Press, 1959.

Fraiberg, S. *The Magic Years.* New York: Charles Scribner and Sons, 1959.

Gordon, B. "A Psychoanalytic Contribution to Pediatrics." In *The Psychoanalytic Study of the Child*, Vol. 25, pp. 521-543. New York: International Universities Press, 1970.

Neubauer, P. "The Third Year of Life: The Two Year Old." In L.L. Dittman (ed.), *Early Childhood Care*. New York: Atherton Press, 1968.

Mahler, M.S. "On the First Three Subphases of the Separation-Individuation Process." In *Annual Progress in Child Psychiatry and Child Development*, pp. 129-138. New York: Brunner/Mazel, 1973.

Schopler, E., and Reichler, R.S. "Parents as Cotherapists in the Treatment of Psychotic Children." *Journal of Autism and Childhood Schizophrenia* 1(1971):87-102.

PART TWO

Handicaps

CHAPTER

Emotional Disturbances in the Mentally Retarded

Frank J. Menolascino

INTRODUCTION

A book which seeks to offer the best that is available in early childhood education for the handicapped must look beyond the immediate subject of discussion. It is necessary to explore the numerous factors which complicate the task of getting the best possible programs to those who most desperately need them.

Among mentally retarded individuals there is high incidence of emotional disturbance (Webster, 1970), and for the most part this subject has been discussed primarily in psychiatric literature. Those who work with the mentally retarded must be well aware of the effect of emotional disturbances in mental retardation.*

HISTORICAL PERSPECTIVE

Professional interest in the personality dimensions of the mentally retarded has fluctuated for almost a century. Students of mental retardation are familiar with and respect the early contributions of such psychiatric pioneers as Itard, Sequin, and Howe. In the United States, the first successful efforts to organize professional services for the mentally retarded and to direct constructive public attention to their needs were largely the work

---

*The most widely accepted definition is: "Mental retardation refers to significantly subaverage general intellectual functioning existing concurrently with deficits in adaptive behavior, and manifested during the developmental period" (Grossman, 1973, p. 11).

FRANK J. MENOLASCINO is a Professor of Psychiatry and Pediatrics at the University of Nebraska Medical Center in Omaha. His major interests are mental retardation and community psychiatry.

of a small but devoted group of psychiatrists.

At the beginning of this century, the differentiation between the symptoms of mental illness and mental retardation in childhood was poorly understood. During the next twenty years, the following three professional viewpoints of mental retardation emerged: (1) it was described as a symptom of fixed neuropathology; (2) the genetic etiologies, with associated hopeless-helpless prognoses, were overemphasized; and (3) the behavioral dimensions of the retarded were alternately viewed as being prosaic or as signals of potential danger to society (e.g., the "eugenic alarm"). For the first half of the twentieth century, professional workers generally abandoned the field of mental retardation. Further, the most desirable recourse (for both society and the individuals) was thought to be the isolation of the retarded in large villages for the "simple minded." Evaluation and treatment of emotional disturbance in the mentally retarded decreased as the object of professional attention. Retardates were viewed as the least ideal candidates for psychotherapy as it was presumed that little could be done for them.

In the 1920s and 1930s the rise of child psychiatry as a separate specialty at first further diminished interest in the emotional dimensions of mental retardation. However, it was the renewed interest in the psychoses of childhood and the emergence of potent parent advocate groups (in the 1950s and 1960s) which returned professional attention to the area in which psychiatrists had been pioneers.

The foregoing brief review of the relative lack of involvement of professionals in the behavioral dimensions of mental retardation may clarify the reason for the scarcity of available professional work and literature until the last twenty-five years. Since 1950, there has been a veritable explosion of interest in the behavioral dimensions of mental retardation, the differentiation between the symptoms of mental retardation and mental illness, and, more recently, the combined challenges of the presence of both symptoms in a given individual.

"AT RISK" BEHAVIORAL CHARACTERISTICS OF THE RETARDED

There are a number of considerations which tend to make the mentally retarded highly "at risk" for developing emotional disorders. It must be remembered that the heterogeneity of the more than 350 causes of the symptom of mental retardation embraces a wide spectrum of disorders which range from disorders in which mental illness is an expected symptom of the disorder (e.g., in the untreated PKU patient), to instances in which the incidence of mental illness approximates the level of the general population (e.g., cultural familial retardation and the "invisible" mildly retarded young adult). Although it is hazardous to generalize across these many etiological determinants of the symptoms of retardation, the author will review (by level of retardation) some of the major personality characteristics which place the retarded individual "at risk" in his vulnerability to emotional disorders.

The Severely Retarded. This group of individuals is characterized by gross central nervous system impairment, multiple physical signs and symptoms, and a high frequency of multiple handicaps (especially special sensory and seizure disorder). These "at risk" considerations directly impair the severely retarded person's ability to assess and effectively maintain ongoing interpersonal-social transactions. Clinically, they manifest primitive behaviors and gross delays in their developmental repertoires. Primitive behaviors include very rudimentary utilization of special sensory modalities with particular reference to touch, position sense, oral explorative activity, and minimal externally directed verbalizations. In the diagnostic interview, one notes much mouthing and licking of toys, and excessive tactile stimulation (e.g., "autistic" hand movements which are executed near the eyes, as well as skin-picking and body-rocking).

From a diagnostic viewpoint, the very primitiveness of the severely retarded individual's overall behavior, in conjunction with much stereotyping and negativism, may be misleading. For example, when minimally stressed in an interpersonal setting, these individuals frequently exhibit negativism and out-of-contact behavior and this behavioral response may initially suggest a psychotic disorder of childhood. However, these children *do* make eye contact and will interact with the examiner quite readily, despite their very minimal behavioral repertoire. Similarly, one might form the initial impression that both the level of observed primitive behavior and its persistence are secondary to extrinsic deprivation factors, (i.e., a functional disorder); however, these children display multiple indices of developmental-biological arrest which are of primary or congenital origins. It should be noted that these children never seem to possess a functional ego at the appropriate chronological age, and there is an amorphic (or minimal) personality structure. The previously noted "at risk" characteristics tend to appear against the backdrop of this amorphic personality.

Recent studies by Chess, Korn, and Fernandez (1971) on severely retarded children with the rubella syndrome, and by Grunewald (1974) on the multiple handicapped-severely retarded clearly document the high vulnerability of these children to psychiatric disorders. It has been noted that without active and persistent interpersonal, special sensory, and educational stimulation (including active support of the parents), these youngsters fail to develop any meaningful contact with reality (i.e., they display "organic autism").

The author has been impressed by the extent of personality development which the severely retarded can attain if early and energetic behavioral, educational, and family counseling interventions are initiated and maintained (Menolascino, 1972). True, they remain severely handicapped as to their cognitive and social-adaptive dimensions; however, there is a world of difference between the severely retarded child who graduates from a standing table to a wheelchair with a wide number of self-help skills and the untrained severely retarded who responds with minimal affect toward any interpersonal contacts. Even in adequately managed severely retarded individuals, one notes that their paucity of language evolution remains as a high vulnerability factor in blocking growth toward more complex personality development. Interestingly, these youngsters tend to be accepted by their parental support systems and peer groups (if adequate evaluations and anticipatory counseling are accomplished), perhaps reflecting empathy for the obvious handicaps which these youngsters display.

The Moderately Retarded. This level of retardation encompasses some of the same etiological dimensions noted above, accompanied by a wide variety and high frequency of associated handicaps. Their slow rate of development and their specific problems with language elaboration and concrete approaches to problem-solving situations present both unique and marked vulnerabilities for adequate personality development. In an outstanding study, Webster (1970) viewed these personality vulnerabilities as stemming from the characteristic postures which moderately retarded individuals tend to utilize in their interpersonal transactions. More specifically, he reported the following clinical features: a nonpsychotic autism (i.e., selective isolation), inflexibility and repetitiousness, passivity, and a simplicity of the emotional life. This simplicity of the emotional life, a cardinal characteristic of the moderately retarded, reflects their undifferentiated ego structures and poses a clinical challenge in attempting to modulate their tendency toward direct expression of basic feelings and wants (e.g., as noted in their obstinancy, difficulties in parallel play situations, etc.). Here again, the high frequency of special sensory and integrative disorders seriously hampers their approach to problem-solving, which makes them more likely to develop atypical or abnormal behaviors in a variety of educational or social settings. The limited repertoire of personality defenses, coupled with their concrete approaches to problem-solving, tends to be fertile ground for overreaction to minimal stresses in the external world. Proneness to hyperactivity and impulsivity, rapid mood swings, and temporary regression to primitive self-stimulatory activities are characteristic of their fragile personality structures. Limitations in language development further hamper their ability to communicate their inter/intrapersonal distress fully.

Lastly, unlike the severely retarded, this group of youngsters tends to be rejected by their parents and peers. Their significant attempts to approximate developmental expectations, coupled with the above noted behavioral traits, appear to alienate them from those very interpersonal contacts which they so desperately need.

The Mildly Retarded. The author is hesitant to discuss the "at risk" personality contingencies of this level of the mentally retarded population because this group has been so harshly treated by professionals in the remote past (i.e., the eugenic alarm period) and in the recent past through indiscriminant labeling and the negative self-fulfilling prophesies of track system approaches in education. In addition, there is confusion over whether to view the mildly retarded as the statistical expression of the polygenic basis of the symptom of mental retardation or as the untutored have-nots of a society which tolerates only minor deviations from the norm (Menolascino, 1972; Eisenberg, 1972). In the author's experience, emotional disturbances in the mildly retarded reflect the well-known residuals of an individual who is labeled as "deviant" and then becomes caught in the dynamic interplay of disturbed family transactions. The typical delay in establishing that these youngsters have a distinct learning disability (usually not confirmed until six to nine years of age) presents the mildly retarded individual with a constant source of anxiety in his inability to integrate the major societal repercussions of being labeled as a "deviant" at a crucial developmental time in his life. Usually, during this quiescent period of psychosexual personality integration, the nonretarded person is firming up his self-concept. Yet, for the mildly retarded person, this period usually brings difficulty in understanding the symbolic abstractions of school work and the complexities of social-adaptive expectations from both his family and peer group. These stresses tend to establish excessive personality defenses against potential dangers to the self-concept, dangers which lurk anywhere and everywhere. The vulnerabilities of the mildly retarded are often not buffered or redirected by loved ones into new interpersonal coping styles to help correct earlier misconceptions about the self-in-the-world (Schechter, 1965; Mowatt, 1970).

Clinically, the entire range of symptoms of emotional disturbances has been noted in the mildly retarded. Most frequently, one notes neurotic depression, character disorders, and the symptom clusters which flow from the reaction-formation type of defense. It has been frequently noted that the mildly retarded experience repeated negative motivational and social reinforcement from their peers and teachers and that they have had many experiences at failure or unfavorable comparisons.

MENTAL RETARDATION AND
THE SEVERE EMOTIONAL DISTURBANCES

Although discrete emotional disturbances have been noted in 25 to 35 percent of the mentally retarded population (Chess, 1970; Menolascino, 1970), it should be noted that, for the most part, there is nothing specific about the psychiatric disorders associated with mental retardation. However, there are specific behaviors (e.g., stereotyped and self-destructive behaviors) and there are some emotional disorders (e.g., infantile autism) which are more frequently associated with the symptoms of mental retardation.

The clinical descriptions of the childhood psychoses, especially the pioneer work of Despert, Kanner, and Bender, have forcefully drawn psychiatric attention to the issue of pseudoretardation. The young child who displays bizarre gestures and postures, whose speech is uncommunicative, who exhibits little (if any) relationship to peers, who shows marked negativism, and who makes little or no discrimination between animate and inanimate objects represents the severe emotional disturbance termed "childhood psychosis." The crucial clinical issues become those of assessing the age of onset (so as to differentiate infantile autism from childhood schizophrenia), assessment of developmental level of language ability (usually a positive prognostic sign), and how to reorient the child to reality-based learning experiences. Although these psychoses are relatively rare (one to two cases per 10,000 children), their rarity does not obfuscate their importance to the evolving knowledge of early personality development and the humanistic concern of helping these children. On the first score, these children clearly have ushered in a prolonged reexamination of the interreactions of cognitive and affective developmental components in early life, and they have cast new light on the possible interrelationships of the early determinants of the symptoms of *both* mental retardation and emotional disturbance. Similarly, the wide range of treatment modalities utilized have been a dramatic advance for the field of child psychiatry, ranging from modified child psychoanalytical techniques (usually in conjunction with a special education program and family therapy) to behavioral modification interventions. Increasingly, one notes less concern with delineating the "real" etiological determinants (which so often becomes an academic debate) and more concern for effectively altering the child's life away from a life of marked confusion, isolation, and developmental arrest.

A COMPREHENSIVE TREATMENT APPROACH FOR THE EMOTIONALLY DISTURBED MENTALLY RETARDED INDIVIDUAL

In recent years, there has been a more enlightened approach toward the welfare and overall adjustment of the mentally retarded. To help the retarded individual utilize his potential, he should be fitted into the world of respectability, productivity, and social ability. What behavioral characteristics are expected from him? Unfortunately, an attempt is usually made to make the retarded person into a nice, quiet, and obedient individual who always does what he is told and continually shows his appreciation. This is no longer the expected behavior of retarded individuals. With the increasing recognition of the wide behavioral dimensions in the general population, the mentally retarded person's physical differences, mental limitations, and social infractions are more readily overlooked as manifestations of developmental delay rather than signs of "differentness and danger."

Although psychiatrists are accustomed to utilizing the reference of the formation of psychiatric symptoms as being the result of a compromise between the expression of an impulse and the defense against its overt expression, they have lagged behind in applying this reference to the mentally retarded (Phillips, 1966). The author has been impressed with the rapid response of retarded individuals, with neurotic and/or character disorders, to both individual and group therapy approaches. Indeed, the rapidity of their responses leads the author to question whether the *extent* of professional attention accorded to them, as persons trying to make it in this world, is not more important than the type or extent of treatment resources utilized.

Ultimately, parental expectations are the primary factors which determine what a mentally retarded individual will be programmed to do. Parents are heavily dependent on professionals for guidelines both for themselves and for their child; therefore, the professional is in an ideal position to help sketch out the expectations for the young mentally retarded member of any family he serves. As previously reviewed, mentally retarded children with an associated emotional disturbance are different from other retarded children, and some of these differences are subtle and perplexing to parents. Parental reaction frequently causes the child to realize he is different, yet he does not know in which specific way nor what he can do about it. A feeling of estrangement may ensue; if the child already perceives the world in a somewhat distorted way, this weakens his anchor on reality so that normal avenues of learning and reality testing undergo interference or even destruction. Accordingly, it is crucial that the family be engaged at an early juncture point in a comprehensive approach to the treatment-management needs of their child.

Principles for comprehensive treatment approaches for mentally retarded children with emotional disturbances are summarized in Chart I, and each of their components will be discussed.

CHART I

Comprehensive Treatment Principles

---

1. Keep an open-minded approach in diagnosis and treatment; reevaluate with the same inquiring attitude.

2. Engage the family through active participation.

3. Early descriptive diagnosis followed by early treatment is essential.

4. Begin with acceptance of each child as he is in all aspects of behavior. Equal acceptance for his family is needed.

5. Focus on what the child can do; lead him step-by-step toward maximal development.

6. Coordinate the services needed for the child; clarity and continuity of communication are of prime importance.

---

1. Open-minded approach. An open-minded approach is the basic principle for the clinician who plans treatment, and it is most important to maintain this approach throughout treatment. The clinician must accept each child as he is at the time of initial contact. The child needs acceptance for what he is, not what he might have been without his problem or what he might have been if therapy had been undertaken sooner. A corollary of this statement is an awareness of the family's feelings and acceptance of them as they are at this time; increasing the parent's guilt feelings is rarely, if ever, desirable in attempting to motivate parents toward therapy. Periodic reevaluation often reveals developmental surprises which emphasize the need for a flexible diagnostic-prognostic attitude.

2. Active participation by family. The family is the key to any effective diagnostic-treatment-management approach in mental retardation (Wolfensberger and Menolascino, 1970). The clinician's attitudes and level of interest are frequently the key to success in this endeavor; thus, future cooperation (or lack of it) may reflect the unspoken, as well as the spoken, attitudes at the time of first contact. The clinician needs to convey to the family his willingness to share with its members the facts he learns, not as an end in itself but as part of the first step in treatment. Treatment plans become a cooperative process which parents and clinician work out over the course of time. It is valuable in an early contact to indicate that treatment planning rarely results in a single recommendation, but that it is something which may shift in focus and alter its course as the child grows and develops. Early implementation of this idea helps develop the concept of the clinician who views the total child, referring to other special sources of assistance as indicated. This approach avoids the "doctor shopping" which may occur secondary to a referral concerning some special or allied problem.

3. *Early diagnosis and treatment.* Early descriptive diagnosis and early treatment intervention include clarification not only of what can, but also of what cannot be actively treated. Full discussion of these considerations can assist families in establishing realistic expectations so mutual frustration is reduced and fewer secondary psychiatric problems are encountered. In this sense, prevention becomes a cohesive part of the continuing work with the child and his family.

The advent of a wide range of psychopharmacologic agents to modify overt behavioral manifestations of cerebral dysfunction has materially increased the range of active treatment for many youngsters. The levels of arousal and motor activity, convulsive thresholds, and general emotional status may be increased, decreased, or altered. Since the reaction of psychopharmacologic agents is often unpredictable, the physician must be prepared to use several drugs sequentially or in combination in any one patient (Donaldson and Menolascino, 1977).

4. *Developmental potential.* To focus on the maximization of developmental potential involves a different type of goal-setting from the usual treatment expectation, since the focus must often be on what the child can do rather than anticipation of a "cure." The goal then becomes how to go about providing the child with the necessary opportunities and support to develop with a minimum of obstacles.

Some crisis situations will be encountered, but a majority can be anticipated and either avoided or minimized. Knowing the child's developmental and emotional needs and what crises are most likely to occur, the psychiatrist can help the parents anticipate and handle emerging adjustment difficulties. After the initial contacts, when rapport with the family has been established, much of the work involves preventative psychiatry. This approach is consistent with the life-planning approaches for other chronically handicapped persons.

5. Coordination of services. The fifth principle is the coordination of the services needed for the child. This requires awareness of the various services available in a given community and an attitude which permits collaboration. It necessitates sharing of the overall treatment plan with the child (when appropriate), the family, and community resources—with a special emphasis on the cooperation of the child's teacher. Close attention to the clarity and continuity of communications is essential.

Services which emotionally disturbed-retarded children may need range from psychotherapy in selected instances, through many types of specialized medical care, to special education, vocational habilitation, and increasing levels of autonomous social functioning.

DISCUSSION

Emotional problems which often complicate the lives of mentally retarded individuals are increasingly being appreciated. Equally important in contemporary thinking is the knowledge that mentally retarded individuals no longer represent a homogenous group in any characteristics: intellectual, physical, social, or cultural. In brief, the mentally retarded individual is a thinking and feeling individual who, like any other person, is prone to similar emotional problems and social difficulties. Like the more normal child, the mentally retarded child may avoid facing his problems and may become anxious, aggressive, hostile, and antisocial. Similarly, he may be responsive, friendly, passive, and cooperative like other children.

It has become apparent that there is no natural line of separation between adequate intellectual functioning and abnormal intellectual functioning. The major differentiation between the retarded individual and his normal peer appears to be his overt, socially judged, adaptive behavior. His limitations can seriously interfere with both his capacity to obtain satisfaction for his own efforts in regard to how he understands the world around him and his capacity to meet environmental demands and expectations. The extent to which he is surrounded by supportive adults becomes the major difference in whether or not he makes a satisfactory emotional adjustment. When adults are inconsistent in their attitudes or support, and are only demanding, undependable, and generally nonsupportive of the mentally retarded individual's efforts, his needs emerge with greater urgency. Such situations may develop in the home or in school and become chronic, even though parents and teachers are aware of the child's retardation. Parents may intellectually accept the problem the child has, but they may have strong emotional reasons which prevent their acceptance of the child for what he is. Some parents react to their child with anger and withdrawal of love and consider their child stubborn, ill-tempered, or lazy; these attitudes increasingly push parents to view their child with nonacceptance or nonrecognition of his capabilities. The overall result is a retarded individual who has to cope with both his intellectual limitations and the psychosocial or emotional handicaps produced by the negative reoccurring interactions with his outside support systems (both in the family and in the general world outside).

In a disturbed family setting in which failure is answered with rejection, the child is continually subjected to increasing insecurity, and he may develop chronic anxiety with fixed pathologic dimensions, such as in a psychoneurosis. He may become diffusely anxious in many areas and may develop phobic phenomena or compulsiveness as defensive responses. Alternately, a child may remain passive and dependent, with particular focus on staying with the "old and safe" approaches to interpersonal relationships; this type of personality defense can drastically interfere with learning opportunities. Both types of disturbance are neurotic structuring of the child's inside world, and both are less likely to yield to environmental manipulation; in these instances, treatment of the child-parent interactional unit must utilize more formal psychotherapy approaches.

Psychiatric aspects of mental retardation become clinically more difficult to apply because of the many causes of mental retardation, the frequently associated multiple handicaps, the rapidly changing psychosocial needs of the developing child, and the complexity of family interactional patterns. The extrinsic factors may also mask, modify, or exaggerate the underlying pathophysiological processes.

A Reflection. Parenthetically, the author has noted neurotic reactions in the mildly retarded, but rarely in any other levels of the mentally retarded. Although a quick answer may be gleaned through reference to the previously noted personality traits and vulnerabilities of the moderate and severely retarded (i.e., level of personality development may preclude the complexities of neurotic symptom formation), the following is another point of view. Perhaps psychiatrists have attempted to fit the current nomenclature systems into their expectations of the behavioral repertoires of the moderately and severely retarded and have attributed mental illness to these stereotypes.

For example, in the past the author studied a group of community-based Down's syndrome youngsters and noted a fairly high incidence of mental illness (Menolascino, 1965); during a later study of an institutionalized sample of Down's syndrome youngsters (1974) he noted that many of them *appeared* happy, overly friendly, and would literally swarm around a visitor on the ward. On reflection, the bulk of the stereotyped *Prince Charming* behavior in this particular subgroup of the mentally retarded appeared to be secondary to *affect hunger*, and a far different set of diagnostic considerations and treatment challenges emerged rather than the initial impression of their behaviors.

It is sobering to note how the past psychiatric stereotype of moderately and severely retarded as the "happy and carefree retardate" may have blinded psychiatrists from serving a lost generation of highly vulnerable retarded youngsters grouped together in institutions. Now their task is one of providing psychiatric services in conjunction with family/home/community opportunities for educational, vocational, and personal-social accomplishments within the mainstreams of society. From this perspective, the goal in approaching the "at risk" personality contingencies of the mentally retarded must focus on helping them to develop more specific psychosocial skills for attaining *interdependence* in society. Previously, there was overattention to the goal of personality *independence*, a task which is extremely complex for the nonretarded. Assisting retarded citizens to understand and manage their needs for *dependent* relationships while simultaneously fostering interdependent experiences with counselors, peers, citizen advocates, and employers will buffer and modify their personality vulnerabilities, thus permitting individuals to develop their social-adaptive potentials more fully. Utilization of this approach can bring about the projection that nine out of ten mentally retarded citizens can be trained to live effectively in the outside world (PCMR, 1973).

SUMMARY

In this descriptive and treatment overview of the most common behavioral reactions noted in mentally retarded individuals, an attempt was made to delineate symptoms which are secondary to cerebral insults, the role of superimposed interpersonal conflicts and their residuals, and those instances in which all of these factors are operative. It was stressed that treatment approaches must first focus on the global nature of the child's interactional problems and only secondarily focus on specific handicaps such as a seizure disorder, motor dysfunction, or speech and language delay. Many behavioral disorders can be helped through widely differing treatment methods and approaches because of the multifactorial complex of forces which are usually present.

No treatment approach is successful unless a continuous working relationship with the family has been established. In comprehensive treatment planning, it is better to focus not on what the child presently is, but also on what he can become. Initial tactful interviews can provide the foothold for the establishment of a good relationship with the family. Within the context of a mutual contract of help, between the therapist and the family, multidimensional treatment needs can be delineated, augmented, and followed through.

The mentally retarded are highly vulnerable in regard to both their intrinsic and extrinsic potentials for maximal developmental progress. The high frequency of allied handicapping conditions, delayed language acquisition, impairments in cognitive function, and the family-societal attitudes toward these specific vulnerabilities, all underscore the need for major inputs of early and continuing psychiatric help for these youngsters and their families. Fortunately, the worldwide interest in the care and management of the mentally retarded remains at a high level because of organized parent-advocate groups and a growing number of highly involved professionals. These individuals *know* what the retarded *can* accomplish as future fellow citizens of this world, and thus give of their interest and compassion.

BIBLIOGRAPHY

Chess, S. "Emotional Problems in Mentally Retarded Children." In Menolascino, F.J. (ed.), *Psychiatric Approaches to Mental Retardation*. New York: Basic Books, 1970.

Chess, S., Korn, S., and Fernandez, P.B. *Psychiatric Disorders of Children with Congenital Rubella*. New York: Brunner/Mazel, 1971.

Donaldson, J.Y., and Menolascino, F.J. "Past, Current, and Future Roles of Child Psychiatry in Mental Retardation." *Journal of Child Psychiatry* 16(1977):38-52.

Eisenberg, L. "Caste, Class, and Intelligence." In Murray, R.F., and Rosser, P.L. (eds.), *The Genetic, Metabolic, and Developmental Aspects of Mental Retardation*. Springfield, Ill.: C.C. Thomas, 1972.

Grossman, H.J. (ed.). *Manual of Terminology and Classification in Mental Retardation* (rev. ed.). Washington, D.C.: American Association on Mental Deficiency, 1973.

Grunewald, K. "International Trends in the Care of the Severely and Profoundly Retarded and Multiply Handicapped." In Menolascino, F.J., and Pearson, P.H. (eds.), *Beyond the Limits: Innovations in Services for the Severely and Profoundly Retarded*. Seattle: Special Child Publications, 1974.

Menolascino, F.J. "Psychiatric Aspects of Mongolism." *American Journal of Mental Deficiency* 69(1965):653-660.

Menolascino, F.J. "The Facade of Mental Retardation: Its Challenge to Child Psychiatry." *American Journal of Psychiatry* 122(1966):1221-1235.

Menolascino, F.J. "The Research Challenge in Delineating Psychiatric Syndromes in Mental Retardation." In author (ed.), *Psychiatric Approaches to Mental Retardation.* New York: Basic Books, 1970.

Menolascino, F.J. "Emotional Disturbance on Institutionalized Retardates: Primitive, Atypical and Abnormal Behaviors." *Mental Retardation* 10(1972):3-8.

Menolascino, F.J. "Changing Developmental Perspectives in Down's Syndrome." *Child Psychiatry & Human Development* 4(1974):205-215.

Mowatt, M.H. "Emotional Conflicts of Handicapped Young Adults and Their Mothers." In Menolascino, F.J. (ed.), *Psychiatric Approaches to Mental Retardation.* New York: Basic Books, 1970.

Phillips, I. "Children, Mental Retardation and Emotional Disorder." In author (ed.), *Prevention and Treatment of Mental Retardation.* New York: Basic Books, 1966.

President's Committee on Mental Retardation. *MR '72: Islands of Excellence.* Washington, D.C.: Government Printing Office, 1973.

Schechter, M.D. "Learning Problems of Handicapped Children." *Lancet* 85(1965):510-515.

Webster, T.G. "Unique Aspects of Emotional Development in Mentally Retarded Children." In Menolascino, F.J. (ed.), *Psychiatric Approaches to Mental Retardation.* New York: Basic Books, 1970.

Wolfensberger, W., and Menolascino, F.J. "A Theoretical Framework for the Management of Parents of the Mentally Retarded." In Menolascino, F.J. (ed.), *Psychiatric Approaches to Mental Retardation.* New York: Basic Books, 1970.

CHAPTER

Emotional and Social Factors in the Neurologically Impaired Child

Nancy R. Haslett

Definitions of normality include attention to the notion of adaptation. An important contemporary example is the coupling of *adaptive deficit* with *intellectual deficiency* in the official diagnosis of mental retardation. Similarly, it is the breakdown in functioning or coping that leads to hospitalization or institutionalization. To understand and help the child with impairment in the nervous system, one must look at how he functions. The way that the preschooler is able to modulate changing states from within and without will be more important in emotional adjustment than any specific deficit or even global disability.

One recalls earlier descriptions of "Epileptic" or "Brain-Injured" personality with disappointment. Even the so-called *distinct categories of disorder* like autism, cerebral palsy, minimal brain damage, or childhood psychosis are more profitably viewed as clusters of associated behaviors with multiple etiologies. Every child is unique and the infant both influences and is influenced by the environment. When children are labeled by their nervous system defects we have often failed to recognize the influence of management on ultimate development, the effect of the child's role in shaping responses to him, and, most important, the plasticity of the interaction between brain function and behavior. Supports for this assertion are the widespread tendency for educational grouping of children by categories of special education, and the wholesale poor prognoses delivered to parents at the birth of children with many types of disabilities. Lack of attention to the dynamic nature of personality has left serious scars on children raised in institutions and homes without provision for an adequate amount of continuity of affection, stimulation,

NANCY R. HASLETT is Clinical Coordinator for the State University Developmental Disability Center for Children in New Orleans. Her major interests are child psychiatry, pediatric neurology, and child development.

and enrichment. The commonest problems in children with neurological impairments are defects in achievement of full emotional maturity, the presence of low self-esteem and poor self-image. They are also vulnerable to the same reactions to which all children are prone. The failure to appreciate and assess accurately deprivation, separation anxiety, maternal depression, phobia, or anxiety may result in failure to intervene, treat, or plan effectively for a child. One must learn to communicate with handicapped children and to recognize their distress signals and the many cues that they are misunderstood or unhappy.

BRAIN MANFUNCTION

There is overwhelming evidence that malfunction in the brain whether grossly obvious or subtle is an important contributing factor in later emotional disability (Richardson and Friedman, 1974), school and vocational failures (Pond, 1961), juvenile delinquency (Hertzig and Birch, 1968), and psychosis. It is true in many epidemiologic studies that children with epilepsy, cerebral palsy, head trauma, meningitis, birth anoxia, and many other conditions have an inordinately high rate of maladjustment and unhappiness throughout their lives (Pond, 1961). The interpretation of these correlations has been based on a misunderstanding of the nature of the relationship between the human mind and brain with the environment. "Organic" factors were assumed to be structural, and therefore fixed and immutable determinants of personality. Too often, educational planning has been determined on IQ level alone or physical examination rather than on considerations of the total life situation of the child. Even more insidious and harmful has been the segregation of neurologically handicapped children from their normal peers at play and at school. Conventional diagnostic and therapeutic interventions have been infrequently applied until recently with a loss of valuable time in the application of modern insights and techniques to these children. Since there is at the present time no study showing that the process of emotional development is any different for the neurologically impaired child, it is inexcusable to continue to ignore their emotional needs for handling, cuddling, affection, education, play, friendship, discipline, sexuality, risk taking, and independent living. Because of pessimism regarding outcome, limit setting has been handled differently from other children. They have been disciplined erratically or with undue severity, and like a self-fulfilling prophesy the child's irritating and frustrating behavior has led to a vicious cycle of pessimism and despair for workers and parents. The beginning of a turnabout often comes when the out-of-control child is accepted as a human being who will respond to limits and frustrations with patience like any other person.

CENTRAL REGULATORY MECHANISMS

It may be helpful to think of the effects of having either a hyperresponsive or an underresponsive mechanism for monitoring and regulating stimuli. Many behavioral deficiencies and excesses are related to problems in these highly important central-control mechanisms for managing attention, activity level, integration of information from various levels of the nervous system, sensory thresholds, frustration tolerance, and various discrimination abilities. There may be subtle alterations in the manner in which the autonomic nervous system functions in these conditions. The children may require considerable help with making compensatory adjustments in these areas.

Many workers have seen that certain infants are more easily startled by changes, show distress with small increments in noise or sound, and react with displeasure to being changed or held. Conversely, an apathetic, hypotonic, seemingly unresponsive infant or child is content to be left alone for hours, perhaps prefers self-stimulation, and is uncomfortable with vigorous handling. Here, the problems are to protect the one child from higher than manageable amounts of stimulation, but not to neglect offering the optimal amount. For the other, it is finding routes of bypassing the troublesome perceptual barriers and gradually introducing changes which can be mastered.

THE CHILD AND THE ENVIRONMENT

Later the hypersensitive or hyperactive child is victimized by his captivation with the many details of his environment. Just as he might experience difficulty in selecting embedded figures from background details, he may not be able to concentrate on the reading lesson in a busy classroom or the command to feed the dog in the disorganized time before the family sits down to dinner. A toddler and preschooler who is constantly nagged and punished often rebels or withdraws. It may be hard at first to appreciate the amount of difficulty some children have in mastering the simplest steps in learning or emotional control. They may be operating at high anxiety levels all the time so that small additional stress can lead to "catastrophic" reactions (Goldstein, 1938) and seemingly mysterious outbursts of aggressiveness and temper. Often simply watching a child attempt to balance as he walks a straight line or tries to form a number helps one to be more patient, tolerant, and helpful.

PROBLEMS SECONDARY
TO NEUROLOGIC IMPAIRMENT

Any combination of behaviors can be seen in the organically impaired child (Eisenberg, 1957). A few classic examples are always listed however: memory defects with a natural tendency to falsify or to hide; intellectual deficiency and its attendant parental disappointment and need for patient education; attention span variations; rambling, slurred, or delayed speech; tremor, gait disturbance, clumsiness, motor incoordination, paralysis, and weakness; emotional lability with rapid mood changes, unpredictable outbursts, easy panics, impulsive acting, and losses of control; sensory differences including indifference to pain, inability to distinguish objects or textures by touch or pressure.

BEHAVIORAL DEVIATIONS

In any particular child, one or more of the specific abnormalities may be aggravated by the general control problems resulting in a number of problems which will be manifested primarily as behavior deviations. These patterns can be summarized in the following ways:
1. Behavior displays attributable to faulty inhibition of emotional or motor functions
2. Behaviors more characteristic of younger children, either in temporary regressions or because of prolonged retention of immature patterns
3. Behavior problems more related to the psychological defenses against the repeated frustrations, the lowered self-esteem, or the anxiety: e.g., bullying or bragging as an overcompensation, avoidance of a difficult task, compulsive rituals which delay getting to work, or admitting problems
4. Behavior which is secondary to faulty development of relationships to other people with relative sensory deprivation, e.g., preoccupation with one's own body or fantasies and constant rocking or other self-stimulating activities

MASKING OF EMOTIONAL
ISSUES BY IMPAIRMENT

In addition to these patterns, neurologically impaired children have every reaction and disturbance to which other children are subject. Often the precipitating environmental event is not recognized because of the masking qualities of the neurological condition: e.g., regression in emotional reactivity in a nonverbal child with institutionalization; hypersexual behavior in a brain-injured child following overstimulation by adults interpreted as a manifestion of brain injury; and increase in disruptive activity with substitute teachers in a child with hyperactivity. It is easy to see how either stern attitudes or reactions which promote infantilization will intensify the problems.

RELATIONSHIP OF MOTOR AND PSYCHOLOGICAL DEVELOPMENT

In the area of motor development, the intimacy of the failure in normal maturation and psychological developments are closely related (Mittelmann, 1954; 1957). For example, delay in development of mechanisms of postural adjustment and the loss of the important role of motor exploration and the sheer joy of motor activity complicate the process of separation and of achievement of independence and predisposes the individual to anxiety. Here again, personal frustration and parental disappointment or overprotection restrict normal personality development. In the preschool years—since motor activity combined with play is the dominant means of mastering anxiety, practicing independence, and expressing most biological urges—motor disequilibria and impairments may in themselves have serious behavioral consequences.

THE CHILD WITH EPILEPSY

The problems of the child with epilepsy highlight another powerful environmental influence. Centuries of prejudice and fear of hereditary taint accompany the diagnosis (Suter, 1954). For every parent, there is a reaction which must be handled. When all goes well, with attention to factual and emotional education, the family and the school are able to treat the child normally. It is still rare, however, to find a family in which there is not some major attitude or fear which is constantly operating to influence and condition the growing child in an emotionally damaging direction (Baird, 1972).

A few common practices include: (1) inadequate limits set for fear of producing anger and seizures, (2) unnecessary restrictions of physical activity, including normal play and organized sports for fear of further head injury and seizures, (3) failure to discuss in age-appropriate terms the nature of the disorder and its implications, (4) failure to treat the child normally in areas having to do with sexual and dating information for fear of the hereditary aspects, (5) failure of the parents to engage in normal sexual lives for fear of bearing other children with epilepsy, (6) failure to allow a child to take usual, normal risks in many areas, (7) overprotection and infantilization often openly and sometimes insidiously present,

(8) deprivation of opportunity for educational experience, (9) stifling, angry dependence of the child on the parents, and (10) formation of unhealthy patterns with siblings because of overprotectiveness, over-indulgence, secret fears, and guilt in regard to the afflicted member. These factors appear in many other handicapping conditions just as vividly and the culture has different biases, legal prohibitions, lack of opportunities, and blind spots for them.

LONG-TERM FOLLOW-UP

It is not then surprising that the "mind-brain" in the "body-family-culture" has important effects on behavior and personality development. Earlier recognition of nervous system involvement is the only way to put the environment ahead in nurturing the vulnerable child. Although the ul-timate outcome of the signs of dysfunction seen in infancy cannot be predicted with absolute certainty, the finding of general tendencies should warrant intervention on the basis of the known high-overall morbidity associated with neurological dysfunction of all degrees of severity. Gabrielle Weiss et al. (1971) studied sixty-four hyperactive children behaviorally, scholastically, and neurologically at adolescence. Although, generally, hyperactivity diminished, these teenagers were now characterized by hav-ing impaired self-images, low estimates of self-value, high degrees of emo-tional immaturity, and poor social adaptation. In the longest follow-up of children grouped as hyperkinetic, Menkes et al. (1967) found only eight of eighteen of his children at the age of twenty-four completely self-supporting. Four were now diagnosed psychotic in institutions for the insane, and two others were living lives of total dependence on their families. Margaret Hertzig and Herbert Birch (1968) studied 204 adoles-cents admitted consecutively to a psychiatric receiving hospital. Boys and girls were found to have an occurrence of neurologic abnormality in excess of control groups. The interesting fact was that in the two sexes, the abnormality was related differently to the psychiatric diag-nosis. In girls the evidence of central nervous system abnormality was more frequently associated with psychosis, while in males it was seen with antisocial behavior. This difference in the relationship of neurological abnormality to diagnosis reaffirms the primary importance of the inter-action between the dysfunction and sociocultural factors.

OUTCOME AFTER HEAD INJURY
AND EMOTIONAL FACTORS

Additional support for the notion of the importance of other factors interacting with neurological injury per se comes from follow-ups of patients with head injury. The postconcussion syndrome, including regressions in already acquired functions, behavioral manifestations of irritability, overactivity, depression, and neurologic characteristics of dizziness, learning difficulties, and EEG abnormalities, has been well-documented to occur, but there is agreement that important factors accounting for the syndrome once again are frequently environmental (Key, Kerr, and Lassman, 1971). A twin study hinted that if premorbid personality was poorly adjusted, then the cranial trauma would be followed by poorer adjustment and in the direction of exaggeration of personality traits and symptoms seen in the uninjured twin (Denker, 1958). Immediate injury effects tend to subside by one year, and ultimate prognosis is more related to the pretraumatic emotional state than to either the nature or severity of the injury.

IMPLICATIONS FOR EARLY IDENTIFICATION AND INTERVENTION

With the growing realization that neurologic dysfunction is not in and of itself the etiologic agent in the behavioral sequelae and personality deviation so often seen, the incentive to identify potential dysfunction is greater than ever before. The Brazelton neonatal behavioral assessment scale (1973) is a very promising instrument for diagnosing central nervous system dysfunction early. This test grades twenty-six behavioral responses to environmental stimuli and twenty reflexes. Its value lies in the attention it gives to social responses and responses to the environment.

SCREAM: AN INFANT MENTAL STATUS EXAMINATION

What follows is an effort to bring together in compact form several historical features known to be associated with later psychiatric and neurologic disability. These signs of disturbance help to identify infants and parents who need help early. They can also be used when eliciting a chronological account of emotional development from the parents of older children. Infancy is the area most often neglected in historical accounts of the neurologically impaired child's emotional development.

"S." Unusual *Sensitivities.* Bergman and Escalona in 1949 published their observations on infants manifesting childhood atypical development. They saw some infants who early manifested unusual sensitivities in several if not all sensory modalities. These infants could be easily upset or easily moved to pleasure. Many of the children were frightened by loud noises or unduly fascinated by music. In their histories, they seemed to precociously prefer particular foods or textures. They might react excessively to color, light, or touch. If one systemically seeks evidence for exaggerated or disturbed sensitivities to sight, sound, touch, smell, taste, movement, temperature, and other stimuli, it is remarkable how frequently there are definite constitutional differences and particularly how these are prominent in children with chronic problems later.

The importance here is that easily visible manifestations of extremes in the sensory thresholds can be appreciated in the first months of life so that measures to modify and bypass, compensate or relieve distress may be begun. In the older child recognition of these constitutional differences can serve as red flags to alert helping personnel to possible future trouble.

"C." *Cuddling.* Dr. Leo Kanner in 1943 described a characteristic lack of response to handling in children that he described as autistic. Today, most researchers agree that the autistic child is constitutionally different. In follow-up, some appear to be severely emotionally disturbed, others more intellectually retarded, or neurologically impaired in later life. Of importance is the potential therapeutic opportunity to intervene. The absence of a social smile, failure to establish warm human relationships, avoidance of eye contact, and resistance to change can also be observed in the first year of life.

"R." *Reactivity.* Stella Chess and Alexandre Thomas in their longitudinal study of individual temperamental differences in children identified nine categories of reactivity which permitted characterizations of children from birth leading to hypotheses about future personality, psychopathology, and adjustment (Chess, Rutter, and Birch, 1963). A mental survey of an infant which includes these areas will sharpen one's selection of high-risk children. These include *activity level, rhythmicity, approach or withdrawal* to new stimuli, *adaptability* to altered environmental structuring, *intensity of reaction* with respect to energy content, *threshold of responsiveness* to sensory stimuli, environmental objects, and social contacts, *quality of mood, distractability* and *attention* span.

Berling (1974) describes how many of the neurologically impaired children fall into the highest risk category for behavioral disturbances. Basic biological functions are altered, and they provide problems to their parents and pediatricians from the beginning. If all involved with a child whose earliested patterns are frustrating and negative realize that these are not personal failures or temporary ("He'll outgrow it.") inconveniences, optimal plans can be devised and individualized approaches attempted.

"E." *Emotional* development. With every child some systematic assessment of level of emotional development is helpful. For the very young child, one should assess the quality and nature of the parent-child relationships. One should note the warmth, degree of attachment, and pleasure in these important relationships. The synchrony of the age and level of maturation is important. An important aspect of emotional development is the ability to experience a range of emotions: love, anger, joy, sorrow, and others. Here, also, a range of coping mechanisms should be apparent. In the infant, an estimate can be made of the ability to deal with inner and outer stresses by observing the child's ease of being comforted, degree of distress when disturbed, and reactions to changes in the environment. In assessing emotional development, specific symptoms can be elicited here.

"A." *Autonomic* nervous system manifestations. Barbara Fish (1957; 1965) was able to predict later emotional disturbance and like many authors before and since pointed to the importance of constitutional factors in later childhood atypical development. The autonomic nervous system was unstable as manifested by feeding, sleep, and skin disturbances. In the child with neurological impairment, often there has been some irregularity in these functions which could alert the parents and doctors that a restless, irritable, or excessively difficult baby needs special management. Kathryn Barnard, R.N., found in the case histories reviewed in children with learning and/or adjustment problems at school age that as infants they had frequent minor illnesses, sleep disturbances, and poor eating (De la Cruz, Fox, and Roberts, 1973). Mothers "knew their baby was different." Prechtl and Therall (1973) documented with polygraphic monitoring distinctly abnormal sleep patterns in infants from high-risk pregnancies.

"M." *Motor Milestones.* In children with a wide variety of neurological problems, milestones are delayed. Barbara Fish (1957; 1965) noted severe but transient lags in attaining milestones and unusual regressions and accelerations in development of motor capacities in children later diagnosed as psychotic.

To summarize the questions one might ask:
SCREAM
    S 1. Are there *unusual sensitivities* to sound, light, touch, taste, smell?
    C 2. What is the response to *cuddling*?
    R 3. What is the *reactivity* of the infant?
    E 4. What is the level of *emotional* development?
    A 5. How does the *autonomic nervous system* function?
    M 6. Are the *milestones* progressing normally and in sequence, without unusual regressions and accelerations?

CONCLUSION

It would appear that neurologic impairment operates from the time of the neonatal period and before interwoven intimately with all aspects of personality development (Rappaport, 1961). There is no time when it can be profitably looked upon as operating separately in the causation of behavior or personality disorder. Data are accumulating to show that earlier recognition and intervention are possible and desirable (Meier, Segner, and Grueter, 1970). Parents and professionals can be helped to understand and plan for these children as never before.

Finally, the boundaries of mind and body are merging. Unnecessary and artificial distinctions between behavior "caused" by either organic or functional factors are disappearing. At the same time we can now do a better job identifying children at risk for difficulty later, our conceptual framework provides a more optimistic and dynamic relationship between the child and his world.

BIBLIOGRAPHY

Baird, Henry W. *A Guide for Parents, Teachers, Counsellors, and Medical Personnel.* New York: Grune and Stratton, 1972. (This useful book answers—in a clear, enlightened way—most questions one is likely to encounter about epilepsy. It is a very practical reference.)

Bergman, P., and Escalona, S. "Unusual Sensitivities in Very Young Children." *The Psychoanalytic Study of the Child*, 3/4(1949):333-352.

Berlin, Irving N. "Minimal Brain Dysfunction Management of Family Distress." *Journal of the American Medical Association* 229(1974): 1454-1456.

Brazleton, T. Berry. *Neonatal Assessment Scale.* London: William Heinemann Medical Books Ltd., 1973.

Chess, S., Rutter, M., and Birch, H.G. "Interaction of Temperaments and Environment in the Production of Behavioral Disturbances in Children." *American Journal of Psychiatry* 120(1963):142-148.

De la Cruz, Felix F., Fox, Bernard H., and Roberts, Richard H. (eds.). *Minimal Brain Dysfunction.* Annals of the New York Academy of Sciences, Vol. 205 (373). New York: New York Academy of Sciences, 1973. (This volume contains the proceedings of the New York Academy of Sciences meeting in February of 1973. It virtually brings one up-to-date on research and clinical issues.)

Denker, S.J. "A Follow-up Study of the 129 Closed Head Injuries in Twins Using Co-twins as Controls." *Acta Psychiatria, Scandinavian Suppl.* 123-126(1958):116-119.

Eisenberg, L. "Psychiatric Implications of Brain-Damage in Children." *Psychiatric Quarterly* 31(1957):72-92.

Fish, B. "The Detection of Schizophrenia in Infancy: A Preliminary Report." *The Journal of Nervous and Mental Diseases* 125(1957):1-24.

Fish, B. "The Prediction of Schizophrenia in Infancy: A 10-year Follow-up Report of Neurological and Psychological Development." *American Journal of Psychiatry* 121(1965):768-773.

Goldstein, K.A. "Further Comparisons of the Moro Reflex and the Startle Pattern." *Journal of Psychology* 6(1938):33-42.

Hertzig, Margaret E., and Birch, Herbert G. "Neurological Organization in Psychiatrically Disturbed Adolescents: A Comparative Consideration of Sex Differences." *Archives of General Psychiatry* 19(1968):528-537.

Key, D., Kerr, T.A., and Lassman, L.P. "Brain Trauma and the Post-Concussional Syndrome." *Lancet* 2(1971):1052.

Meier, John H., Segner, Leslie, L., and Grueter, Barbara B. "An Educational System for High Risk Infants: A Preventive Approach to Developmental and Learning Disabilities." In Hellmuth, H. (ed.), *Disadvantaged Child*, Vol. 3. New York: Bruner-Mazel, 1970. (This is an excellent review of developmental and educational research on early intervention with children at risk because of socioeconomic deprivation and with the infant who has a high potential for neurologic damage.)

Menkes, M., Rowe, J.S., and Menkes, J.H. "A Twenty-five Year Follow-up Study on the Hyperkinetic Child with Minimal Brain Dysfunction." *Pediatrics* 39(1967):393.

Mittlemann, B. "Motility in the Therapy of Children and Adults." *The Psychoanalytic Study of the Child* 12(1957):284-319. (This article and an earlier one by the same author review the importance and relevance of the musculo-skeletal apparatus in psychological development.)

Mittlemann, B. "Motility in Infants, Children, and Adults: Patterning and Psychodynamics." *The Psychoanalytic Study of the Child* 9(1954): 142-177.

Pond, D.A. "Psychiatric Aspects of Epileptic and Brain Damaged Children." *British Medical Journal* 2(1961):[a]1377-82, [b]1454-59. ([a]About one-quarter of 100 surveyed children with epilepsy showed psychological disturbances. Two main determinants of changes in the conditions of the children were attributed to environmental factors and the nature of the epilepsy. [b]Pond emphasizes the extraordinary variation in behavioral symptoms in brain-damaged children. Only when the whole situation is considered can the contribution of the intrinsic handicap be assessed.)

Prechtl, H.F.F., and Therall, K. "Behavioral Cycles in Abnormal Infants." *Developmental Medicine and Child Neurology* 15(1973):606-615.

Rappaport, Sheldon R. "Behavior Disorder and Ego Development in a Brain-Injured Child." *The Psychoanalytic Study of the Child* 16(1961): 423-501. (This paper brings together the thesis that organic functions and logical functions use the same apparatus for expression—the ego. Results of treatment of a child with serious developmental problems illustrate the practicality of the approach. Excellent paper.)

Richardson, Donald W., and Friedman, Stanford B. "Psychosocial Problems of the Adolescent Patient with Epilepsy." *Clinical Pediatrics* 13(1974):121-126.

Suter, A. *Psychological Factors in Epilepsy.* Edited by Murphy Garner and Arthur J. Bachrach. New York: Random House, 1954.

Weiss, Gabrielle et al. "Studies on the Hyperactive Child." *Archives of General Psychology* 24(1971):409-414.

SUPPLEMENTARY RESOURCES

Brain Dysfunction

Box, Martin, and MacKeith, Ronald (eds.). *Minimal Cerebral Dysfunction Clinics.* In Developmental Medicine, No. 10. London: William Heinemann Medical Books, Ltd. (This is a good review of diagnosis and has chapters on family dynamics and problems of development. Also contains reports on recognizing minor cerebral palsy syndromes and clumsiness.)

Brutten, Milton, Richardson, Sylvia O., and Mengel, Charles. *Something's Wrong with my Child: A Parent's Book about Children with Learning Disabilities.* New York: Harcourt, Brace, Jovanovich, 1973. (This is a practical, readable, and hopeful book for parents and others involved with children with learning problems.)

Shaffer, D., McNamara, N., and Pincus, J.H. "Controlled Observations on Patterns of Activity, Attention, and Impulsivity in Brain Damaged and Psychiatrically Disturbed Boys." *Psychological Medicine* 4(1974):4-18. (Findings suggest that overactivity and impulsivity are also components of conduct disorder syndrome. They failed to show a relationship between those behaviors and frank brain dysfunction. The study supported the presumption that there is increased vulnerability to psychiatric disorder in the brain injured.)

Stone, Frederick H. "Psychodynamic of Brain-Damaged Children: A Preliminary Report." *Child Psychology and Psychiatry* 1:203-214. (Stone points out the high anxiety level, outbursts of rage followed by emotional collapse, augmented signs of neurological dysfunction during these outbursts, and obsessions and retreats in many children with organic brain disease.)

Walzer, Stanley, and Wolff, Peter H. (eds.). *Minimal Cerebral Dysfunction in Children.* New York: Grune and Stratton, 1973. (A distinguished group of contributors present new data on the relationship between neuroanatomic causes and behavioral characteristics.)

Werry, John S. "Developmental Hyperactivity." *Pediatric Clinics of North America*, 15(1968): Chapter 13. (A critical review of the concept suggesting that developmental hyperactivity is a pseudo syndrome, but nonetheless an important clinical problem because of associated behavioral and academic problems.)

Cerebral Palsy

Bobath, Berta. "The Very Early Treatment of Cerebral Palsy." *Developmental Medicine and Child Neurology* 9(1967):373-390. (This article suggests that sensorimotor deprivations and lack of early stimulation contribute to adaptive failure and secondary mental retardation. Program for early treatment is outlined.)

Bowley, Agatha. "A Follow-up Study of 64 Children with Cerebral Palsy." *Developmental Medicine and Child Neurology* 9(1967):172-182. (Highlights the need for adequately meeting educational needs of severely physically handicapped and noncommunicating children, and the need for practical help and counseling for the parents.)

Molnar, Gabrielle, and Taft, Lawrence. "Cerebral Palsy." In Joseph Wortis (ed.), *Mental Retardation and Developmental Disabilities Annual Review*, Vol. 5. New York: Bruner/Mazel, 1973.

Epilepsy

Gottschalk, L.A. "Effects of Intensive Psychotherapy on Epileptic Children." *Archives of Neurology and Psychiatry* 70(1953):361-384. (This article provides evidence for improvement in seizure frequency with psychotherapy in three cases. It also gives evidence supporting the hypothesis that interpersonal events as well as intrapersonal conflicts can activate epilepsy.)

Gottschalk, L.A. "Psychologic Conflicts and Electroencephalographic Patterns." *Archives of Neurology and Psychiatry* 73(1955):656-662. (This paper tries to correlate EEG rhythms, suppression of abnormal activity, and specific conflicts in interviews. He reviews briefly the subject of reduced seizure frequency with psychotherapy.)

Hutt, S.J. "Experimental Analysis of Brain Activity and Behaviors in Children with 'Minor' Seizures." *Epilepsia* 13(1972):520-534. (Minor seizures appear to reduce the child's capacity to process information.)

Neurology and Behavior

Pincus, Jonathan H., and Tucker, Gary. *Behavioral Neurology.* London: Oxford University Press, 1974. (Here is a book which explores the traditional border zone between neurology and psychiatry. There are chapters on seizures, organic syndromes, schizophrenia, and anxiety.)

CHAPTER

The Hearing-Impaired Preschooler

Hilde S. Schlesinger

ROLE OF HEARING

Hearing serves many functions throughout the life span of man. It serves a crucial role in cognitive and affective development. Sound announces danger and the arrival of the caretaker; it brings the distant world nearer where things can be heard and not seen, seen and not touched. Most importantly, sound and hearing are crucial in the normal acquisition of language.

There are youngsters who, due to irreversible nerve damage, have inadequate auditory contact with the environment. Some are oblivious to loud sounds like traffic noises; some miss out on all, some only on certain, conversational sounds; some may miss out only on whispers. Early profound hearing loss is more than a medical and audiological diagnosis; it is a cultural phenomenon in which social, linguistic, and intellectual patterns and problems are inextricably bound together (Schlesinger, 1969). Despite the normal potential of the deaf infant and vast advances in the fields of medicine, audiology, and education, academic retardation and psychological uniqueness remain frequent among deaf children and adults.

IMPACT OF DEAFNESS

Studies of educational achievement almost universally indicate a three-to-four-year lag between deaf and hearing youngsters; the average deaf adult

*Acknowledgment is made to Gallaudet College for the Powrie V. Doctor Chair of Deaf Studies Award which helped make this work possible.

HILDE S. SCHLESINGER is Director of Mental Health Services for the Deaf at the Langley Porter Neuropsychiatric Institute in San Francisco. Her areas of special interest are child and community psychiatry and early parent-child interaction.

reads at a fifth-grade level or below; only 12 percent are said to achieve true linguistic competence in English, and only 4 percent are proficient speech readers or speakers (Furth, 1966). Despite these deficiencies, there is an increasing body of evidence that nonlinguistic cognitive tasks are performed at age level (Furth, 1970).

Psychologically, the most frequent generalization about deaf individuals is that they seem to reflect a high degree of "emotional immaturity." Levine (1956) describes this complex in terms of pronounced under-development, substantial lag in understanding the dynamics of inter-personal relationships and of the world about them, a highly egocentric life perspective, a markedly restricted life area, and a rigid adherence to the book-of-etiquette code rather than an inner sensibility as a standard for behaving and even for feeling. Myklebust (1960) finds that the deaf are immature in caring for others. Altshuler (1964) characterizes the deaf as showing egocentricity, a lack of empathy, gross coercive dependency, impulsivity, and an absence of thoughtful introspection. The consistency of these observations by independent investigators working with popula-tions of varying ages and backgrounds is impressive. Nevertheless, we must be careful to see if these generalizations refer to the impact of the deficit per se or to the impact the deficit has on the intricate relationships bet-ween the deaf child and significant others.

Previously the hearing-impaired child and the deaf adult were studied without clear delineation of a number of important variables that marked-ly affect the character of the deficit. Schlesinger and Meadow (1972a) postulate that varying auditory and environmental conditions can signifi-cantly affect the cognitive and emotional development of the hearing-impaired child. Variables such as etiology of deafness, extent, shape and onset of the hearing loss, hearing aid usage, parental hearing status, paren-tal involvement, and school environment have all been shown to dif-ferentially influence the impact of the hearing loss (Meadow, 1975). It may be that the most crucial variables promoting optimal adaptation are related to a successful resolution of the impact of the diagnostic crisis and to an opportunity for early parent-child communication (Schlesinger, in press-a).

The Diagnostic Crisis. Most parents of deaf children are hearing, and the diagnosis of deafness precipitates a crisis. The defect is usually unexpected and invisible. The infant is seen and identified as normal, and expecta-tions for normal growth develop. At varying times in the child's life, suspicions about his hearing loss develop; suspicion is accompanied by anx-iety. Unfortunately, the type of defect, its uniqueness, infrequency, and invisibility frequently delay the diagnosis. The symptoms produced by deafness—delayed speech and lack of attentiveness—are ubiquitous and often mimic other childhood disorders such as mental retardation, developmental lag, and emotional disturbance.

During the process of suspecting, recognizing, and identifying the handicap, fear, anger, guilt, bewilderment, and resentment can be seen in the most normal of parents. Physicians in the past have often compounded the anxiety by denying the diagnosis or by false assurance (Meadow, 1968). The medical expert is hampered by ignorance about deafness, a repugnance toward giving "bad news," a frequent reluctance to deal with a so-called irreversible defect, and a vast array of conflicting ideologies surrounding deafness in the young child (Schlesinger and Meadow, 1972a). Distress about the diagnosis or lack of authoritative support may lead to overly rigid adherence to therapeutic regimens, vacillations between overprotection and rejection and/or self-sacrifice and martyrdom for the child's sake. Many parents desire to induce an impossible normalcy, intactness, and conformity and the elimination of the defect itself and any differences it might cause. Throughout life the deaf child of hearing parents will be "different." In infancy he may show the difference in obvious ways by not reacting, and in more subtle ways now being studied. Later the deficit may become visible through hearing aids and sign language, and audible through the "deaf voice." Parents wish to have children who are similar to them, and the desire to force normalcy occasionally leads to a search for miracles or to a temporary paralysis in parenting.

Deaf parents appear to expect the diagnosis and to accept it when the child is at a much earlier age. The children are like them and the parents have more experience with deafness. Deaf parents cope with the crisis easily and quickly, while their hearing counterparts prolong and intensify it (Meadow, 1967).

Preschool teachers usually note that the primary task of imparting new skills to children can be more effective by constructively involving the parents of their young charges. The diagnostic crisis described above is often followed by a treatment crisis, for parents must carefully evaluate advice given by experts—experts in audiology, speech therapy, and deaf education. Frequently the advice is, or is seen as, overwhelming, conflicting, or incompatible, for experts continue to disagree on the role of hearing aids, auditory training, and sign language. The successful resolution of the treatment crisis tends to depend upon certain characteristics of the helping professional, who frequently, but not necessarily, is the initial teacher of the deaf child. A sensitive teacher can, through empathy, reduce the burden of overwhelming advice, and can, through respect for divergent opinions, reduce the conflict for parent and child. Furthermore, the teacher of young deaf children can sensitively enlarge the parental role, rather than usurp it, by carefully clarifying the myriad of prescriptions and proscriptions, but leaving the choice to the parents (Schlesinger and Meadow, 1972b).

Early Language Interchange. The second crucial variable may be related to an opportunity to establish an early, largely meaningful, reciprocal and enjoyable language interchange between parent and child. This can happen when the hearing loss occurs after language acquisition, when the residual hearing is extensive, when the curve of the hearing loss is propitious, and when early and appropriate amplication is provided. All the above increase the auditory contact with the environment and thus better enable the infant to acquire the basic linguistic tools within the usual time and through the usual auditory route.

Deaf children of deaf parents, and some hearing parents, also establish successful communication early through the visual modality of sign language. Without this early linguistic interchange through either auditory-vocal or visual-motor modalities, or both to their optimum levels, the deaf child suffers a cumulative linguistic deficit which affects most areas of his life. Such a view corroborates an impression that some of the characteristics of deaf children should be examined in terms of the basic clash between the child and the environment (Chess, Korn, and Fernandez, 1971), a clash which is affected by linguistic restraints during the early years.

THE DEAF CHILD FROM 0 TO 6

The Infant. Evidence is accumulating that the intact infant utilizes sound early. Even *in utero* the fetus is surrounded by sound, will react to sound, and can be conditioned to sound. The newborn reacts responsibly to speechlike signals and even moves synchronously to human speech (Schlesinger, in press-b).

Sound is among the first stimuli implicated in the process of attachment behavior, most recently considered to be a crucial step in child development. *Attachment behavior* can be defined as the tendency of the infant to be preferentially soothed by particular people (usually the mother), to approach them more by clinging or by reaching, to be more delighted by their arrival and more distressed by their departure, and to vocalize and explore the environment more freely in their presence. The presence of the human is also critical in the usual acquisition of language.

What about the deaf infant? There is a plethora of studies of normal audition, a dearth of studies regarding the impact of hearing loss. The observational studies that do exist indicate that the deaf infant looks normal and vocalizes normally until the age of about six or eight months, at which age a decrease of vocalizations occurs in the absence of effective intervention. Some clinicians have noted some differences as early as three months (Akin, 1974). Retrospectively, deaf infants have been described as lying more quietly in their cribs.

The above are the sparse data. The following is speculation based on clinical observations of intact infants. The deaf infant may have some delay in cognitive development and a delay in his attachment behavior, for visual attachment follows auditory attachment. His caretakers may react to his distress speedily, but the infant will not note the bustle of caretaking activity as speedily as his hearing counterpart. Prior to the diagnosis, the parents may interpret his lack of reaction to sound as obstinacy and negativism. They may react by over- or understimulation. More specific statements for the infancy period must await further research.

The Deaf Preschooler. The competent infant makes tremendous strides in a number of areas and in very short time lapses. He develops both through maturational responses, i.e., those that need no formal tutoring, and through learned responses, i.e., those that are acquired through the interaction with his maturational stage and the environmental stimuli. These strides occur in the general areas of motor development, cognitive and linguistic development, and affective development. The hearing-impaired child may have difficulties and/or delays in all of the above areas. Although the hearing-impaired child is beset with all the usual vicissitudes of child development, there appears to be a superimposed cluster of symptoms which seems specifically related to language development and a general air of *differentness* which may elicit differential treatment from the environment.

The deaf preschooler has been described as immature, impulsive, and showing a lower level of autonomy even in areas where skills were available (Chess, Korn, and Fernandez, 1971). Other studies indicate that deaf preschoolers have more social interaction in terms of physical contact, approval and negative interaction (Van Lieshout, 1973), while their hearing counterparts engage in more social interactions in the categories of verbal interaction and mutual attention, and that hearing youngsters are more able to use highly organized communication to gain control of the situation without arousing either aggression or withdrawal (Heider, 1948).

Our own work in comparing deaf and hearing preschool-age children and their mothers (Schlesinger and Meadow, 1972a) indicates that as a group the mothers of deaf children were less flexible, less permissive, less encouraging, and less creative; they were more frequently didactic and intrusive. As a group the deaf children were less buoyant, less compliant, showed less enjoyment of their mothers and less pride in their own achievement. However, within this group of deaf children, some revealed a more successful, meaningful, and gratifying communication with their mothers. These understanding and understood youngsters had a higher level of communicative competence and more closely resembled hearing children and their parents.

As we followed these youngsters for five years, we noted that as their communication skills improved, their mothers more and more resembled mothers of hearing children, and the deaf children themselves more and more resembled their hearing peers. For the deaf children whose communication continued to be poor, the gap between them and their hearing peers grew wider as they grew older; they were seen as enjoying the interaction even less, to appear less independent, creative, and happy, and to exhibit even less pride in mastery (Meadow and Schlesinger, 1976).

How do we explain that language-delayed children show a similarity of behavioral symptoms whereas language development diminishes the difference between hearing-impaired youngsters and their hearing counterparts? There are two areas of child development which appear to progress within the relatively normal range.

Motor development: This appears to be primarily maturational in nature, and deaf children without additional handicaps achieve within the norm. There are, however, some who, along with their nerve deafness, also suffer from some motor impairment (probably on a neurological basis), resulting in delays in development, awkwardness, difficulties with rail walking, coordination, and some possible abnormalities on the Bender (Meadow, 1975). On the other hand, deaf infants have revealed an advanced ability to use their hands for purposeful activity, and these youngsters perform feats of intricate hand movements to express a sign in advance of their hearing counterparts' ability to express the spoken word. While the motor development itself progresses normally, there is some indication that deaf children seem to be more hyperactive and have a greater difficulty inhibiting motor activity when appropriate. This is more closely related to linguistic deprivation and will be discussed below.

Cognitive and linguistic development: A number of cognitive abilities can develop in the absence of audition and language. Cognitive abilities utilizing the combination of visual and motor learning can occur in the normal sequence. This particularly applies to concepts of size, form, function, and causality—all of which the deaf child can comprehend fully without possessing the linguistic competence to communicate this understanding by means of spoken words.

Language acquisition is the most crucially deficient area for the deaf child. The hearing child achieves linguistic competency even with relatively low intellectual ability. The hearing-impaired child shows vast delays that become cumulative as he grows older in the absence of optimal intervention. We postulate that this linguistic impoverishment directly affects the affective component in many areas of early childhood development as symbolic and linguistic communication assume a more crucial role in childhood socialization.

According to the cognitive view of early development, most early learning consists of the reduction of ambiguity, the ordering of the "buzz-ing of confusion" that surrounds the child. Language plays a critical role that is still under investigation. The youngster is now expected to learn how to forego, delay, substitute, or prohibit satisfaction of his own urges. The outer controls designed to help the child are more and more accom-panied by linguistic symbols and communication. A number of studies indicate that clarity of communication between parent and child is crucially important in a number of competent childhood behaviors. Baumrind (1967) indicates that clarity of communication relates to the young child's competence in terms of self-reliance, social responsibility, independence, achievement motivation, and vitality. It has also been shown (Hill and Sarason, 1966) that highly defensive children typically do not have adequate communication with their parents about either emotional or cognitive matters.

The deaf child can frequently understand intricate relationships bet-ween objects through visual representation and manipulation. Intricate relationships between people are more difficult to grasp when language is delayed and communication hampered. It also appears that the deaf child can learn about space concepts quite easily, but time concepts are vastly more difficult to understand without language. When time concepts are not internalized, delay of gratification is difficult to achieve, for it is im-portantly associated with the mother's verbalizations. For example, children learn that their dependency needs cannot be fulfilled, at the exact moment they want something, through repeated statements that mother is busy now but will manage later; thus their needs and feelings are recognized, but the action is delayed. When explanations do not take place, the child may misinterpret the interaction to represent rejec-tion of a deeply held feeling or of his own person.

Deaf youngsters frequently show signs of negativism, impulsive aggres-siveness, fearfulness of adult disapproval, provocation of adult nurturance and overprotection—all of which can be seen as sequelae of an unresolved crisis of autonomy (Schlesinger and Meadow, 1972a). There are also fre-quent clinical reports of delayed toilet training, of feeding problems, and of imposition of stringent safety measures.

How does the deaf child learn who he is and how others see him? He feels early that his hearing parents want to force him into a normalcy which is not available to him; he feels early that language which others learn easily is to him a laborious task, the result of which seems terribly important to his parents. The self-esteem of deaf children has been found to be significantly less accurate than that of hearing children (Craig, 1965). It is inaccurate both in the direction of superiority and inferiority. Most deaf children are in a unique position in regard to identity information. Born to hearing parents into a "hearing world," they appear to travel on an inexorable path toward the "deaf world." During their early years they are characteristically deprived of contact with successful deaf adults, a fact that may deeply influence self-concept. The children are aware very early that they are different and that their difference is seen as negative by the people around them. Very young infants smile with delight when others wear hearing aids, and very small children are fascinated with others who use sign language.

There appears to be increasing evidence that language development is highly correlated with a number of optimal solutions of developmental stages. A number of studies summarized by Meadow (1975) indicate that deaf children of deaf parents have significantly better scores on reading and written language, with no statistical differences on tests of speech and lipreading skills. These findings also tend to correlate highly with a more optimal adjustment in terms of maturity, responsibility, independence, popularity, and adjustment to deafness (Schlesinger and Meadow, 1972). This superiority of deaf children of deaf parents has been postulated to depend on the early onset of manual communication as well as the less conflict-filled acceptance of the deaf child by his deaf parents.

More recently, because of shifting educational philosophies, it has been possible to study deaf children with hearing parents who also utilize some form of manual communication and thereby also implicitly accept the deafness of the child more realistically. Moores et al. (1972) have reported initial results of an ongoing study of preschool children. He found that the more successful children were found in programs that had five elements in common: a strong cognitive and academic orientation, a concomitant usage of manual and oral communication, structured and organized classroom activities, auditory activities included in ongoing class-room events, and parents who viewed the program as a combination of oral and manual activities and felt comfortable with the communicative mode. Brasel and Quigley (1975) found that deaf parents using manual communication closely approximating English, had youngsters who consistently outscored youngsters "whose parents do not use any form of manual communication even when those parents expend large amounts of time, effort, and money in obtaining early, intensive and continuous oral training for their children and work intensively with them at home during the pre-school years" (p. 135).

Our own longitudinal studies of deaf children of hearing parents may shed some light on optimal intervention. The parents were informed that in our experience the early use of sign language in a nonconflicted (untroubled) setting and in conjunction with auditory and speech training will enhance and promote the acquisition of language and speech and will contribute to the social and emotional development of the deaf child. The parents then elected to use manual communication. They elected to use one of the newer forms more closely approximating English and they elected to pay careful attention to the auditory and vocal components of their youngsters' language. The children in turn revealed that the milestones in sign language acquisition generally paralleled the milestones of spoken language acquisition. Knowledge of sign language at these early ages has not interfered with speech acquisition; on the contrary, the number of spoken words and lipreading facility increased with sign language acquisition. Finally we were struck with the decreased level of communicative frustration and the increased level of gratification (Schlesinger and Meadow, 1972a&b; Schlesinger, 1972). In general, it would appear that deaf children who are able to establish a meaningful and joyful communication with their parents through whatever modality are more likely to resolve the developmental crises more successfully.

PRACTICAL HINTS

Prior to the Diagnosis. One of the most important things to remember about a hearing-impaired youngster in the preschool setting is that he may as yet be undiagnosed. You may encounter a quiet or a hyperactive youngster who seems oblivious to speech but aware of environmental sounds or a youngster who is oblivious to both. You might encounter a youngster who is delayed in his speech development. However, such a nonreaction to sound or a delay in speech does not necessarily indicate a hearing loss; both may be encountered in emotional disturbances, developmental lag, or mental retardation. The differential diagnosis is difficult to make and cannot be achieved by ticking watches, tuning forks, or handclapping behind the child. The procedures are highly sophisticated and require the assistance of a highly trained audiologist competent to work with young infants.

Children who do not react to parental voices frequently elicit powerful feelings. Parents who feel "he is not paying attention to me" may out of irritation with themselves or the child resort to active chin jerking, body poking, or foot stomping to reach the child. Some parents give up communication altogether. The child in turn may learn to poke excessively or come to resent the intrusive quality of his caretakers and practice eye avoidance. Even when attention is focused the transmission of the message is enormously difficult. People need to be understood and to understand others, and an inability to send messages brings forth communicative impotence and frustration.

Following the Diagnosis. Under ideal conditions the diagnosis will not be unduly delayed, and the infant will be wearing hearing aids and receiving auditory training (training designed to teach him how to use whatever hearing may be available to him). There seems to be a magical hope that hearing aids will restore normal hearing; unfortunately, this is not the case. Nevertheless, most hearing-impaired youngsters can benefit early from hearing aids. Depending on the severity of the hearing loss, some youngsters will learn to appreciate environmental sounds; some will learn to discriminate between speech and environmental sounds, between male and female voices, between cheerful and angry voices; and some will eventually be able to repeat words, even unfamiliar ones, with good approximation.

Hearing aids on young infants can elicit strong feelings. A tiny infant with occasionally bulky hearing aids can evoke feelings of discomfort or pity; they serve as a visible indication of the handicap. The very young infant can object to the foreign objects in his ears and to them getting in his way; however, patient training can help quicken acceptance and enjoyment. The slightly older infant can sense the adult's feelings of rejection of the hearing aid and "learns" to reject it himself.

Hearing aid receivers are connected in the outer ear with a mold which needs a tight fit, as a loose fit will produce an irritating, squealing noise. Parents need to be informed about the functioning of the hearing aid, and again the competent audiologist can be helpful to both parent and teacher about information and practical hints.

Communicating with a deaf child can challenge ingenuity and tax resources. Deaf children learn early that a nod pleases adults and will use it, appropriately or not. Speaking at the child's physical level enhances the likelihood of understanding. Repeating or speaking more forcefully is not likely to be helpful. A turned back, cigarettes dangling from the mouth, mustaches, or lips which move too much or too little interfere greatly with a child's understanding of speech. Changing words, using gestures, acting out a story through puppets or pantomime can enhance understanding.

Enhanced understanding will promote optimal development for the deaf child. An intricate relationship of understanding between the qualified teacher for the deaf, the qualified preschool teacher, the parent, the deaf adult, the hearing child, and the deaf child can lead to an alliance of benefit to all.

BIBLIOGRAPHY

Akin, J. "Unpublished Research." In Northern, J.L., and Downs, M.P. (eds.), *Hearing in Children*. Baltimore: Williams and Wilkins, 1974.

Altshuler, K.Z. "Personality Traits and Depressive Symptoms in the Deaf." In Wortis, J. (ed.), *Recent Advances in Biological Psychiatry*, Vol. VI. New York: Plenum Press, 1964.

Baumrind, D. "Child Care Practices Anteceding Three Patterns of Preschool Behavior." *Genetic Psychology Monographs* 75(1967):43-88.

Brasel, K.E., and Quigley, S.P. *The Influence of Early Language and Communication Environments on the Development of Language in Deaf Children.* Urbana: Institute for Research on Exceptional Children, University of Illinois, 1975.

Chess, S., Korn, S.J., and Fernandez, P.B. *Psychiatric Disorders of Children with Congenital Rubella.* New York: Brunner/Mazel, 1971.

Craig, H.B. "A Sociometric Investigation of the Self-Concept of the Deaf Child." *American Annals of the Deaf* 110(1965):470.

Furth, H.G. *Thinking Without Language: Psychological Implications of Deafness.* New York: Free Press, 1966.

Furth, H.G. "A Review and Perspective on the Thinking of Deaf People." In Hellmuth, J. (ed.), *Cognitive Studies.* New York: Brunner/Mazel, 1970.

Heider, G.M. "Adjustment Problems of the Deaf Child." *Nervous Child* 7(1948):38-44.

Hill, K.T., and Sarason, S.B. "The Relation of Test Anxiety and Defensiveness to Test and School Performance Over the Elementary-School Years: A Further Longitudinal Study." *Monographs of the Society for Research in Child Development* 31(1966):No. 2.

Levine, E.S. *Youth in a Soundless World: A Search for Personality.* New York: New York University Press, 1956.

Meadow, K.P. The Effect of Early Manual Communication and Family Climate on the Deaf Child's Development. Unpublished Ph.D. Dissertation, University of California, Berkeley, 1967.

Meadow, K.P. "Parental Responses to the Medical Ambiguities of Deafness." *Journal of Health and Social Behavior* 9(1968):299-309.

Meadow, K.P. "The Development of Deaf Children." In Hetherington, E.M., et al. (eds.), *Review of Child Development Research*, Vol. 5. Chicago: University of Chicago Press, 1975.

Meadow, K.P., and Schlesinger, H.S. *Studies of Family Interaction, Language Acquisition, and Deafness: Final Report.* Maternal and Child Health, No. MC-R-060160, March, 1976.

Moores, D.F., McIntyre, C.K., and Weiss, K.L. *Evaluation of Programs for Hearing Impaired Children:* Report of 1971-1972. Washington: Department of Health, Education and Welfare; U.S. Office of Education; Bureau of Education for the Handicapped; 1972.

Myklebust, H.R. *The Psychology of Deafness: Sensory Deprivation, Learning, and Adjustment.* New York: Grune and Stratton, 1960.

Schlesinger, H.S. "Beyond the Range of Sound." *California Medicine* 110(1969):213.

Schlesinger, H.S. "Meaning and Enjoyment: Language Acquisition of Deaf Children." In O'Rourke, T.J. (ed.), *Psycholinguistics and Total Communication: The State of the Art.* Washington, D.C.: American Annals of the Deaf, 1972.

Schlesinger, H.S. "The Deaf Child." In Noshpitz, J.D. (ed.), *Basic Handbook of Child Psychiatry.* New York: Basic Books, in press(a).

Schlesinger, H.S. "Hearing and Vision Problems." In Noshpitz, J.D. (ed.), *Basic Handbook of Child Psychiatry.* New York: Basic Books, in press(b).

Schlesinger, H.S., and Meadow, K.P. *Sound and Sign: Childhood Deafness and Mental Health.* Berkeley: University of California Press, 1972a.

Schlesinger, H.S., and Meadow, K.P. "Emotional Support to Parents: How, When, and By Whom." In Lillie, D.L. (ed.), *Parent Programs in Child Development Centers.* Chapel Hill: University of North Carolina, 1972b.

Van Lieshout, C.F.M. The Assessment of Stability and Change in Peer Interaction of Normal Hearing and Deaf Preschool Children. Paper presented at the 1973 biennial meeting of the International Society for the Study of Behavioral Development, Ann Arbor, Michigan, 1973, unpublished.

CHAPTER **8**

The Blind

David A. Freedman

The experiences of several independent workers (Blank, 1957; Keeler, 1957; Norris et al., 1958; Fraiberg and Freedman, 1964) make it clear that the fact of congenital blindness carries with it a high risk for serious behavioral pathology. Without appropriate interference from the environment, at least 25 percent of individuals so afflicted will develop a psychotic syndrome which in many respects mimics the condition known as the autistic psychosis of childhood. This extraordinarily high incidence of an otherwise very rare condition has given an importance to the study of the congenitally blind which goes well beyond the problems posed by the blind themselves. In addition to helping to clarify the reasons for their vulnerability to psychosis, investigation of the early life of the blind has added significantly to our understanding of the developmental process in all infants. In the paragraphs which follow, I shall review the theoretical basis for these studies and consider their impact on our understanding of the development of both the blind and the sighted infant.

It is fair to say that had the incidence of psychosis among the blind been 100 percent rather than 25 percent, we would have been much less likely to have attempted to analyze the basis for their emotional disturbance. The 25 percent figure, however, proved provocative. Inevitably it led to the two questions: (1) Why so high an incidence of a syndrome which otherwise occurs in a small fraction of 1 percent of the population? and (2) If the fact of congenital blindness is indeed associated with a propensity for autism, what else is involved such that it is possible for approximately 75 percent of congenitally blind individuals to avoid becoming autistic?

In considering these questions, we came to the hypothesis that the

DAVID A. FREEDMAN is a Professor of Psychiatry at Baylor College of Medicine in Houston, Texas. His major interests include psychoanalysis and the effects of sensory deprivation on psychological development.

fact of congenital blindness could be considered as analogous to an inherited gene factor of limited penetrance. That is, the blindness can be viewed as an element in the individual's congenital equipment which has some fixed and invariable effects which will become manifest no matter what the postnatal environment may be like, and other effects which depend very much on the nature of the environment. To illustrate the principle involved in this hypothesis, I cite the relation between the inherited propensity to be tall and success as a basketball player. There is no doubt that among successful practitioners of the game, great height is very common. On the other hand, (1) not all tall people become outstanding basketball players, and (2) occasionally, perhaps in less than 1 percent of cases, a short man is able to play basketball of professional caliber. Clearly the genes which result in tallness are highly, but not completely, penetrant for ability in basketball and absence of such genes, while they render it unlikely that an individual will be professionally competent in the sport, do not entirely preclude the possibility. Viewed from this standpoint, it is possible to consider the state of congenital blindness as an experiment of nature which by heightening susceptibility to autistic reactions also throws into relief other aspects of the infantile experience which are relevant to healthy psychological development.

The research of Mrs. Selma Fraiberg* has been particularly significant with respect to our efforts to clarify these issues. In a series of studies which have focused on the first two to three years of the life of congenitally blind infants, she has done much to clarify the nature of the vicissitudes to which such children are exposed. Her own results (no autistic outcomes in a series of ten cases) stand as testimony to the validity both of her analysis of the problems of blind infants and of the prophylactic measures she has undertaken.

LENNIE

Like many seminal insights, the observations which led to her later work came almost as an accident. During the very early investigations of the development of the congenitally blind which were carried out in collaboration with the present author (Fraiberg and Freedman, 1964) we had occasion to make a home visit to a nine-month-old infant. He was the youngest member of a sibship of fourteen. The child, who had been kept in a darkened room since birth, had by family consensus been considered to be blind since his third month. When we examined him, however, it was apparent that he was capable of regarding our faces and tracking our movements. Mrs. Fraiberg was particularly impressed with certain aspects of her

---

*For specific references to some of Mrs. Fraiberg's publications, see the bibliography.

reaction to this child as they contrasted to her response to Toni, the congenitally blind baby whom we were then studying intensively. These were all the more striking because Toni was a responsive, attractive, and endearing child, while both she and I experienced a certain repugnance in handling Lennie. Despite this difference in her "gut" reaction, she found herself engaging in a monologue with Lennie. By contrast she rarely found herself attempting to sustain a conversation with Toni or, as her subsequent experience indicated, with other congenitally blind infants. I think it can be confirmed by anyone who has worked intensively with congenitally blind infants that this discrepant experience is not unique for her. *Rather, it would appear to be generally the case that adults are not inclined to engage in social exchanges with blind infants and children.* In making this statement, I have chosen my words very carefully; I do not wish to convey the impression that the adult's lack of response is due to some antipathy on his or her part.* Rather, the adult's failure to attempt to induce an oral dialogue appears to be secondary to the infant's inability to make visual contact. The failure, furthermore, to establish a vocalizing relation is only the most obvious manifestation of a failure to establish appropriate parenting behavior.

Both positive and negative evidence in support of this analysis can be adduced. For example, infants suffering from retrolental fibrous dysplasia show no external evidence of their blindness. Their mothers however, tend to find them unusually quiet and unresponsive babies. As a consequence they tend to be handled and played with very little during the early months of their lives. It is only when they are approximately six months old that their behavior comes to be seen as so atypical that even the least experienced mothers consult their physicians. As in other congenitally blind infant populations, there is a 25 percent or greater incidence of autistic reaction among retrolental babies. By contrast, the work of both Decarie (1965) and Roskies (1972) shows that sighted thalidomide babies with gross skeletal deformities, whose mothers establish a dialogue with them, experience normal early psychological development. When the mother's reaction to the defect is one of rejection, on the other hand, deviant emotional development similar to that observed in the blind is seen. Bennet (1971) has stated the situation most succinctly. In a study of the reactions of attendants in a nursery to babies who were being held for adoption, he found that "of all the baby's cues, the most compelling were offered by his eyes. Wide bright eyes, especially with search movements were seen as signs of intelligence and curiosity" (p. 330).

---

*Affective reactions to the fact of blindness do, of course, complicate the problem.

THREE KINDS OF LANGUAGE

Her recognition of the breakdown in the mother-infant dyad, which results from lack of eye contact, led Mrs. Fraiberg to search for other cues in the infant which, if recognized by the mother, could lead to those maternal responses which in turn make healthy psychological development possible. She identified three alternative avenues of expression through which the mother could gain insight into the internal state of the baby. These she designated as "smile language, hand language, and vocalization." Since the mother's ability to attune herself to these modes of communication are critical for the prevention of deviant development in the blind, I shall go into some detail in considering each.

The smile language. Our understanding of the smiling response has undergone a progressive evolution since Spitz and Wolf (1946) called attention to its role as an early manifestation of the reaction of the infant to the environment. It has been clearly established, for example, that both blind (Fraiberg, 1974) and sighted (Wolff, 1963) infants as young as four weeks old smile *selectively* to the sound of their mothers' voices. Six weeks later, however, when the sighted baby smiles to the visual stimulus of a face, the blind child of necessity remains unresponsive. It is ironical that this latter smiling response which does so much to cement the mother's relation to her sighted infant is actually nonspecific. It can be elicited by any moving face presented full view to the baby or even by a balloon with a pair of eyes painted on it. Nonetheless, the sighted baby's response is interpreted by the mother as a mark of individual recognition and a specific social communication. For the mother of the blind baby to elicit an equivalent response demands that she make a great deal of effort. In addition, at times, to repeated vocal exhortations she must resort to gross tactile and kinesthetic stimulation. Repeated jiggling, bouncing, tickling, and nuzzling were required, in Fraiberg's experience, to elicit even an approximation of the smile which comes so automatically to the face of the sighted baby in response to the appearance of the constellation of a face. It is not surprising that many mothers tend to interpret the infrequency of the smile, and the general lack of expressiveness of the blind baby's face, as evidence of a lack of interest. Whether a mother will redouble her efforts to get the baby to respond or give up in discouragement will be a major factor in determining whether the barrier blindness poses to access to the infant's psyche will be bypassed.

A recognition of the significance of this barrier to communication—i.e., a clarification for the mother of the blind child that her baby's unresponsive behavior *does not* mean the absence of a potentiality to respond and *does* make it imperative that she find alternative methods for engaging the infant (e.g., increased physical activity)—would appear to be a first step in the effort to prevent the emergence of deviance in the blind.

Hand language. In the course of her analysis of the barriers to communication posed by blindness and the correlated search for an alternative indicator of the psychic state of the blind infant, Mrs. Fraiberg came to the study of the behavior of blind children's hands. As we consider her analysis and the very significant results of her efforts, it may be important to keep in mind that what blind infants do with their hands is not necessarily different from what sighted children do. Rather, it appears to be the case that the emphasis we find it necessary to place on the manual activity of the blind reflects the extent to which communication with the blind baby (as well as that insight into the inner states of the baby which must precede communication) is dependent on clues which are at best minor and often ignored adjuncts to the communication systems of the sighted.

In order to understand the mental processes of the blind child as they are reflected in his manual activity, it will be necessary to review the process by which the hand gradually emerges as a purposefully functioning (and, therefore, communicating) organ in normal infants. McGraw (1945) has described the transition through which manual activity passes during the first three years. According to her, the sequence begins with the passive, automatic grasp reflex and progresses through a series of six steps to skilled manipulative behavior. It is an eloquent commentary on the problem of the blind that McGraw views each stage after the initial reflex stage from the standpoint of the child's response to a *visual* stimulus. Other studies, however, have shown that the emergence of hand/eye coordination and hand/ear coordination results from separate maturational events (Freedman et al., 1971). It was observed by these authors that blind babies who, at ten weeks and younger, gave evidence of discriminating their mothers' voices from all other voices made no effort to reach for a sound-making object when they were five months old, the age at which sighted babies reach for objects. In an effort to explain this paradox, they undertook to investigate the response of sighted babies to sound-making objects when the visual cue was eliminated. They found (as had both C. Darwin and J. Piaget before them) that sighted babies also do not use sound for cognitive purposes. In both sighted and blind babies, the emergence of sound as a cue to the existence of an object occurs at roughly ten months. Further confirmation of this finding has come from the work of Yakovlev and LeCours (1971) who have shown that the deposition of myelin in the auditory system follows a two-phase process.* The lower auditory pathways—i.e., those which may be related to emotion and some simpler forms of selective response—are fully myelinated by birth. However, the higher

---

*The deposition of myelin can be regarded as an indicator of the capacity of the system to function.

pathways,—i.e., those presumably associated with cognition and the ability to conceptualize—do not begin to gain myelin until after birth and actually are not completely myelinated until the third year.

From the standpoint of the mother of the blind child who can only observe her baby with expectations based on her experience with the behavior of sighted children, this fact of normal development can only result in concern and frustration. Ignorant of the process by which the nervous system matures, she inevitably regards her baby's failure to respond as evidence of apathy or, even worse, of rejection of herself. Certainly a major aim of the advisor of such a person would be to help her to understand that the *apparent* lack of interest in her five- to ten-month-old blind baby does not necessarily portend a dire psychologic future. Nor, as will be shown below, does it mean that the blind baby has failed to distinguish his mother as a special person. While there is a hiatus in behavioral evidence of progress because of the absence of age-appropriate visual stimulation, the maturation of the infant's brain is proceeding normally. Once the auditory system is useable as an apparatus of cognition, the youngster will show an appropriate interest in sounds and their implications.

The use at roughly ten months of the hand in response to auditory stimuli is only the most dramatic evidence of the blind child's increasing awareness of the world outside himself. It is by no means the only indicator that the capacity for mental functioning is maturing in the blind infant just as it does in the sighted. Thus, some three months earlier (at seven months), the blind child can use tactile cues to differentiate strange from familiar individuals. In the course of our early work with Toni, Mrs. Fraiberg and I (Fraiberg and Freedman, 1964) were able to demonstrate typical seven-month stranger anxiety. When she was being held by Mrs. Fraiberg, Toni reached up and stroked her face. Immediately she became stiff and began to cry bitterly. She continued to do so until her mother took her, whereupon (having felt her mother's cheek) she quieted and became content.

A few months later (at ten months), it was possible to document Toni's ability to differentiate by touch among a series of toys we offered her. She carefully explored each of several stuffed animals, discarding one after the other, until she found the one she wanted. A month later (at eleven months), she would reach out into space and open and close her hand to indicate she wanted a toy that had been taken away from her. Subsequently Toni, like all blind children who successfully negotiate the barriers posed by the problems of the period between five and ten months,*

---

*That is, the period during which the normally developing baby is using preponderantly visual stimuli to learn about and relate to the world.

showed increasing ability to use her hands alone and in combination with her hearing to make progressively more refined tactile and auditory discriminations of objects.

How, once the barrier is passed, the blind child's conceptual and cognitive abilities can parallel those of the sighted was illustrated by one of my own subjects. When he was nineteen months old, Stevie searched through a large assortment of pot covers to find one he particularly enjoyed. The procedure he followed was to feel the covers carefully and test those which seemed likely candidates by listening intently to the sound they made after he banged them on the floor. He discarded them one by one until, by a combination of touch and hearing, he found precisely the one he sought.

These evidences of discrimination and active exploration may occur while the blind infant's face remains void of those manifestations of attention and active interest we are accustomed to see in the face of a similarly occupied sighted youngster. Clearly it is important for the mother of the blind infant to learn to attend to his manual activity and to understand that it may have the same expressive connotations as do the looks of interest, of rapt attention, of puzzlement, etc., on the face of the sighted. How difficult a task this is, Mrs. Fraiberg (1974) describes very eloquently.

Vocalization. The two-phase process by which infants come to use auditory stimuli as indicators of the events occurring around them is only one of the complexities of the process which culminates in the coordinated use of our hearing and vocalizing equipment. That to begin with the development and functioning of these two aspects of our basic communications equipment involves independently developing processes is indicated by the studies of Lenneberg (1969). He showed that during the first 100 days of postpartum life, the sounds made by deaf babies and babies of deaf parents who were being reared in soundless environments were identical in amount and quality with those made by normal babies being reared in normal environments. Only when he is about ten weeks old does the *normally* hearing baby begin to apprehend that he is producing the sound he hears. Obviously for him to understand this is a necessary precursor of the events which culminate in his being able to use the same sounds for purposes of communication. At the same time it is important to emphasize that the maturational processes which make it *possible* for him to achieve this understanding constitute only a part of the story—i.e., they are a necessary but not a sufficient condition for the emergence of meaningful vocal communication. Equally important is the condition under which the development occurs. It is with respect to this second factor that the specific vulnerabilities of the congenitally blind child become most dramatically apparent. Delay in, or failure ever to develop, useable language skills has been reported by nearly all workers with congenitally blind children. It constitutes one of the more dramatic aspects of the autistic syndrome to which they are so prone. Even among those youngsters who ultimately do not become autistic, a delay in the evolution of communication by speech has been noted. Particularly impressive in this regard has been the frequently noted lag in the appearance of the first person pronoun. It is not unusual for congenitally blind children to continue to refer to themselves either in the third person or by their proper names until their third year. Among the deviant population, the persistence of the phenomenon of echolalia is often very striking. This is a condition in which an individual is able to repeat words and phrases, or even long sentences and paragraphs in his own or a foreign language without any understanding of what he is saying. At the same time he may be unable to use his speaking apparatus for even the simplest communication.

It is again impressive, and a commentary on the effectiveness of the techniques she developed, that none of Mrs. Fraiberg's ten subjects showed a significant departure from the pattern of speech development we are accustomed to anticipate in normally developing babies. This proved to be the case even though during the first year, the blind babies did not seem to engage in as much spontaneous vocalization as do sighted infants. Mrs. Fraiberg suggests that this difference may be related to the fact that the combination of sound and kinesthetic stimuli to which the blind infant is competent to respond is less readily available than are visual stimuli. The sighted child need only open his eyes to be exposed to a wealth of visual stimuli which might evoke interest and a vocal expression of his feelings. The relatively passive position of the blind child is, of course, complicated by the already noted tendency, even among sophisticated adults, not to initiate communication in the absence of the visual exchange.

Clearly, if deviant speech development is to be avoided, yet another burden is placed on the mothering one. In the absence of the reinforcement of her impulse to communicate which is typically preferred by the baby's visual response, she must engage in a pattern of vocalizing which she may well experience as entirely one-sided. With the passage of time, however, she will again discover that the critical processes which lead to self-differentiation and normal mental development have been proceeding even in the absence of vision and those reassuring behavior patterns which are dependent on vision. Despite his apparent impassivity, her baby will have heard and have registered both her sounds and the feelings they connote. He will furthermore develop a healthy ego structure even in the face of the massive barrier imposed by his blindness.

CONCLUSIONS

A prophylactic program along the lines indicated in the foregoing paragraphs should, as Mrs. Fraiberg's results indicate, sharply reduce the incidence of deviant development among the congenitally blind. The extent to which the principles involved are applicable to the child who has already become deviant remains, however, an open question. One note of optimism in this regard is found in the recently adduced evidence that the unstimulated brain may retain a considerable degree of plasticity as late as the fourth year. The observations of both Skeels (1966) and Kagan and Klein (1973) on sighted, environmentally deprived children give us reason to assume that until that age the deviant processes which result from *lack* of stimulation may be reversed by appropriate parenting. There is no a priori reason to assume that their findings coupled with an appreciation of the specific problems of the blind should not be applicable to the rearing of very young deviant blind children.

Regrettably, it does not seem likely that we would be justified in being similarly optimistic with regard to older children, whether sighted or blind. By age four, it would seem that deviant patterns are set. The possibility of reversing or even mitigating such deviance thereafter becomes increasingly unlikely. The specific problems of the congenitally blind are, in brief, best dealt with by preventive measures.

Finally, it should be clear that throughout this chapter I have been dealing with the developmental problems posed by congenital blindness. Acquired blindness whether in the child or adult raises entirely different theoretical and practical questions. To the extent that the individual suffering from acquired blindness has learned about the world through the medium of vision, he will continue to think and relate to others like a sighted person. To that extent, the fact of his blindness will be of psychological relevance as a loss—a stress to which he must adapt. Obviously this poses very different problems for the caretaker. Grief reactions, depressions, secondary neurotic reactions, analogous to those one might anticipate in the presence of any other major loss or traumatic event are to be anticipated in connection with acquired blindness. No such problems are relevant to the congenitally blind. Never having experienced vision, he cannot readily conceive of what he lacks. For him, the alternative routes of communication I have discussed are not alternative; they are the only ones he is capable of knowing. Perhaps in this sentence I have characterized most succinctly the conceptual problem posed for the worker with the congenitally blind. For him, for all of us who are sighted, vision is so dominant a modality that all others seem substitutive. For the blind individual, this is simply not the case. That which is all important to the rest of us simply does not exist for him.

BIBLIOGRAPHY

Blank, H.R. "Psychoanalysis and Blindness." *Psychoanalytic Quarterly* 26(1957):1-24.

Bennet, S. "Infant Caretaker Interaction." *Journal of the American Academy of Child Psychiatry* 10(1971):321-335.

Decarie, T. "A Study of the Mental and Emotional Development of the Thalidomide Child." In Foss, B.M. (ed.), *Determinants of Infant Behavior*, Vol. IV. New York: Wiley, 1965.

Fraiberg, S. "Parallel and Divergent Patterns in Blind and Sighted Infants." *Psychoanalytic Study of the Child* 3(1968):264-300.

Fraiberg, S. "Smiling and Stranger Reaction in Blind Infants." In Helmuth, J. (ed.), *Exceptional Infants.* New York: Brunner/Mazel, 1971.

Fraiberg, S. "Intervention in Infancy." *Journal of the American Academy of Child Psychiatry* 10(1971):381-405.

Fraiberg, S. "Blind Infants and their Mothers: An Examination of the Sign System." In Lewis, M. (ed.), *Origins of Human Behavior.* New York: John Wiley, 1974.

Fraiberg, S., and Freedman, D.A. "Studies in the Ego Development of the Congenitally Blind Child." *Psychoanalytic Study of the Child* 19(1964):113-169.

Fraiberg, S., Siegel, B., and Gibson, R. "The Role of Sound in the Search Behavior of the Blind Infant." *Psychoanalytic Study of the Child* 21(1966):327-357.

Freedman, D.A., Fox-Kolenda, B.J., Margileth, D.A., and Miller, D.M. "The Development of the Use of Sound as a Guide to Affective and Cognitive Behavior: A Two Phase Process." *Child Development* 40(1971):1099-1105.

Kagan, J., and Klein, R. "Cross Cultural Perspectives on Early Development." *American Psychologist* 28(1973):947-961.

Keeler, W.R. "Autistic Patterns and Defective Communication in Blind Children with Retrolental Fibroplasia." In Hoch, P., and Zubin, J. (eds.), *Psychopathology of Communication.* New York; Grune and Stratton, 1957.

Lenneberg, Eric H. "On Explaining Language." *Science* 164(1969):635-643.

McGraw, M. *The Neuromuscular Maturation of the Human Infant.* New York: Columbia U. Press, 1945.

Norris, M., Spaulding, P., and Brodie, F. *Blindness In Children.* Chicago: U. of Chicago Press, 1958.

Roskies, E. *Abnormality and Normality: The Mothering of Thalidomide Children.* Ithaca: Cornell U. Press, 1972.

Skeels, H.M. "Adult Status of Children with Contrasting Life Experiences." *Monographs of the Society for Research in Child Development* 31(1966): No. 3.

Spitz, R., and Wolf, K.M. "The Smiling Response." *Genetic Psychology Monographs* (1946):No. 34.

Wolff, P.H. "The Early Development of Smiling." In Foss, B.M. (ed.), *Determinants of Infant Behavior*, Vol. II. London: Methuen, 1963.

Yakovlev, P.I., and LeCours, A.R. "The Myelogenetic Cycles of Regional Maturation of the Brain." In Minkowski, A. (ed.), *Regional Development of the Brain in Early Life.* Oxford: Blackwell, 1971.

PART THREE

Treatment

CHAPTER

The Psychiatric Model

Robert G. Aug

The multidisciplinary team (psychiatrist, psychologist, social worker, educator, and pediatrician) was the matrix from which child psychiatry arose, especially during the second and third decades of this century. Of course, being a medical specialty, child psychiatry also bears the stamp of the physician's role and identity, and the physician's models of conceptual formulation and intervention; likewise, child psychiatry carries the imprint of current ferment and changes in our methods of serving children. These influences notwithstanding, today's child psychiatrist still functions in the context of collaboration with other disciplines; his diagnostic understanding of the child and his intervention efforts are informed by what happens in the other sectors of the child's life (particularly at home with parents and sibs, and at school with teachers and peers). Thus, the "psychiatric model" overlaps considerably with the psychoeducational model and the parent model in the aspects of the child's life to which it addresses itself, despite various differences in emphasis, theoretical viewpoint, method, and terms in which one views one's goals in helping children.

Even in regard to differing theoretical frameworks (e.g., the behavior-modification approach in contrast to the child psychiatrist's subtly ingrained traditional use of psychoanalytic theory and the "medical model"), there is currently much rapprochement and combined application of these differing rationales for intervention with children in need. Thus, in order to evaluate and to help real children, the child psychiatrist must use the behavioral model (together with the psychoanalytic and medical models), just as he must integrate family and educational setting with his "just-between-you-and-me" dyadic relationship with the individual child he is evaluating or treating.

ROBERT G. AUG is Professor of Psychiatry and Director for the Division of Child Psychiatry at the University of Kentucky Medical Center. His major interests include childhood psychosis, Anorexia Nervosa, and adolescent-parent interaction.

All this is by way of preparing the reader for abridged and compressed accounts of such things as the psychiatrist's work with parents and teachers, and his incorporation of behavior-modification techniques with a "psychodynamic" approach. Every effort will be made to avoid repetition of ideas conveyed in chapters on these particular approaches (i.e., behavioral, psychoeducational, and via-parent); but the unavoidable duplications should serve to remind us that the whole child consists of more than the image we create in the process of applying a particular approach, method, or conceptual framework.

THE APPROACH IN CHILD PSYCHIATRY

What, then, is the particular approach of child psychiatry? Key aspects are:

1. The process of reaching a diagnosis.
2. The implications of two kinds of diagnosis, their uses and misuses or limitations.
3. Formulation and implementation of a comprehensive treatment plan *based on diagnosis*.
4. Integration of "organic" or biological with psychological and social aspects of both diagnosis and treatment.
5. Inclusion of subjective, experiential data along with objective "behavioral" data in both diagnosis and treatment.
6. Inclusion of emotions and feelings (of both patient and doctor) in diagnosis and treatment; avoiding the limiting of professional consideration to purely cognitive, rational, or explicitly verbalized material.
7. A developmental perspective, which includes awareness of the normal *emotional* vicissitudes of each developmental stage.
8. The acquisition and use of special interviewing skills with children, adapted to the language and modes of communication of each age group (e.g., play, making up stories together, drawing, and the like). These interviewing skills also involve awareness of, and skill in, the *use of oneself* in interacting with the child.

To elucidate these "key aspects," we begin with the following material:

CASE I: Cathy, two years and ten months of age, was referred because of her tantrums, which were reportedly totally refractory to any method of handling. The tantrums occurred primarily with mother, and especially when mother and Cathy were on outings, such as shopping trips; and they usually were over the issue of Cathy's insistence on doing something in her own particular way, and tenaciously insisting on going back and doing it over again whenever she felt it wasn't done properly. One case in point occurred when Cathy and her mother were returning to their car in a shopping center parking lot. At a point where they had to cross a rather busy and dangerous roadway, Cathy insisted that mother *not* take her hand, that she (Cathy) could do it herself. Mother overtly complied, but surreptitiously placed her hand lightly on the top of Cathy's hat, maintaining contact which Cathy didn't notice . . . until just after they crossed the roadway, at which point Cathy sensed the hand being taken away, realized what had happened, and insisted on going back and crossing the street without contact. At this point mother decided this would be going too far, refused, and dragged the screaming Cathy the rest of the way to the car. Cathy continued her tantrum (and insistence on going back and doing it over) during the entire trip home, and for a considerable period of time after arriving home. Mother reported she was several times on the verge of giving in and actually going back, but "this time" she did not yield (she had yielded on other occasions to similar demands from Cathy).

After hearing this episode described in the initial telephone call from the mother, but before actually seeing any member of the family, the psychiatrist envisioned the therapy as consisting mainly of a systematic behavior-modification program in which the mother would be instructed in consistently avoiding inadvertent reinforcement of the tantrums, the use of "time outs," "catching" Cathy in good behavior in order to give her attention, etc. This tentative plan seemed all the more fitting following the diagnostic interview with Cathy, which yielded the diagnosis: "normal toddler."

However, in the follow-up interview with mother, when discussing the prospect of standing firm no matter how intensely displeased and unhappy Cathy became, the slightest hint of increased moisture appeared in mother's eyes. The tone and content of what she was saying remained matter-of-fact; and this slight hint of tears would have been passed over had it not been for the importance the psychiatrist placed on emotions as legitimate data for professional inquiry. The psychiatrist commented on the possible tears, to which mother responded with more definite tears, saying that during a tantrum Cathy seems to be expressing a desperate *plea*, rather than just anger. Mother said she herself felt like expressing the same kind of desperate plea because she felt so hopelessly trapped by her life situation.

Mother was a part-time graduate student, married to a physician who was continuing his post-M.D. training in a medical specialty (which demanded all of his time, energy, and interest, and which provided very limited income). Cathy's mother had interrupted her own studies in order to take a very ungratifying job to support her husband's medical education. Following his graduation, the couple spent two years in the military service. Cathy was born early in this two-year period; this was a planned pregnancy in which mother had reluctantly submitted to the wishes of husband and grandparents.

After Cathy's birth, mother felt doubly hemmed in and alienated from any life of her own: (1) by the demands of caring for the infant; and (2) by the fact that the only social contacts she could find were other young mothers, whose only interests were in housekeeping and raising children. After leaving the service to return to her present situation as a mere adjunct to her husband's career and nursemaid for Cathy, mother felt the same constriction and alienation, with no possibility for change.

All this material emerged in a single interview, as a result of inquiry about possible tears in mother's eyes, which was part of the inquiry into how she would feel while carrying out the behavior-modification program. In essence, mother's ambivalent response to seeing Cathy's look of frustration would very likely undermine the behavior-modification program in the same way it had made mother ineffective in handling Cathy's tantrums previously. Mother said that most of the times she thwarted Cathy's will, she "read" the look in Cathy's eyes as a poignant expression of the same yearning mother herself felt, and mother just ". . . couldn't bring myself to do to her what life was doing to me."

Mother felt her husband was too brittle, too conservative, and under too many heavy work pressures to enter conjoint couple therapy with her, or even to be exposed to the knowledge of her discontent. However, he was able to accept this "news" and entered conjoint couple therapy, which became a vital and necessary context for the behavior-modification program with Cathy.

CASE II: Five-year-old Tommy was referred for long-term inpatient treatment because of being diagnosed as "psychotic." This diagnosis was made on the basis of his sustained chaotic behavior both at home and at school. His behavior seemed to lack any goal-directed quality, especially with his very frequent shifts in attention and type of activity. He had been expelled from several kindergartens because his impulsive behavior (talking loudly out of turn, hitting other children, aggressively breaking toys) and off-task behavior disrupted the class beyond tolerable limits. All attempts by adults to command, persuade, or punish Tommy into changing this behavior failed, leaving the adults with the strong feeling that "you just can't get through to him"; this, plus his frequent falls and other self-injuring "accident-prone" impulsive acts led adults to describe him as "out of touch with reality," hence psychotic (a diagnosis which many workers regard as requiring lengthy inpatient treatment).

The examining psychiatrist of the inpatient unit found Tommy to be very impulsive, refractory to control, and giving a strong impression of chaos and disorganization. However, Tommy did *not* have the cardinal, essential signs of childhood psychosis, viz: he made good eye contact, reacted (uncooperatively) to what the psychiatrist said, and altogether showed flexible, reciprocal social contact (albeit obnoxious social contact); Tommy's use of language for social communication was quite competent (albeit disrespectful); and Tommy's mood and emotional states were clearly communicated and congruous with the situation (albeit an unpleasant situation most of the time).

Not only did Tommy lack these cardinal symptoms of childhood psychosis, but he showed hyperactivity, short attention span, easy distractibility, and impulsivity in a way which fit the picture of the "hyperkinetic syndrome" (also known as "minimal brain dysfunction"). This latter condition usually responds well to medication and can be managed without hospitalization, even with attendance at a regular school (especially if any specific learning disabilities are taken into account). This outpatient course of action was followed successfully with Tommy.

CASE III: Six-year-old Jeff, a first-grader, was referred for behavior somewhat similar to Tommy's: disruptive, defiant rule-breaking behavior, off-task behavior, and learning far below his potential. He also was described as hyperactive, restless, and impulsive, altogether resembling the "minimal brain dysfunction" symptom-picture. However, this diagnosis was not supported by the history given by the mother, by psychological testing, or by neurological examination. Indeed, the family history gave abundant information suggesting an emotional cause: Jeff's parents had divorced about a year ago, and the cold war between them (disparaging and depreciating each other in ways Jeff could sense, disputing each other's discipline of Jeff) had been going on for years before, during, and after the divorce. The mother told Jeff: "Now that Daddy's out of the house, you'll be the man of the family, . . . open doors for me, . . . seat me at the table, [etc.] ."

In the first diagnostic interview with the psychiatrist, Jeff spent much of the time playing with the farm animals; and much of the verbal exchange between Jeff and the psychiatrist pertained to the animals. Jeff showed a rich imagination in the many adventures he put the animals through, and he readily answered most of the psychiatrist's questions about why the animal was doing something, how the animal felt, and what if the animal did something else instead.

Throughout these many animal adventures, a basic theme appeared over and over again: two animals fighting to be the one-and-only best friend (or spouse) of a third animal, or fighting over the position of boss of the herd. Repeatedly the loser suffered banishment into being all alone and friendless, plus bodily mutilation (e.g., losing part of a leg). The winner eventually suffered a similar fate, or was killed, by way of punishment for his previous aggressive victory.

During all this animal play, Jeff showed no hyperactivity or distractibility, and demonstrated quite a long attention span and well-sustained "on-task" behavior. Also, he was free of any rule-breaking or impulsive behavior. However, when the psychiatrist finally stated it was time to end the animal play, Jeff refused; when the psychiatrist insisted, Jeff angrily counter-insisted, then threw toys around the room as the psychiatrist moved in to restrain him by gently-but-firmly holding Jeff's arms. Jeff shouted: "You can't tell me what to do ... I can beat you up ... I can kill you." But as the psychiatrist continued to hold him firmly and repeated that he wouldn't let Jeff hurt anyone or hurt himself, Jeff gradually simmered down (and even seemed relieved and became somewhat amicable again).

In the context of the total body of diagnostic information, it appeared that the above excerpt reflected Jeff's key problem: he was lagging behind on an important emotional developmental task, which psychoanalysts call "resolution of the Oedipus complex."

With apologies to those already familiar with the term, "Oedipus complex" refers to a particular combination of intense feelings which the child has toward his parents during the "preschool" years (i.e., age three to about five-and-a-half or six), in which the child feels a kind of romantic, erotic attachment toward the opposite-sex parent, and a kind of rivalry toward the same-sex parent. According to psychoanalytic theory, these feelings are accompanied by fears of retribution in the form of bodily injury, loss of the parents' love, etc. In the normal course of development, the child decides: "Since I can't beat 'em, I'll join 'em." The five-year-old who sees one parent as a rival, hopelessly bigger and smarter, and both parents as police, feels he has nothing to fear when he joins their side. He joins up in several ways: (1) He becomes his own policeman in the sense that he "internalizes" and carries within himself the parents' rules and regulations; his conscience is formed. (2) He becomes strongly motivated to learn and acquire the abilities and attributes of the parents (especially the same-sex parent), and the skills of other adults he encounters in school, on television, etc. (3) He gives up his claim to exclusive possession of Mommy or Daddy and displaces much of his intensity of emotional involvement from family to the "outside world" of school and peers.

One need not subscribe to this psychoanalytic theory of the mechanisms of this developmental change in order to observe that such a change in behavior and attitude does indeed normally occur around this age, a change which makes the child so much more ready for school (where he has to be reliably controlled from within and motivated to learn). Further, it is easy to see how this developmental change can be delayed or hindered when there is not a strong parental coalition, when the child is neither faced with the futility of "beating 'em" nor encouraged to "join 'em."

When this is the case, the child quite predictably shows poorly controlled, rule-breaking behavior and rather weak motivation to learn (especially by sustained effort in school), as was indeed the case with Jeff.

Thus, although the presenting problem in Jeff's case bore many descriptive similarities to that in Tommy's (impulsive rule-breaking, restlessness, off-task behavior, underachievement, etc.), diagnostic inquiry revealed quite a different total picture, which called for a different treatment approach. There was no need for medication for Jeff; and Jeff had a greater and more specific need for *psychotherapy* to help him deal with his conflicting feelings in more successfully adaptive ways and to free him to resume normal emotional development, together with as much modification as possible of his "real-life" situation outside the therapeutic hours (e.g., mother's style of relating to him), with the aim of optimizing conditions for the same goal of fostering a resumption of normal emotional development.

The psychotherapy with Jeff was in the form of weekly individual sessions with the psychiatrist in which verbal communication in the context of play constituted a principal method. In this joint play, after Jeff would have two bulls fighting to the death to be boss of the herd, the psychiatrist would say: "Let me tell the story another way," and designate one bull as younger and smaller, comment that he must be frightened over the prospect of fighting an adult bull, over the possibility of being hurt (or at best all alone) if he lost, and full of regret if he won at the expense of hurting the other bull, who had been his friend. The psychiatrist's variations on this plot (which Jeff wanted to play over and over again) also included the younger bull and the older bull reaching an agreement whereby they would be good friends, the younger bull would abide by all the rules of the herd, and the older bull would help him become stronger, grow up, and have a herd of his own some day. There was much discussion about a version of the story in which the younger bull found himself the one-and-only leader of the herd, and really felt quite uneasy and afraid that he wasn't big enough and didn't really know how to lead the herd.

DISCUSSION

From the foregoing clinical material, what should we underscore as vital to the psychiatric model?

First of all, the *comprehensiveness* of approach, both in terms of all facets of the particular patient and his situation, and in terms of the use of multiple, different theoretical points of view and methods is important. Precision is sought, but not by narrowing our approach, nor be excluding certain kinds of variables or data (e.g., excluding subjective and emotional data, or excluding "organic" data) from consideration or from use in a treatment program.

Secondly, this comprehensiveness helps make possible the principle of tailoring the treatment program to fit the individual patient (rather than excluding patients who don't fit a particular method, or dealing only with those aspects of the patient which do fit the method).

Thirdly, this tailoring of treatment to fit the patient depends upon making a diagnosis which is accurate and complete enough. This calls for an explanation of the two kinds of diagnosis in psychiatry: (1) "clinical diagnosis" (or "nosologic classification"), and (2) "dynamic diagnosis" (or "dynamic formulation").

The "clinical diagnosis" is parallel to the use of diagnosis in any other medical specialty: it is much like asking, "Is this a case of measles, meningitis, pneumococcal pneumonia, leukemia, [etc.]?" It amounts to a way of *classifying* the child's behavior. Is it normal or abnormal? If abnormal, does it belong in the class of the neuroses, mental retardation, psychosis, benign developmental lag, antisocial personality, [etc.]?

There has been much criticism of this kind of diagnosis: it means putting a label on the child which may stigmatize him; it fails to treat him as an individual person; it often tends to be thought of as a *static* "disease entity" rather than as an ongoing *process*; and it inclines us (and the patient) to think of him as passive victim of his condition rather than active agent of his own behavior.

However, as long as we can be alert to avoid these misuses of clinical diagnosis, we can benefit from a very important advantage it gives us. Making the correct clinical diagnosis opens up a tremendous amount of additional information to us, information which has been collected on thousands of similar cases by many other workers. This information concerns the usual causes that have been found for this class of illnesses, the most effective treatment, the natural course or outlook for the future (what the child and his parents can expect to be the outcome) as it has turned out in thousands of other cases in the same diagnostic category.

Thus, the clinical diagnosis tells us a lot about a patient, but it does not tell us everything. It tells us about objective qualities which he shares with all other members of the same category, but it does not tell us about him as an individual with his unique combination of subjective feelings. It helps us understand the patient as object, but not as subject.

Therefore, in order to understand the patient not only as object, but also as subject, we complement our "clinical diagnosis" by seeking out a "dynamic diagnosis" or "dynamic formulation": What *in particular* is this individual child defending himself against, what scares him, what is he angry about, and why does he handle his anger or his fear in this particular way? In what way do the answers to these questions fit in with or explain the symptoms or complaints about the patient?

In both the clinical diagnosis and the dynamic formulation, the psychiatrist uses a *developmental* perspective in which the patient's behavior and expressions of feeling are viewed in terms of a "sliding scale" of normal developmental phenomena at different ages. For example, consider the behavior of Cathy (Case I), in which her very intense concern with doing things in just a certain way (and doing it over again if it wasn't done properly) would seem eccentric and irrational in light of the commonsense unimportance of such things. However, an awareness that toddlers *normally* have a peak of emotional investment in rituals (and normally go to some excess in exercising the newly acquired function of asserting a will of their own) helped greatly in evaluating both the parents' complaints and Cathy's behavior in the psychiatric examination.

Here in a chapter on intervention we have put this much emphasis on diagnosis because our choice of methods of intervention and "systems-level" of intervention (e.g., family, school, peer group, individual person, organ-system or molecular level within the person, etc.) depends on the accuracy and completeness of diagnosis, of evaluating just where the problem(s) lie. This may seem self-evident, but it bears repeating because in actual practice many workers have followed a policy of doing only a very brief and incomplete evaluation (just enough to assess whether the child is a good psychotherapy candidate, or just enough to identify problem behaviors and establish a baseline for a behavior-modification program).

At any rate, in accordance with his total diagnostic picture, the child psychiatrist attempts to map out a total plan of intervention, which may include: (1) individual psychotherapy with the child; (2) psychotherapy with one or both parents; (3) coaching the parents on child-rearing techniques in general or in a specific system which may or may not use systematic behavior modification; (4) collaboration with teachers, liaison teachers, and other school personnel to obtain and share information about the child and make specific applications of the psychiatrist's understanding of the child to the classroom setting (which may or may not include a systematic behavior-modification program); (5) medication for the child when indicated; (6) referral for remediation of specific handicaps (e.g., in vision, hearing, speech, etc.) and for special training in those areas when indicated; (7) consultation with a wide variety of agencies in the community which deal with children, focusing either on a client of the agency or upon problems of interaction among agency personnel.

From among these various modes of intervention, perhaps we should single out psychotherapy for further elaboration, since it has traditionally constituted such a major part of the actual work of most child psychiatrists.

Without attempting a complete definition of psychotherapy, we can say that it involves a process of relating and communicating between therapist and patient, with the aim of altering certain maladaptive and/or distress-producing behaviors and/or feelings of the patient. Psychotherapy was first conducted with adults, and later adapted to use with children. This adaptation involved finding more concrete and vivid modes of communication (e.g., via play, telling stories together, and generally more active use of the therapist's whole person, such as active physical limit-setting); and it also involved dealing with the fact that the child's behavior, his personality, is much more plastic and chameleonlike in response to the current environment than is the adult's, so that the "gap" between the therapist's office and the rest of the child's world posed much more of a problem.

In addition to calling for more intervention in those other parts of the child's world, this "gap" accentuated the problematic fact that office psychotherapy involves creating a replica or representation of the patient's problems (which can then be worked on in the psychotherapy setting). This creating a representation of the problem holds true even for the use of play to give concrete embodiment to the communication: it still is a type of representation. Whatever healthier solutions and better adaptations are worked out in the psychotherapy sessions, the problem still remains of generalizing or carrying over such solutions to other settings in the child's life.

This difficulty can be surmounted most easily with adults and adolescents, somewhat less easily with older school-age children, and with increasing difficulty as one descends the chronological age scale through early school-age and preschool children. Fortunately, what this calls for is not abandoning psychotherapy for these younger children, but rather including the child's other care-giving adults in a psychotherapeutic approach.

Perhaps the best way to convey the general tone of a psychotherapeutic approach is by the "two-layer" concept. We look upon the child's personality as involving two levels: an "outer" one, consisting of his overt behavior; and an "inner," not-so-readily-observable one consisting of underlying causes and reasons for the overt behavior. In general, the underlying causes of symptomatic, maladaptive behavior can be classified as either (1) some form of deficit, or (2) some form of emotional conflict, which causes anxiety, against which the child tries to defend himself by his overt symptomatic behavior. In either case, we can look upon the symptomatic behavior as an understandable method of defense called on to cope with underlying distress.

The purpose of visualizing symptomatic behavior this way is to enable us to feel genuine empathy for the underlying distress, and communicate a nonjudgmental attitude toward the child experiencing such distress, at the same time that we set limits on the overt behavior, and even communicate a judgmental attitude toward obnoxious or destructive overt behavior.

For example, it would be absurd to try to be totally nonjudgmental toward a child who starts hitting you in the face with a heavy metal toy; but you can handle the situation constructively by firmly grasping his arm and expressing your anger over his actions, while reminding yourself of his underlying problems with which you can feel genuine empathy. If one genuinely feels such empathy, it will get across to the child without elaborate verbal explanation; and this may constitute a corrective emotional experience for the child in which he encounters the natural consequences of his (aggressive) actions, yet is helped to control his behavior and does not reexperience total abandonment.

Another principle of the psychotherapeutic management of children is to offer (whenever feasible) some alternative outlet or gratification at the same time that one sets limits on some behavior, e.g., directing the child to pound a pounding toy instead of you, or to throw a ping-pong ball or ball of socks around the room (at windows or at other people) instead of a hard object. Metaphorically, one might say: present the child with a "detour" sign instead of a "dead-end" sign.

CHAPTER 10

The Psychoeducational Model

Mary M. Wood

A RATIONALE FOR MERGER

Psychoeducation has been so broadly defined by individuals and theories that perhaps it is best viewed as a generic term rather than as a single intervention approach. The term has been used to describe many combinations of psychological and educational theories and practices. Broadly, when a psychological construct or theory is translated into an educational or preschool setting, it becomes a psychoeducational strategy. The characteristics of any one psychoeducational model depend primarily upon the balance between the psychological and educational constructs involved. For example, psychoeducational practices with heavy emphasis on learning theory become characterized as behavioral interventions (Hewett, 1975); while practices drawing upon ego theory become psychodynamic models (Long, Morse, Newman, 1971); those with foundations in psychoanalytic theory generally make distinctions between educational activities and treatment although both are recognized as important (Furman and Katan, 1969); and those influenced by ecological theory often are characterized as transactional or reality therapies (Rhodes and Head, 1974). Whatever blend of psychological and educational effort is used, results indicate that both are significant aspects of effective intervention with young handicapped children. There is also considerable agreement that compartmentalized efforts, produced in isolation and separated by professional vocabulary, training, philosophy, or agency setting, seem to work against effective progress. Long, Morse, and Newman (1971) describe some of the adverse effects:

MARY M. WOOD is a Professor of Special Education and Director of the Developmental Therapy Institute at the University of Georgia. Her major professional interest is developmental curriculums for emotionally disturbed children and the preschool handicapped.

> . . . The child-guidance approach created as many problems as it solved. For example, when a child was taken out of a classroom for individual therapy, the child's problem was placed outside the teacher's jurisdiction. The teacher's role was devaluated when the therapist, because of severe time limitation or a lack of interest, was unable to maintain a cooperative and continuous flow of information. Under these conditions, the teacher was relegated to a passive role, where his insights and concerns were not considered (p. 224).

Newton and Brown (1967) put the same idea another way: "The teacher has no choice! She must be involved in the mental health of children and the developement of their adequacy" (p. 525ff). They call attention to the deliberate or inadvertent influence of a teacher on children: "She stands on the front lines of stress and potential disordered behavior as she daily confronts a child's crises and growing pains" (p. 525ff). Recognizing the unique needs of emotionally disturbed children and the effect of the school environment on them, Pate (1963) stresses the need for "psychotherapeutic experiences in an educational framework" (p. 255). He describes the emerging role of such teachers as "therapeutic educators" (p. 255). He also emphasizes that this new therapeutic education should not be considered psychotherapy.

The concept of therapeutic education has been interpreted in many ways, but all can be generally classified as psychoeducational models. Kirk (1972) puts a particular parameter around the concept of therapeutic education with three convincing arguments that psychoeducational intervention can contribute to improved adjustment of children. First, coping skills can be taught to children. Second, teachers can become skillfully trained to use crisis management techniques suitable to the emotional needs of individual children at times of crisis. Third, interpersonal adult-child and child-child relationships, essential for effective treatment, can be developed in school settings. There are strong implications in these statements to support the inclusion of teachers in planning intervention strategies for emotionally disturbed young children.

One of the original demonstrations of the psychoeducational approach to intervention with seriously disturbed children began in 1953 at the League School. Fenichel (1971) describes this approach which keeps children in their communities and substitutes a day treatment school and home involvement for the traditional mental hospital.

> We began with the hypothesis that behavioral changes could be achieved by the use of special educational techniques in a therapeutic setting without individual psychotherapy. This hypothesis was based on the assumption that a properly planned and highly individualized educational program with interdisciplinary clinical participation could result in social and emotional growth as well as in educational achievements (p. 337).

Since that time, the psychoeducational model has received increasing attention from both psychiatric and special educational sources. Long,

Morse, and Newman (1971) summarize characteristics which seem to be unique to most psychoeducational models, as applied to school-age children:

1. An educational milieu must be developed in which careful psychological attention is given to everything that affects the pupil as he interacts with the school, staff, peers, and curriculum.
2. An understanding of the teacher-pupil relationship is important.
3. All learning must be invested with feelings to give it interest, meaning, and purpose.
4. Conflict can be used productively to teach new ways of understanding and coping with stress.
5. Each pupil has his own learning style.
6. Relearning follows a cyclical process making temporary regression in behavior a normal part of the process.
7. The teacher works at the child's current level of functioning, which may or may not be related to his IQ, aptitude, or age (p. 330).

In support of psychoeducational strategies with preschool children, Glasscote and Fishman in their report, *Mental Health Programs for Preschool Children* (1974), describe the Dubnoff School in California:

It is, if one had to construct a hierarchy, primarily educational, but with significant leavening of developmental theory, a "systems approach" of family contact and involvement, and a frequently mentioned need for parallel psychotherapy from some other source. It includes even, or perhaps inevitably, social reinforcement which would qualify as "behavior modification" . . . with a special valuation of the educational approach, in the most sophisticated meaning of that concept (p. 36).

This program description represents a significant step toward recognizing the contribution of educational constructs to a model of intervention for the seriously disturbed young child. However, it is evident that there remains some reluctance to throw off the traditional dependence upon psychotherapy.

THE "FIRST CHANCE" MODELS

The most recent trends in psychoeducational models for preschool children can be followed by reviewing strategies and models developed by more than 150 First Chance demonstration projects funded by the Bureau of Education for the Handicapped, U.S. Office of Education, under the Handicapped Children's Early Education Assistance Act, P.L. 91-230, Part C. In these projects, the various curriculum designs and their organization around a particular rationale often reveal the philsophy for intervention. Among these projects there appear to be five basic ways of expressing a rationale: (1) a deficit-ameliorative approach which begins with individual problems; (2) a basic-skills approach, teaching processes for skill development; (3) psychological constructs to guide the intervention strategies; (4) an educational content approach which identifies academic content areas to be taught; or (5) a developmental approach built upon sequences of normal development (Wood and Hurley, 1975). Each approach, or combination, reflects a psychoeducational orientation with varying degrees of emphasis upon psychological or educational constructs. The psychological constructs most often included were: self-concept, identity, divergent thinking (creativity), motivation, and body image. At the other end of the continuum, educational content areas most frequently included were prereading, number, music, art, dance, play, storytelling, social studies, and nature. The content areas included most often by projects of all orientations were language, cognition, auditory and visual perception, and gross and fine motor skills.

A trend in these projects suggests an increasing use of developmental constructs as the basis for many models. This developmental emphasis represents an exciting potential for psychoeducational intervention which is only beginning to emerge.

DEVELOPMENTAL THEMES
IN PSYCHOEDUCATIONAL MODELS*

With a developmental approach, a variety of psychological, psychiatric, pediatric, and educational procedures can be translated into a common language which focuses upon characteristics in the developing young child which are growth inducing. Such an approach would be in contrast to more clinical strategies which focus upon maladaptive behavior or pathological conditions. This idea is reflected by Glasscote and Fishman (1974), citing the Institute of Human Development (at the University of California—Berkeley) study of infants and children followed for twenty-five years. This study reports a surprisingly high incidence of satisfactory adjustment among adults for whom poor forecasts had been made as children. Glasscote and Fishman quote from the report, "the investigators gave too much weight to the troublesome and pathogenic elements in a child's life—quite naturally, in view of the studies that have traced neuroses and psychoses to such elements—and too little weight to the healthful, maturity-inducing elements" (p. 25).

Theoretical support for the developmental approach can be drawn from the fields of child development, psychoanalytic theory, learning theory, and developmental psychology. The existence of hierarchical progressions of developmental skills related to cognition and adjustment has been well

*A portion of this discussion of developmental themes in psychoeducational models appeared originally in "A Developmental Approach to Educating the Disturbed Young Child," an article written by M. M. Wood and W. W. Swan and published in *Behavioral Disorders*, Spring 1978.

documented. In particular, maturational sequences in communication, games and play, socialization, adaptive behavior, creativity, and sensori-motor and self-help skills have been the focus of much recent research. It is surprising that greater attention has not been given to the relation-ship between these normal developmental milestones and the processes of development in handicapped children. Developmental strategies offer promising potential for designing psychoeducational models to serve the preschool and school-age handicapped populations (Biber and Franklin, 1967).

Several contributions to the professional literature specifically con-cerning the emotionally disturbed child have been made from this develop-mental perspective. Hewett (1968) was the first to introduce and evaluate the effect of a developmental hierarchy of educational goals on the achievement of emotionally disturbed school-age boys. His developmental sequence includes attention, response, order, and exploratory and mastery skills. Refinement of this model resulted in the generalization of Hewett's model to other areas of special education (Hewett, 1975; Taylor, Artuso, and Hewett, 1970; Hewett, 1976). This model illustrates the changes that can occur in children receiving a carefully sequenced, developmen-tally oriented program. It also underscores the necessity for the class-room design, the curriculum, and materials to change as the child changes, reflecting new developmental stages.

Dupont (1975) recognized the importance of including many aspects of psychological and affective development in the curriculum for the emotionally disturbed. In summarizing the current status of curriculum planning he stated:

> Ego development and the development of competence as concomitants of psychoaffective development have been left almost entirely to chance. In the cognitive-developmental model, cognitive and affective processes are assumed to interact as the child's development moves through hierarchical stages as he/she experiences and interacts with the environment. Patterns of feeling and behavior are symbolized, organized, and integrated through cognitive processes and structures (p. 437).

Loevinger (1976) further elaborates on the complexity of this idea: "What changes during the course of ego development is a complexly inter-woven fabric of impulse control, character, interpersonal relations, con-scious preoccupations, and cognitive complexity, among other things" (p. 26).

Using a slightly different emphasis, several investigators have examined the concept of the developmental crisis. That is, certain critical age points in the development of all children tend to produce certain types of emo-tional and behavioral problems. The nature of the resolution of these events, or stages, will significantly influence the course of emotional development at the next stage.

A number of authorities have identified fairly consistent age trends for developmental crises. Clarizio and McCoy (1976) have summarized the extensive longitudinal investigation of MacFarlane, Allen, and Honzik (1954), concerned with behavior problems for children between one and three-quarters years and fourteen years. This investigation noted the existence of age-referenced problems and asserted that in general the following five developmental patterns of problems can be identified on an age continuum, declining with age:

1. Elimination
2. Fears
3. Thumbsucking
4. Destructiveness
5. Temper outbursts

Clinical observations have corroborated the statistical trend studies. Herbert (1974) organized problem syndromes into four corresponding stages of normal development: infancy, the toddler, the preschooler, and middle childhood. While the concept of clustering clinical problems by stages may hold true in some respects, this approach fails to accommodate the idea that the hierarchy of development is interactive, with elements of one stage influencing the characteristic behavior of the subsequent stage.

Swap (1974) uses this idea to describe emotionally disturbed children as those who "are seen as having difficulty negotiating developmental crises. . ." (p. 169). She suggests operationalizing intervention programs based upon this definition and emphasizes the importance of adapting teaching environments and adult roles to the particular stage of a child's development.

Others also suggest the importance of adapting to developmental differences in curriculum planning. Working with learning-disabled children ages seven to ten years, Carter and Miller (1975) attempted to improve perceptual-motor coordination, self-awareness, self-image, interest span, and identification with experiences using art activities. They reported the need to change their original experimental lessons to adapt to various developmental levels in their group in order to ensure success and motivation. In the treatment of young children with cerebral palsy, Bobath (1966) has emphasized intervention at the early stages of motor development. In particular, he advocates techniques based on the sensation of movement as the basis for a sequence of developmental steps which enhance advantageous movement patterns and postures.

Two other illustrations of developmental curriculum are those described by Lavatelli and by Lillie. Lavatelli (1970) developed a preschool curriculum based upon Piaget's theory of cognitive development, with a specific emphasis on the sequence of development of classification, space and number, and seriation. Piaget's work was used by Lillie (1975) in a different way. His "Developmental Task Instructional System" was built upon the theoretical constructs of Piaget's organization of cognitive development and the Thurstones' factor analytic studies of intellectual functioning. It includes sequences of tasks for the development of motor skills, perceptual reasoning, and language skills for children ages three through five years of age. Although Lillie has constructed the developmental tasks on the assumption of an invariant sequence of development, he makes an important differentiation between *acquisition* and *practice*. The simultaneous occurrence of these two steps compounds the difficulties in research into developmental sequences because a child may be refining one skill while starting the active mastery of a subsequent skill. Kohlberg and Hersh (1977) call these same processes *hierarchical integrations* and Piaget and Inhelder's (1969) terms are *assimilation* and *accommodation*.

These basic developmental constructs have been applied in a developmental approach to group counseling by Gazda (1971). Drawing upon the theoretical works from counseling, group psychotherapy, child development, personality development, and group dynamics, Gazda has formulated four stages for counseling groups: Exploratory, Transition, Action, and Termination. He has summarized the rationale for a developmental approach in this way:

> The needs of a child, preadolescent, adolescent, and adult can be related to his developmental stages of growth and the developmental tasks that confront him. How he copes with or fulfills the tasks is related directly to his level of adjustment and well-being. The developmental tasks with their appropriate coping behaviors serve as excellent guideposts or signals for all those who are responsible for facilitating growth and development (Gazda, 1971, p. viii).

The challenge is unmistakable. If we are to assist emotionally disturbed young children, we must have greater knowledge of how these many complex factors interact to produce the evident signs of disturbance. Or, put in a more positive way, we must understand the many factors which contribute to the social and emotional growth of children who have been identified as disturbed. Behind the impressive array of theory and research centered around normal development, one implication for intervention seems to predominate: that *maturation* may be the single most powerful force to be harnessed in therapy with young children. If this can be done, the healthy aspects of growth may override emotional problems impeding progress.

DEVELOPMENTAL THERAPY

A major effort to implement this idea in a psychoeducational model has been made at the Rutland Center in Athens, Georgia. There, a psychoeducational curriculum called Developmental Therapy (Wood, 1975; Wood and Swan, 1978) has been pilot-tested, demonstrated, and evaluated over a seven-year period. Applicable for children from two to fourteen years of age, this curriculum is based upon the idea that adjustment of young children is an ever-changing process, involving significant experiences with adults and the sequential mastery of developmental skills which aid children in successfully coping with demands of a particular age and the unique circumstances of each child. The skills needed by a young child in order to cope effectively are those which assist him in *doing, saying, caring,* and *thinking.* Translated into practice, these processes can be taught in sequential steps using the Developmental Therapy objectives. These objectives represent milestones in the curriculum areas of behavior (doing), communication (saying), socialization (caring), and (pre)academics (thinking). Figure 1 illustrates this schema.

IDENTIFYING CHILDREN WITH SPECIAL NEEDS

One important aspect of a psychoeducational strategy for young handicapped children is its potential kinship with preschool and day-care programs. It is here, in the many child-care institutions, that early identification and intervention can be realized. This assumes, of course, that teachers and other child-care workers are alert to children who may have special needs. By sensitizing teachers to recognize such children, the first step in implementing a psychoeducational model begins. The Rutland Center Early Childhood Project (NTAO, 1974) uses an audio-slide presentation illustrating sixteen key problems which may help a teacher recognize a child with a special need.* The key items are those which have recurred repeatedly over a five-year period in the referrals of young children at the center. A short brochure accompanies the visual presentation; in it, the teacher is asked:

> As a teacher have you come across a child who seems to have a harder time in school than others? Have you noticed children who seem to need something special to help them along? Sometimes a child's problem may be a handicap you can easily see. But for other children the handicap may be hidden. . . . If a child in your class has any one of these characteristics ask yourself, "Is his behavior making things so hard for him that he is not progressing?"

The sixteen key items for the teacher's reference are then listed:

---

*The National Technical Assistance Office assists agencies and school systems in using the Rutland Center Developmental Therapy model to treat severely emotionally disturbed and autistic preschool children. This project is funded by the Bureau of Education for the Handicapped/Division for Innovation and Development under the Handicapped Children's Early Education Program.

FIGURE 1

**THE ELEMENTS OF EMOTIONAL DEVELOPMENT
SHOWN IN STAGES OF
THE DEVELOPMENTAL CURRICULUM***

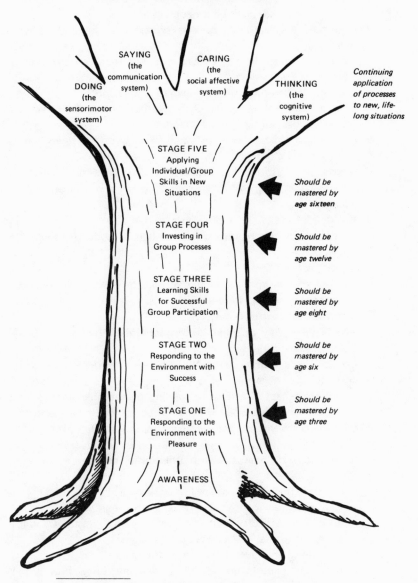

SAYING
(the
communication
system)

DOING
(the
sensorimotor
system)

CARING
(the
social affective
system)

THINKING
(the
cognitive
system)

*Continuing
application
of processes
to new, life-
long situations*

STAGE FIVE
Applying
Individual/Group
Skills in New
Situations

*Should be
mastered by
age sixteen*

STAGE FOUR
Investing in
Group Processes

*Should be
mastered by
age twelve*

STAGE THREE
Learning Skills
for Successful
Group Participation

*Should be
mastered by
age eight*

STAGE TWO
Responding to the
Environment with
Success

*Should be
mastered by
age six*

STAGE ONE
Responding to the
Environment with
Pleasure

*Should be
mastered by
age three*

AWARENESS

*Modified from Wood, M.M. "Developmental Curriculum for Social And Emotional
Growth." In D. Lillie, *Early Childhood Education: An Individualized Approach to
Developmental Instruction*. Chicago: Science Research Associates, 1975.

1. *Short attention span; unable to concentrate:*
   —not able to pay attention long enough to finish an activity.
2. *Restless or hyperactive:*
   —moves around constantly, fidgets; doesn't seem to move with a purpose in mind; picks on other children.
3. *Does not complete tasks; careless, unorganized approach to activities:*
   —does not finish what is started; does not seem to know how to plan to get work done.
4. *Listening difficulties; does not seem to understand:*
   —has trouble following directions, turns away while others are talking; does not seem to be interested.
5. *Avoids participation with other children or only knows how to play by hurting others:*
   —stays away from other children; always plays alone; leaves a group of children when an activity is going on; bites, hits, or bullies.
6. *Avoids adults:*
   —stays away from adults; does not like to come to adults for attention.
7. *Repetitive behavior:*
   —does some unusual movement or repeats words over and over; cannot stop activity himself.
8. *Ritualistic or unusual behavior:*
   —has a fixed way of doing certain activities in ways not usually seen in other children.
9. *Resistant to discipline or direction (impertinent, defiant, resentful, destructive, or negative):*
   —does not accept directions or training; disagreeable, hard to manage; destroys materials or toys deliberately; temper tantrums.
10. *Unusual language content (bizarre, strange, fearful, jargon, fantasy):*
    —very odd or different talk with others or in stories.
11. *Speech problems:*
    —rate: speech that is unusually fast or slow
    —articulation: difficulty making clear speech sounds
    —stuttering: difficulty with flow of speech; repeating sounds, words, or phrases; blocking words or sounds
    —voice: unusually loud, soft, high, or low; scratchy
    —no speech: chooses not to talk or does not know how to talk so that others can understand.
12. *Physical complaints:*
    —talks of being sick or hurt; seems tired or without energy.

13. *Echoes other's speech:*
    --repeats another person's words without intending for the words to mean anything.
14. *Lack of self-help skills:*
    —unable to feed self, unable to dress self, unable to conduct toilet activities unaided, or to carry out health practices such as washing hands, brushing teeth, etc.
15. *Self-aggressive or self-derogatory:*
    —does things to hurt self
    —says negative things about self.
16. *Temperamental, overly sensitive, sad, irritable:*
    —moody, easily depressed, unhappy, shows extreme emotions and feelings.

This approach is not an attempt to make a diagnostician of the teacher, nor to expect a referral to carry a categorical label such as "mentally retarded with emotional problems." Rather, it is a sensitizing process oriented to the individual needs of children and to the notion that the teacher has much to contribute in meeting the special needs of special children.

PARENT PARTICIPATION IN PSYCHOEDUCATIONAL MODELS

Every model of intervention has an option to include a parent component. The nature of such involvement should be a direct outcome of the theory behind the model. Types of parent participation programs range from formalized parent appointments for counseling at one end of the continuum all the way to programs conducted entirely by parents with their children at home (Ora, 1970; Shearer and Shearer, 1972; Karnes and Badger, 1969). Almost all clinically oriented programs view parent participation in some form as an essential aspect of treatment. The Julia Ann Singer therapeutic nursery uses "family demonstration" and "parent education" as means to enhance parents' abilities to conduct therapeutic programs (Glasscote and Fishman, 1974). "Parents as partners" or "parents as cotherapists" are other phrases used to describe this concept of parent involvement in providing therapy and teaching (Schopler and Reichler, 1972).

At the Rutland Center, parents may be involved in a variety of progams, depending upon their own needs (Wood, *Developmental Therapy*, 1975). These programs are:

1. *Parent Conferences:* weekly appointments to discuss the child's progress at school, home, and center. These conferences can serve to facilitate the partnership aspect of the treatment program.

Both the treatment team and the parents share information to the end that the child's development will be enhanced in both settings.

2. *Parents' Association:* an organization of Rutland Center parents which meets in the evening once a month at the center. All parents are welcome. This program offers parents an opportunity to meet and get to know other parents whose children are enrolled in the Rutland Center program. Information may be shared, programs to help the center may be planned and implemented, and the feeling of isolation which may be felt by the parents of an emotionally disturbed child may be reduced at these meetings. The group also is involved in a number of helping activities. Parents report that this is a significant way that they can reciprocate and "do something for the center."

3. *Observation:* learning about the Rutland Center program by observing the class through a one-way mirror with staff who are also working with the child. For many parents, observing may be their first opportunity to see their child interacting successfully in a group situation. Observation may be of help to a parent who wants to see a particular objective being implemented. Also, observation provides parents the opportunity to really know what is going on with their children at Rutland Center.

4. *Home Program:* the teacher and parents plan new management routines for parents to use at home. Often these planning sessions are conducted in the home. It is difficult for a staff person to understand the home situation of which parents speak until he actually sees the family members on their own ground. Parents may feel that the home contact is the best way to explain themselves. In this case, the Home Program may be chosen.

5. *The Parent Training Program:* parents learn the skills used by the Rutland Center staff by working as support teachers with treatment teams at the center. The amount of time required will depend upon the parents' time and interest. This program carries the observation program a step farther. It can be very useful to the parent who actually feels the need to use Developmental Therapy techniques and wants to learn them in a monitored situation. The feedback on the parents' progress is then immediate.

As part of the initial program-planning phase, when children are enrolled at the Rutland Center, a tentative recommendation is made concerning the amount of parent involvement and the type of parent program which seems to suit the parents' current situation. A realistic appraisal is essential. Parents with low-income jobs are not advised to leave their work to participate in parent programs during working hours. Also, parents with great distrust of agencies are advised to "wait and see" if they notice any changes for the better before they become involved. For these parents, the monthly Parents' Association meeting may be all that is recommended at first. Or, a parent unable to mobilize psychic energy for the day-to-day family routines may be encouraged to come into the therapeutic classroom as an assistant teacher for the purpose of directly modeling the teacher's management style. Regardless of the initial approach, parents are informed of the variety of programs available and are encouraged to become increasingly involved as their child progresses.

In general, parents of children enrolled at the Rutland Center seem to go through the same Developmental Therapy stages as do the children:*

Stage I   *Responding and Trusting.* The phase in which the center's credibility is established and a parent comes to trust the center personnel to understand and support him.

Stage II   *Learning Individual Skills.* Based upon previously established trust, this phase emphasizes enhancing the parent's own skills as a person and as a parent. Successful management of daily routines is the focus.

Stage III   *Learning Skills for Successful Group Participation.* With a repertoire of basic skills for personal routines and child management established at the previous stage, parents are encouraged to extend these skills in their family constellation, in their neighborhood, and with other parents at the center.

Stage IV   *Investing in Group Processes.* This stage is not reached by all parents before their children are terminated. However, for some parents it represents a phase of active participation and leadership in groups.

Stage V   *Applying Skills in New Situations.* Designed to be a follow-up phase, emphasis at Stage V is put on independent ventures into new group situations, often confronting situations previously avoided.

This model highlights the dynamic changing nature of parental needs as well as the increasing capacity of parents to contribute to the therapeutic and learning process. There are a number of implications in this for parental involvement in psychoeducational programs. Perhaps most obvious is the concept that *sequence* of development and *rate* of progress for effective parenting are important variables to be incorporated into program planning. Bronfenbrenner (1974) offers a similar series of provocative conclusions, which he calls "Stages of Intervention," designed to differen-

---

*For a description of each of these five stages of Developmental Therapy as applied to children see Wood (*Developmental Therapy*), 1975.

tiate developmental levels of families. In his report, a careful review of longitudinal research on preschool intervention for the disadvantaged, he also concludes that effects of parental involvement are inversely related to the age of the child. Thus, the critical years before age five seem to indicate the need for programs which pivot around family-centered intervention.

WAYS TO DELIVER
PSYCHOEDUCATIONAL SERVICES

After an intervention theory has been translated into content and practices, procedures for effectively delivering such services must be designed. There are numerous ways to deliver psychoeducational services to young children. To date, no one service model has proven more successful than another. There are many issues to consider, such as geographic distances, transportation, availability of professional manpower, parent life-styles and economic conditions, availability of suitable day-care and preschool programs, and the characteristics and needs of the children to be served. At least six general styles for psychoeducational service delivery, at present, are being used to service young children; often, they are used in combination.

1. *Direct Service in Regular Preschool Classroom*—intervention on a scheduled basis directly with the child in his regular day-care class, individually or in small groups.
2. *Direct Service in Special (Resource) Classroom*—intervention in small, special groups in the regular preschool setting. Throughout the day groups are scheduled for special intervention according to needs and then returned to regular classroom. (The number of children needing this service is too small at some preschools to justify this service model.)
3. *Direct Service at Home*—intervention directly with child at home, involving the parent through observation, planning, and participation.
4. *Indirect Service at Home*—intervention directly with parent and indirectly, through the parent, with the child; on a regularly scheduled basis in the home.
5. *Indirect Service at School*—intervention through consultation with the teacher and indirectly, through the teacher, with the child; on a regularly scheduled basis.
6. *Psychoeducational Center Service*—intervention at a treatment center away from the preschool for a specified time daily with groups of children of similar developmental needs. Both children and families must travel to the center for services. However, the

greatest pooling of professional expertise is possible with this service model. For this reason, the psychoeducational center may be best suited for children with severe forms of emotional and behavioral disabilities.

DOCUMENTING CHILDREN'S PROGRESS

Psychoeducational models lend themselves to evaluation and accountability. In general, such evaluation falls into two categories: documentation of service effectiveness and experimental research. The former is recommended as the more viable strategy for demonstration and service projects, although it does not answer the question, "Is this model more effective than that model?" The experimental research approach does attempt to answer this question, but the current methodological problems are enormous. Bronfenbrenner (1974) reviews a number of such problems in experimental design including:

IQ as a Criterion of Selection
Insuring Parental Motivation
The Factor of Age
Differences in Degree of Deprivation
Forming Experimental and Control Groups
    Randomized local control groups
    Non-random local control groups
    Geographically randomized control groups
    Non-randomized distal control groups (pp. 8-18)

He cautions against blanket generalizations from experimental studies and recommends careful consideration of findings in light of these issues.

Deutsch, Taleporos, and Victor (1974) make several suggestions for improving future methodology:

... the development and utilization of more relevant measures ... properly standardized and validated ... which have the intrinsic capacity to measure the child's responsiveness, and also to measure the ability of the system to respond to the child.

... devising experimental designs which take into consideration all the extra-school and uncontrolled variables which have influenced the children's behavior and development.

... an interplay of innovation, training, evaluative feedback and parental as well as community participation (p. 60).

Perhaps the most productive approach to the problems of advancing both knowledge and practice in the field of early childhood education for the handicapped lies in careful, systematic studies of exacting developmental specifications based on theory and refined through empirical evidence of the interactive nature of behavioral and environmental factors with development processes. Bijou (1976), Loevinger (1976), Wohlwill (1976), and others have discussed the problems and the benefits which can be obtained from such research. In time, such functional-analytic studies should provide a body of useful principles and technological advances which will be of significant use to practitioners in solving the problems of the emotionally disturbed preschool child.

In studying the development of any group of handicapped preschool children, postulates can be made about the nature of developmental stages. Such information raises inquiry into the interaction of historical antecedents with present environmental conditions which produce developmental changes in the characteristics of each child. Such an approach offers an array of opportunities for a program of research which rigorously seeks to answer the question, "How is a child progressing?" (Blake and Allen, 1976).

First, the dimension of time (age) can be studied as a significant variable in the development of handicapped children, just as it has been studied as a force in the development of nonhandicapped children (e.g., Bayley, 1970; Gesell and Amatruda, 1973; and so on). Longitudinal studies are important; yet alone they are not sufficient for the current needs because they leave unidentified the variable, interactive relationships among psychological, biological, and environmental conditions which produce disturbance.

To expand upon the information gained from studies of time effects, a second level of effort is needed: normative studies. These allow us to conduct functional analyses of patterns of development in groups of emotionally disturbed children at the several stages of development.

Third, to make judgments about the significance of developmental changes of handicapped children as a function of an intervention program, we must know two things: (1) the rate and pattern of progress before, during, and after the program; and (2) the expected rate and pattern of comparable nonhandicapped children. These data enable us to compare developmental trends and extrapolate the short- and long-term effects of intervention.

Fourth, correlational studies will be needed to add the dimension of interaction effects among variables influencing developmental trends.

Finally, if refinements in classroom practices and curriculum are to be ensured, we must be able to take the data resulting from such studies and organize them into meaningful constructs which can connect theory and application, each enriching the other in a reciprocal relationship. This will give us directions for the question, "What do these research results mean for the classroom teacher and parent?"

To benefit fully from a program of research such as the one outlined above, investigators must have formulated goals and objectives during the model-planning phase and must have reliable and valid instruments for gathering information which is pertinent to these goals and objectives.

FIGURE 2

**A MODEL FOR DETERMINING TREATMENT
EFFECTIVENESS, USING A CRITERION-REFERENCED
SYSTEM APPLIED TO DEVELOPMENTAL THERAPY***

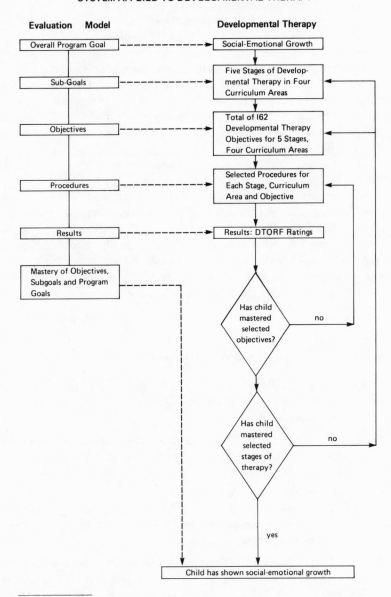

*From Wood, M.M. *Developmental Therapy.* Baltimore: University Park Press, 1975.
Printed here by permission of the author.

Finally, the data obtained must be interpreted in view of the original goals and objectives. Huberty and Swan (1975) describe this process in a three-phase model involving *planning, monitoring,* and *appraising.* In short, evaluation in this context means asking pertinent questions based upon thorough knowledge of the intervention model and then obtaining reliable answers which can be used to draw relevant conclusions.

Behind this approach is a strong implication for carefully constructed relationships between goals, objectives, procedures, documentation of outcomes, and documented conclusions. One example of evaluation as an integral part of a psychoeducational model is shown in Figure 2 (Swan and Wood, 1975). In this figure, the general evaluation outline is presented on the left side and the application of a specific model, Developmental Therapy, is shown on the right.

Such specificity and continuity between model building and practice should be expected from any exemplary program of intervention. This expectation permeates the present social/political climate and is reflected in the federal government's determination to implement fully Public Law 94-142, The Education for All Handicapped Children Act of 1975. The Individualized Education Program (IEP) mandated by this legislation for each handicapped child can become a positive force, involving teachers, evaluation personnel, and parents who develop a common understanding of what is desired for a child, what will be done, and how it will be documented.

BIBLIOGRAPHY

Bayley, N. "Development of Mental Abilities." In Mussen, P.H. (ed.), *Carmichael's Manual of Child Psychology*, Vol. 1. New York: John Wiley and Sons, 1970.

Biber, B., and Franklin, M. "The Relevance of Developmental and Psychodynamic Concepts to the Education of the Preschool Child." *Journal of the American Academy of Child Psychiatry* 6(1967):5-24.

Bijou, S.W. "Ages, Stages, and the Naturalization of Human Development." In Endler, N.S., Boulter, L.R., and Osser, H. (eds.), *Contemporary Issues in Developmental Psychology*, 2nd Edition. New York: Holt, Rinehart, and Winston, 1976.

Blake, K.A., and Allen, J.C. "Conducting Longitudinal Research in Reading." In Parr, R., Weintraub, S., and Tone, B. (eds.), *Improving Reading Research*. Newark, Delaware: International Reading Association, 1976.

Bobath, K. *The Motor Deficit in Patients with Cerebral Palsy.* Suffolk, England: The Lavenham Press Ltd., 1966.

Bronfenbrenner, U. "Is Early Intervention Effective?" In *A Report on Longitudinal Evaluations of Preschool Programs*, Vol. II. Washington, D.C.: Children's Bureau; Office of Child Development; U.S. Department of Health, Education, and Welfare; DHEW Publication No. (OHD) 74-25; 1974.

Carter, J.L., and Miller, P.K. "Creative Art for Minimally Brain-Injured Children." *Academic Therapy* 6(1975):245-252.

Clarizio, H.F., and McCoy, G.F. *Behavior Disorders in Children*, 2nd Edition. New York: Thomas Y. Crowell, 1976.

Deutsch, M., Taleporos, E., and Victor, J. "A Brief Synopsis of an Initial Enrichment Program in Early Childhood." In Ryan, S. (ed.), *A Report on Longitudinal Evaluations of Preschool Programs*, Volume 1. Washington, D.C.: Children's Bureau; Office of Child Development; U.S. Department of Health, Education, and Welfare; Publication No. (OHD) 74-24, 1974.

Dupont, H. (ed.) *Educating Emotionally Disturbed Children*, 2nd Edition. New York: Holt, Rinehart, and Winston, 1975.

Fenichel, D. "Psycho-Educational Approaches for Seriously Disturbed Children in the Classroom." In Long, N.J., Morse, W.C., Newman, R.G. (eds.), *Conflict in the Classroom*, 2nd Edition. Belmont, California: Wadsworth Publishing Co., Inc., 1971.

Furman, R.A., and Katan, A. *The Therapeutic Nursery School*. New York: International Universities Press, Inc., 1969.

Gazda, G.M. *Group Counseling: A Developmental Approach*. Boston: Allyn and Bacon, 1971.

Gesell, A., and Amatruda, C. *Developmental Diagnosis*, 3rd Edition. New York: Harper and Row, 1973.

Glasscote, R., and Fishman, M.E. *Mental Health Programs for Preschool Children*. Washington, D.C.: The Joint Information Service of the American Psychiatric Association and the National Association for Mental Health, 1974.

Herbert, M. *Emotional Problems of Development in Children*. New York: Academic Press, 1974.

Hewett, F. *Education of Exceptional Learners*. Rockleigh, N.J.: Allyn and Bacon, Inc., 1975.

Hewett, F. *The Emotionally Disturbed Child in the Classroom*. Boston: Allyn and Bacon, 1968.

Hewett, F.M. *Teaching the Disturbed Child: The Orchestration of Success*. (Abstracts from presentation at the Advanced Institute for Trainers of

202

Teachers for Emotionally Disturbed Children, Conference on Socialization.) Minneapolis: The University of Minnesota, (November) 1976.

Huberty, C.J., and Swan, W.W. "Evaluation of Programs." In *Early Childhood Education for Exceptional Children—A Handbook of Ideas and Exemplary Practices*. Arlington: Council for Exceptional Children, 1975.

Karnes, M.B., and Badger, E.E. "Training Mothers to Instruct Their Infants at Home." In Karnes, M.B. (ed.), *Research and Development Program on Preschool Disadvantaged Children:* Final Report. Washington, D.C.: U.S. Office of Education, 1969.

Kirk, S. *Educating Exceptional Children*, 2nd Edition. Atlanta: Houghton Mifflin Co., 1972.

Kohlberg, L., and Hersh, R.H. "Moral Development; A Review of the Theory." *Theory into Practice* 16(1977):53-58.

Lavatelli, C.S. *Piaget's Theory Applied to an Early Childhood Curriculum.* Boston: Center for Media Development, Inc., 1970.

Lillie, D.L. *An Individualized Approach to Developmental Instruction.* Chicago: Science Research Associates, 1975.

Loevinger, J. *Ego Development.* San Francisco: Jossey-Bass, 1976.

Long, N.J., Morse, W.C., and Newman, R.G. (eds.). *Conflict in the Classroom*, 2nd Edition. Belmont, California: Wadsworth Publishing Co., Inc., 1971.

MacFarlane, J., Allen, L., and Honzik, M. *A Developmental Study of the Behavior Problems of Normal Children Between Twenty-One Months and Fourteen Years.* Berkeley: University of California Press, 1954.

NTAO. *A Child's Way of Asking* (audio-slide training package). Athens, Ga.: National Technical Assistance Office, 698 North Pope Street, 1974.

Newton, M.R., and Brown, R.D. "A Preventive Approach to Developmental Problems in School Children." In Bower, E.M. and Hollister, W.G. (eds.), *Behavioral Science Frontiers in Education.* New York: John Wiley and Sons, 1967.

Ora, J.P. *Regional Intervention Project for Preschoolers and Parents*, Final Report. Washington: HEW, 1970. (Eric Number, ED 043179).

Pate, J.E. "Emotionally Disturbed and Socially Maladjusted Children." In Dunn, L.M. (ed.), *Exceptional Children in the School*, 1st Edition. Atlanta: Holt, Rinehart, and Winston Inc., 1963.

Piaget, J., and Inhelder, B. *The Psychology of the Child.* New York: Basic Books, 1969.

Rhodes, W.C., and Head, S. *A Study of Child Variance.* Ann Arbor: The University of Michigan, 1974.

Schopler, E., and Reichler, R.J. "Parents as Co-therapists in the Treatment of Psychotic Children." In Chess, S., and Thomas, A. (eds.), *Annual Progress in Child Psychiatry and Child Development.* New York: Brunner/Mazel, 1972.

Shearer, M.S., and Shearer, D.E. "The Portage Project: A Model for Early Childhood Education." *Exceptional Children* 39(1972):210-217.

Swan, W.W., and Wood, M.M. "Making Decisions About Treatment Effectiveness." In Wood, M.M. (ed.), *Developmental Therapy.* Baltimore: University Park Press, 1975.

Swap, S.M. "Disturbing Classroom Behavior: A Developmental and Ecological View." *Exceptional Children* 41(1974):163-172.

Taylor, F.D., Artuso, A.A., and Hewett, F.M. *Creative Art Tasks for Children.* Denver: Love Publishing Company, 1970.

Wohlwill, J.F. "The Age Variable in Psychological Research." In Endler, N.S., Boulter, L.R., and Osser, H. (eds.), *Contemporary Issues in Developmental Psychology*, 2nd Edition. New York: Holt, Rinehart, and Winston, 1976.

Wood, M.M. *Developmental Therapy.* Baltimore: University Park Press, 1975.

Wood, M.M. "A Developmental Curriculum for Social and Emotional Growth." In Lillie, D., *Early Childhood Education: An Individualized Approach to Developmental Instruction.* Chicago: Science Research Associates, 1975.

Wood, M.M., and Hurley, L.O. "Curriculum and Instruction." In *Early Childhood Education for Exceptional Children—A Handbook of Ideas and Exemplary Practices.* Arlington: Council for Exceptional Children, 1975.

Wood, M.M., and Swan, W.W. "A Developmental Approach to Educating the Disturbed Young Child." *Behavioral Disorders* Spring 1978 (in press).

CHAPTER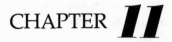

Intervention: The Behavioral Model

Thomas Stachnik

A behavioral intervention model for the preschool child includes at least the following assumptions and emphases:

I. Maladaptive emotional and social behavior not attributable to some organic condition is strengthened or weakened via the same learning processes which account for the strengthening or weakening of adaptive behavior. Thus, utilizing those learning processes (particular child-environment interactions) during intervention constitutes an appropriate strategy, and places the responsibility for change on the child's environment, not on the child.

II. Regardless of the specific intervention procedure employed, some measure of the maladaptive behavior must be taken prior to and during intervention so that a continual assessment of the efficacy of the procedure is available.

III. Intervention will be most effective if it occurs in the setting where the maladaptive behavior occurs, as opposed to a clinic or other outpatient facility. Thus, for the preschooler, the optimal intervention site will most often be the home or nursery school.

IV. Intervention procedures should emphasize the use of positive reinforcement to strengthen appropriate behaviors and extinction to weaken inappropriate behaviors. Aversive techniques should always be a procedure of last resort when all else has failed and the well-being of the child is in jeopardy.

V. Once maladaptive behavior has become habitual, it is often difficult to modify—even in the preschooler where, in terms of absolute time, it has a relatively short history. Thus, large-scale, systematic attempts to *prevent* behavior problems in the preschooler must be given a high priority.

THOMAS STACHNIK is an Associate Professor in the Department of Psychiatry at Michigan State University. His main professional interest is applied behavior analysis.

The text that follows explicates these five points and includes examples of how a behavioral model might be employed in attempting to resolve various maladaptive behaviors in a preschool child.

LEARNING PROCESSES

Unless attributable to some organic condition, a behavioral intervention model assumes that a child who demonstrates maladaptive emotional or social behavior has been taught to do so. Saying it that way is not meant to imply that the teaching has been deliberate or systematic, but to emphasize that the all-powerful adults in a preschooler's life have arranged the environment, albeit inadvertently, in a way that strengthened inappropriate behavior. For example, consider a mother at the supermarket with her four-year-old boy who is told that he may not have the candy bar he has taken from the display rack because "it's almost lunchtime and it will spoil your appetite." The boy's initial displeasure grows quickly into sobbing and then a full-blown temper tantrum. Mother now begins to feel uncomfortable because curious people in the store are staring with looks that she interprets as "what kind of mother are you?" When her discomfort level has risen even further, she relents and gives the child the candy bar with the admonition, "I'm going to let you have it this time, but don't you ever do this again!"

Will the boy do it again? Very likely he will because his environment has taught him to do it, i.e., provided a satisfying state of affairs (candy bar) subsequent to a behavioral episode (temper tantrum). This process is called *positive reinforcement* and is one of the most common ways in which behavior, both adaptive and in this instance maladaptive, is strengthened. A second strengthening process, termed *negative reinforcement*, is operating relative to the mother's behavior. For her, the boy's tantrum constituted an unpleasant state of affairs and thus the behavior (giving the candy bar) that succeeded in terminating the unpleasantness is strengthened. Note that the behavior of the boy and the behavior of the mother have both been strengthened, although by different processes, and that we would expect both to behave in a similar fashion under similar circumstances in the future.

The environment also responds to behavior in ways which weaken it, i.e., make it less likely to occur in the future. In the supermarket example, had the mother ignored the tantrum (let the boy scream but paid no attention to it and above all not provided the candy bar) the probability of future tantrums would have been lessened. This process of ignoring undesirable behavior is termed *extinction*. It is a very useful, effective procedure to weaken inappropriate behavior, particularly when used in conjunction with a procedure like positive reinforcement to strengthen a response which will compete effectively with the undesirable behavior.

Two other processes that weaken behavior are *positive punishment* and *negative punishment.* Like positive reinforcement, positive punishment involves the occurrence of an event subsequent to some behavior, but in positive punishment the event is aversive rather than pleasant. In the supermarket example, the mother positively reinforced the temper tantrum by providing a candy bar. Had she verbally reprimanded (or spanked) the boy for the tantrum it would have been an example of positive punishment. Negative punishment, like negative reinforcement, involves the termination of an event subsequent to some behavior, but in negative punishment the event is pleasant rather than aversive. In the supermarket example, remember that the mother's relenting was negatively reinforced (strengthened) because it terminated an unpleasant event (tantrum plus people staring). Negative punishment weakens behavior because a pleasant event is terminated; e.g., a child's favorite television program is turned off because he refuses to negotiate the use of the television set with his brother or sister. Or, in the supermarket, the mother might have returned to the display rack five packages of Kool-Aid which she had earlier agreed to purchase at the child's request. The table below summarizes the four learning processes discussed above which specify a particular relationship between some behavior and the environment in which it occurs.[*]

| | | Environmental event | |
		Presented	Terminated
Nature of environmental event	Pleasant	Positive reinforcement (strengthens)	Negative punishment (weakens)
	Unpleasant	Positive punishment (weakens)	Negative reinforcement (strengthens)

[*]Extinction (ignoring) is not included in the table because unlike the other four processes it does not include both a behavior and an environmental event. Extinction includes only a behavior, e.g., tantrum, and stipulates that no environmental event, pleasant or unpleasant, follows the behavior closely in time.

A behavioral intervention model assumes that these learning processes account for the development of much of a preschooler's behavior, both adaptive and maladaptive. They emphasize the consequences provided by the child's environment over which the child ordinarily has little or no control. In this specific sense, then, the preschooler is not responsible for his behavior, and the responsibility for the success or failure of intervention rests squarely and unequivocally on the child's environment.

MEASUREMENT

Asking a person working with a preschooler to obtain a *measure* of the child's disturbed behavior prior to and during intervention is almost invariably an unpopular request. Usually the person asked to do so feels it is unnecessary, i.e., that he will surely be able to tell if his intervention procedure is having a particular effect without actually recording the behavior in question. For that person, the following anecdote is relevant (Harris, Wolf, and Baer, 1964):

> A boy in the laboratory preschool frequently pinched adults. Attempts by the teacher to ignore the behavior proved ineffective, since the pinches were hard enough to produce at least an involuntary startle. Teachers next decided to try to develop a substitute behavior. They selected patting as a logical substitute. Whenever the child reached toward a teacher, she attempted to forestall a pinch by saying, "Pat, Davey," sometimes adding, "Not pinch," and then strongly approving his patting, when it occurred. Patting behavior increased rapidly to a high level. The teachers agreed that they had indeed succeeded in reducing the pinching behavior through substituting patting. Then they were shown the recorded data. It showed clearly that although patting behavior was indeed high, pinching behavior continued at the previous level. Apparently, the teachers, were so focused on the rise in patting behavior that, without the objective data, they would have erroneously concluded that development of a substitute behavior was in this case a successful technique (p. 17).

An error in the opposite direction can also occur, i.e., judging that an intervention procedure has not been effective when in fact it has been. Wolf, Risley, and Mees (1964) worked in an inpatient setting with a very disturbed preschooler for whom it was crucial to wear glasses. Unfortunately, the boy developed a pattern of throwing and often breaking them. To discourage his doing so, attendants were instructed to put him in his room for ten minutes after each throwing episode. After a few days, when the attendants were asked how the procedure was working, they reported that the glasses-throwing had not diminished. However, a check of the records showed that there had been a significant decrease, and subsequently dropped to zero within five days.

The moral of these anecdotes and a key emphasis in a behavioral intervention model is that while intuition may be a useful tool in diagnosis or treatment design, it ought not be relied upon to assess the efficacy of treatment.

INTERVENTION LOCATION

In a behavioral intervention model, the question of *where* intervention is to occur is at least as important as the nature of the intervention. Historically, treatment for the preschooler has entailed the parent(s) and/or child going somewhere to receive it, e.g., a child guidance clinic, the office of a private practitioner, etc. This going-somewhere-for-service probably was a direct outgrowth of delivering other health care on an outpatient basis, e.g., taking a child with a broken arm to a clinic to have the arm set and placed in a cast. Mending a preschooler's broken arm at an outpatient clinic makes perfectly good sense, but attempting to resolve behavior problems with that model may be a less than optimal procedure.

One disadvantage of the clinic setting is that the therapist does not see the quality of parent-child interaction in a natural setting. The unusual, artificial environment of the clinic may well preclude the occurrence of characteristic interchanges between parent and child, and it may prompt unusual, artificial behavior. While the behavior seen in the clinic may be interesting, it will usually be the child's characteristic behavior in characteristic settings (home, nursery school, at play with peers, etc.) which is of greatest concern.

Depending on the type of therapist consulted and the therapist's theoretical orientation, in some instances the parent(s) of a preschooler who exhibits deviant behavior may be involved in psychotherapy in order to change parental behavior toward the child. While the logic of such a strategy is sound, the chief disadvantage is that the therapist sees little or no interaction between the parent(s) and child—important data in a behavioral intervention model. Furthermore, the therapist must rely on the parent's description of the child's problem behavior, a notoriously unreliable source for an objective, accurate report. The alternative strategy of treating the child at a clinic in the absence of the parent(s), e.g., in play therapy, also appears to have some important limitations. Again, there is little opportunity to observe the nature of child-parent(s) interactions. Also, there is the additional, often tenuous, assumption that whatever gains the child makes in the play therapy will in fact transfer to other settings—home, nursery school, etc.

In an attempt to avoid some of these assumed limitations, *a behavioral model holds that intervention should occur in the setting where the problem behavior is occurring, and that the role of therapist be filled by the parent(s) or teacher or other significant adult in the child's environment.* The following case illustrates the approach very well (Hawkins, Peterson, Schweid, and Bijou, 1966):

> The child in this study was a four-year-old boy, Peter S. He is the third of four children in a middle-class family. Peter had been brought to a university clinic because he was extremely difficult to manage and control. His mother stated

she was helpless in dealing with his frequent tantrums and disobedience. Peter often kicked objects or people, removed or tore his clothing, called people rude names, annoyed his younger sister, made a variety of threats, hit himself, and became very angry at the slightest frustration. He demanded attention almost constantly, and seldom cooperated with Mrs. S. In addition, Peter was not toilet trained and did not always speak clearly.

Peter had been evaluated at a clinic for retarded children when he was three years old and again when he was four and a half. His scores on the Stanford Binet, form L-M were 72 and 80, respectively. He was described as having borderline intelligence, as being hyperactive, and possibly brain-damaged.

Two therapist/observers, observing the mother and child in the home, noted that many of Peter's undesirable behaviors appeared to be maintained by attention from his mother. When Peter behaved objectionably, she would often try to explain why he should not act thus; or she would try to interest him in some new activity by offering toys or food. (This "distraction" method is often put forth by teachers as a preferred technique for dealing with undesirable behavior. Behavior theory suggests, however, that while distraction may be temporarily effective in dealing with such behaviors, repeated employment of such a procedure may increase the frequency of the unwanted set of responses.) Peter was occasionally punished by the withdrawal of a misused toy or other object, but he was often able to persuade his mother to return the item almost immediately. He was also punished by being placed on a high-chair and forced to remain there for short periods. Considerable tantrum behavior usually followed such disciplinary measures and was quite effective in maintaining mother's attention, largely in the form of verbal persuasion or argument (p. 99).

After identifying nine of Peter's behaviors which were most objectionable (designated "O" behaviors), Peter's mother was instructed in the use of those processes described earlier in this chapter which strengthen or weaken behavior, i.e., positive reinforcement, negative punishment, etc. At the outset of intervention, two therapist/observers were in the home with Peter and his mother. They used three gestural signals to indicate how she was to behave toward Peter. Signal "A" meant she was to tell Peter to stop whatever O behavior he was engaged in. Signal "B" meant she was immediately to place Peter in his room and lock the door. Signal "C" meant she was to give him attention, praise, and affectionate physical contact. The first time Peter demonstrated an O behavior his mother was signaled to tell him to stop. If he did not do so, or if he repeated the same behavior later, she was signaled to put him in his room where he had to remain for a minimum of five minutes. (Previously, all items that might have served as playthings were removed from the room so that he had little opportunity to amuse himself.) Occasionally, when the therapist/observers noticed that Peter was behaving appropriately, signal "C" was given and his mother responded to him with attention and approval. When Peter's mother reported that she "felt sure of herself," the therapist/observers no longer came to the home. During a follow-up visit some forty-five days later, the therapist/observers noted an enormous decrease in the rate of Peter's O behaviors, and his mother reported that it was necessary for her to send him to his room only about once a week.

As presented here, the case is obviously incomplete. The matters of Peter's toilet training, his speech, and an analysis of the entire family dynamics would all have to be addressed. But one point is clear: a parent can be readily taught to use specific, relatively simple procedures that will have an immediate, positive, and often dramatic impact on a preschooler's behavior.

AVERSIVE TECHNIQUES

There are times when the use of an aversive procedure, i.e., positive punishment, can be justified in intervention with a young child. Whaley and Tough (1970) report using electric shock with a six-year-old severely retarded boy who banged his head against the wall and pounded his ears with his fists. Others (Lovaas, Schaeffer, and Simmons, 1965) have experimented with electric shock in both positive punishment and negative reinforcement procedures to help build social behavior in autistic children who were unreachable by any other means. Note that in both these instances the children involved were either extremely disturbed and thus not amenable to the usual array of intervention techniques, or were engaging in behavior which clearly jeopardized their physical well-being.

In all but these extreme, relatively rare cases, a behavioral intervention model precludes the use of aversive procedures. Apart from the obvious ethical and humanitarian considerations, there is ample evidence, both from animal data in controlled laboratory studies and clinical observations of children, that aversive techniques often generate a host of undesirable side effects. Furthermore, a skilled therapist can use a combination of nonaversive procedures, e.g., positive reinforcement and extinction, in such a way that aversive procedures are unnecessary. The following case illustrates the point (Harris, Johnston, Kelley, and Wolf, 1964):

> The study dealt with a three-year-old girl who had regressed to an excessive amount of crawling. By "excessive" is meant that after three weeks of school she was spending most of her morning crawling or in a crouched position with her face hidden. The parents reported that for some months the behavior had been occurring whenever they took her to visit or when friends came to their home. The teachers had used some conventional techniques in an attempt to build the child's "security."

> Observations recorded in the third week at school showed, however, that more than 80% of the child's time was spent in off-feet positions. The records also showed that the crawling behavior frequently drew the attention of teachers. On-feet behaviors, such as standing and walking, which occurred infrequently, seldom drew such notice.

> A program was instituted in which the teachers no longer attended to the child whenever she was crawling or crouching, but gave her continuous warm atten-

tion as long as she was engaging in behavior in which she was standing, running, or walking. Initially the only upright behaviors that the teachers were able to attend to occurred when the child pulled herself almost to her feet in order to hang up or take down her coat from her locker, and when she pulled herself up to wash her hands in the wash basin. Within a week of the initiation of the new attention-giving procedure, the child acquired a close-to-normal pattern of on-feet behavior.

In order to see whether the change from off- to on-feet behavior was related to the differential attention given by the teachers, they reversed their procedure, making attention once again contingent only upon crawling and other off-feet behavior. They waited for occasions of such off-feet behavior to "reinforce" with attention, while not attending to any on-feet behavior. By the second day the child had reverted to her old pattern of play and locomotion. The observational records showed the child was off her feet 80% of the class session.

To see whether on-feet behavior could be re-established, the teachers again reversed their procedure, giving attention to the child only when she was engaging in behaviors involving upright positions. On-feet behavior rose markedly during the first session. By the fourth day, the child again spent about 62% of the time on her feet. Once the child was not spending the greater portion of her day crawling about, she quickly became a well-integrated member of the group (p. 8).

This same contingent use of adult social reinforcement has also been used with great success (Harris, Wolf, and Baer, 1964) to help preschoolers who cried or whined excessively, to teach preschoolers to play cooperatively rather than always in isolation, and to teach assertiveness to an excessively passive preschool boy. Again, the point to note is that successful intervention in relatively difficult behavior problems can be achieved without resorting to aversive procedures of any kind (which includes nagging, scolding, shaming, etc.).

PREVENTION

Placing a high priority on the prevention of behavior problems is certainly not a feature unique to a behavioral intervention model. In fact, it is axiomatic in all intervention models that prevention is preferable to remediation. But the distressing fact is that each year a large number of five-year-olds begin their formal education with serious behavior problems. Many of these children experience anxiety when faced with any challenging task, others have disabling language deficits, some are uncooperative, others have great difficulty getting along with their peers, and the list could go on. For these children, the school experience is going to be unsatisfying for all concerned—the child, parents, teacher, and peers.

If we ask what steps are being taken to reduce the number of such children and the severity of the disorders, there are many hopeful signs. The recent, rapid expansion of preschool programs has the potential for a solid preventive effort. The consultation offered by community mental health centers, coupled in some communities with screening programs to detect behavior problems as early as possible are also important preventive developments. However, a behavioral model would judge these efforts incomplete unless another element is added: a serious national effort in parenthood training.

Hawkins (1971) has proposed in some detail how such an effort might be conceptualized and implemented. He contends that instruction in child rearing should occur in our secondary schools since they represent an institution that has access to virtually every person who will become a parent and also has the capacity to provide the training. As part of his proposal he suggests that every high school include a nursery school or day-care center which would serve as a laboratory where students could carry out certain exercises in working with children. There are provocative elements in his proposal as well, e.g., that at some point it may become feasible to begin certifying persons suitable for parenthood.

While perhaps few people would agree with all of these suggestions, the need for effective, large-scale parenthood training can be attested to by anyone who regularly must deal with children damaged by ignorant, inept parents. If such a program were undertaken, the parent training would likely focus on three questions: (1) what behavioral and physical development is it reasonable to expect of a child; (2) what behavior (including attitudes and values) should a parent attempt to strengthen in a child; and (3) how, specifically, can a parent proceed to strengthen those behaviors. While a behavioral model may have no special contribution to make relative to the first two questions, it can contribute significantly, perhaps uniquely, to the third. Several decades of applied research have produced a set of effective, specific, easily teachable procedures which speak directly to the question of how behavior is established, strengthened, maintained, or weakened. Furthermore, there have been repeated demonstrations that parents can be taught to be effective in altering problem behavior of their children. It surely is time that these same, effective procedures be made available to parents *before* behavior problems develop. While it may require a considerable effort to do so, increasing the number of happy, productive children would make such an investment seem trivial.

BIBLIOGRAPHY

Harris, Florence, R., Johnston, Margaret K., Kelley, C. Susan, and Wolf, M.M. "Effects of Positive Social Reinforcement on Regressed Crawling of a Nursery School Child." *Journal of Educational Psychology* 55 (1964):35-41.

214

Harris, F., Wolf, M., and Baer, D. "Effects of Adult Social Reinforcement on Child Behavior." *Young Children* 20(1964):8-17.

Hawkins, Robert P. "Universal Parenthood Training: A Proposal for Preventive Mental Health." *Educational Technology* 11(1971):28-35.

Hawkins, Robert P., Peterson, R.F., Schweid, E., and Bijou, S.W. "Behavior Therapy in the Home: Amelioration of Problem Parent-Child Relations with the Parent in a Therapeutic Role." *Journal of Experimental Child Psychiatry* 4(1966):99-107.

Lovaas, O.I., Schaeffer, B., and Simmons, J.Q. "Building Social Behavior in Autistic Children by Use of Electric Shock." *Journal of Experimental Research in Personality* 1(1965):99-109.

Whaley, Donald L., and Tough, Jerry. "Treatment of a Self-Injuring Mongoloid with Shock-Induced Suppression and Avoidance." In Ulrich, R., Stachnik, T., and Mabry, J. (eds.), *Control of Human Behavior*, Vol. 2. Glenview, Illinois: Scott, Foresman, and Co., 1970.

Wolf, M.M., Risley, T., and Mees, H. "Application of Operant Conditioning Procedures to the Behavior Problems of an Autistic Child." *Behavior Research and Therapy* 1(1964):305-312.

Supplementary References

The following books are good sources for further examination of behavioral *intervention techniques* with preschoolers. All three are available in paperback from the Research Press, Box 31775, Champaign, IL 61280.

For parents:
Parents Are Teachers by Wesley Becker, 1971.

For preschool teachers:
Teaching Social Behavior to Young Children by William Sheppard, Steven Shank, and Darla Wilson, 1973.

For parents or preschool teachers:
Living With Children by Gerald Patterson and Elizabeth Gullion, 1971.

The following includes a good discussion of various *philosophical issues* relative to a behavioral intervention model:

Ullman, L., and Krasner, L. *Case Studies in Behavior Modification*. New York: Holt, Rinehart and Winston, 1965.

Index